# On the Trail
# of the Indian Tiger

# ON THE TRAIL OF THE INDIAN TIGER

BY
TOBIAS J. LANZ, PH.D.

Safari Press

*On the Trail of the Indian Tiger* © 2009 by Tobias Lanz. No part of this publication may be used or reproduced in any form or by any means, electronic or mechanical reproduction, including photocopying, recording, or any information storage and retrieval system, without permission from the publisher.

The trademark Safari Press ® is registered with the U.S. Patent and Trademark Office and in other countries.

Lanz, Tobias

First edition

Safari Press
2009, Long Beach, California

ISBN 1-57157-328-3

Library of Congress Catalog Card Number: 2008927484

10 9 8 7 6 5 4 3 2 1

Printed in the United States of America

Readers wishing to receive the Safari Press catalog, featuring many fine books on big-game hunting, wingshooting, and sporting firearms, should write to Safari Press Inc., P.O. Box 3095, Long Beach, CA 90803, USA. Tel: (714) 894-9080 or visit our Web site at www.safaripress.com.

# Table of Contents

Acknowledgments .......................................................................................................................... vii

Introduction .................................................................................................................................. ix

Chapter One            William Blane, *Cynegetica; or Essays on Sporting* (1788). ........................................ 1

Chapter Two            Thomas Williamson, *Oriental Field Sports* (1807). ................................................ 9

Chapter Three          Daniel Johnson, *Sketches of Indian Field Sports* (1822). ...................................... 22

Chapter Four           Godfrey Mundy, *Pen and Pencil Sketches, Being the Journal of a Tour of India* (1832). ........ 32

Chapter Five           Thomas Bacon, *First Impressions and Studies from Nature in Hindostan* (1837). ............... 45

Chapter Six            Edward Napier, *Scenes and Sports in Foreign Lands* (1840). ................................... 57

Chapter Seven          William Rice, *Tiger Shooting in India* (1857). ................................................ 67

Chapter Eight          Walter Campbell, *My Indian Journal* (1864). ................................................... 80

Chapter Nine           James Forsyth, *The Highlands of Central India* (1871). ........................................ 94

Chapter Ten            Gordon Cumming, *Wild Men and Wild Beasts* (1871). ............................................ 108

Chapter Eleven         George Sanderson, *Thirteen Years among the Wild Beasts of India* (1882). ..................... 119

Chapter Twelve         Arthur Pollock, *Sporting Days in Southern India* (1894). ..................................... 134

Chapter Thirteen       Alexander Glasfurd, *Rifle and Romance in an Indian Jungle* (1905). ........................... 146

Chapter Fourteen       Alfred Watson, *King Edward VII as Sportsman* (1911). ......................................... 156

Chapter Fifteen        Charles Gouldsbury, *Tiger Land* (1913). ...................................................... 169

Chapter Sixteen        Robert Baden-Powell. *Memories of India* (1915). .............................................. 179

Chapter Seventeen      Nigel Woodyatt, *My Sporting Memories* (1923). ................................................ 193

Chapter Eighteen       Bernard Ellison, *HRH The Prince of Wales's Sport in India* (1925). .......................... 207

Chapter Nineteen       Arthur Stewart, *Tiger and Other Game* (1928). ................................................ 218

Chapter Twenty         James Best, *Tiger Days* (1931). .............................................................. 228

Chapter Twenty-One     Reginald Burton, *The Tiger Hunters* (1936). .................................................. 239

Chapter Twenty-Two     Jim Corbett, *Man-Eaters of Kumaon* (1946). ................................................... 249

Chapter Twenty-Three   James Sleeman, *From Rifle to Camera: The Reformation of a Big Game Hunter* (1947). ..263

Chapter Twenty-Four    Olive Smythies, *Tiger Lady* (1953). .......................................................... 274

Chapter Twenty-Five    Kenneth Anderson, *Nine Man-Eaters and One Rogue* (1954). ..................................... 284

Chapter Twenty-Six     Kesri Singh, *One Man and a Thousand Tigers* (1959). .......................................... 301

Chapter Twenty-Seven   Robert Ruark, *Use Enough Gun* (1966). ........................................................ 312

Glossary ................................................................................................................................... 325

Bibliography ............................................................................................................................... 331

# Acknowledgments

My first bit of gratitude goes to the many people of India who gave me information about tigers and tiger hunting during my travels there over the last ten years. I also want to thank my old friend Rob Somers who first introduced me to hunting literature, for it was his introduction that got me interested in the many people who wrote these books and made hunting their pastime.

I also want to thank the various people and departments at the University of South Carolina. First there is the interlibrary loan department that helped locate so many rare books for me. Special thanks also goes to the Rare Book Collection for owning those few rare books that are too precious to circulate. University photographer Phil Sawyer deserves all the credit for preparing the photographs in the book. Finally, special thanks to Jennifer Almeda, my graduate assistant, who spent many tedious hours scanning and re-typing the various chapters of the book.

*A Mogul tiger hunt.*

Thanks also to Lionel Leventhal, owner of Greenhill Books in London, who helped track down rare volumes. He also proved information on authors and many small and defunct publishers. I must also praise the many people working for various publishers who diligently searched for old titles and copyright holders for me. Special thanks to Trophy Room Books in Agoura, California, for its guidance and expertise and for the use of two pictures from *Someone of Value: A Biography of Robert Ruark* by Hugh Foster. I must thank Ludo Wurfbain for accepting my proposal, which made this whole project possible, and his staff who plodded through my manuscript and dealt with the painstaking details of getting this work into print.

My greatest thanks is reserved for my wife for first accompanying me in my travels across South Asia and then for diligently and patiently supporting me as I worked on finishing this project.

## Introduction

Men have hunted tigers since the beginning of time. But nowhere were tigers hunted more fervently than in India* Both Indian royalty and simple villagers alike hunted tigers for centuries and developed a complex set of rituals and methods that varied based on culture and region. But it was the British who became the greatest of tiger hunters. Their pursuit of "field sports," or shikar, was unparalleled even by India's traditional rulers, the Moguls and maharajas, who invented the sport. The British shot tigers in more ways and in more locales and wrote more on their hunting exploits than any people in history. All told, about forty thousand tigers were bagged and hundreds of hunting books and articles published between 1850 and 1950, the height of British influence in India.

Today this seems almost unbelievable, as there are only a few thousand tigers remaining in India. But in those haughty days of empire the world seemed without limits, and so it was with hunting. Few hunters ever thought the tiger could be eradicated because they, and other wild creatures, were so abundant. Tigers lived on the periphery of villages, towns, and even large cities well into the twentieth century. Rogues frequently killed livestock and even human beings. The tiger was a political and religious symbol throughout the land because it was bold and adaptive, as well as beautiful and mysterious. The great cat was synonymous with India itself.

The country's large tiger population and its massive and striking specimens are the result of its geography. India is one of the world's most ecologically diverse lands, with habitats ranging from deserts and swamps to grasslands, woodlands, and rain forests. It was a natural haven for many wild animals, but it was the adaptive tiger that was found everywhere except the far western deserts and the frigid highlands of the upper Himalayas. As a result, there was no better place to shoot tigers.

India's most famous tiger lands were the Himalayan foothills, or Terai, a land of densely forested hills interspersed with rivers that border the swampy

---

*India, later the British Indian Empire or Raj, was the general name for all of South Asia, including the present-day countries of India, Pakistan, Bangladesh, Bhutan, Sri Lanka, Nepal, and Myanmar. The Indian tiger *(Panthera tigris tigris)* is the tiger subspecies that historically range across this territory

grasslands of the northern plains. In terms of hunting and wildlife, this rich habitat was the Indian equivalent of East Africa. Swamp deer, or barasingha, formed herds that numbered in the hundreds that grazed alongside elephant, rhinoceros, and water buffalo. Leopard, bear, and other deer species were also abundant. But most important, the Terai was home to the famous "royal Bengal tiger," known for its size and rich color.

Western India was another favored hunting ground. It is an arid land of rolling hills and scrub forests offset by fields and rocky outcroppings left behind by ancient volcanoes. The landscape is punctuated by numerous ravines and escarpments and is dotted with the crumbling fortifications of local warrior clans, all of which provide hideaways for the cat. The tiger shared this rugged landscape with hyenas, vultures, and antelope. And during the long dry season the tiger blended perfectly with the brown and yellow grasses, allowing it to hide from hunter and hunted alike.

There were also many tiger haunts scattered across the Deccan Plateau, the landmass that constitutes the bulk of the Indian subcontinent. Tigers were particularly abundant in the central highlands, a land of mountain ranges, woodlands, and broad river valleys. That is the classic India made famous by Rudyard Kipling's *Jungle Book,* and it is there that the remote and mysterious forests are shared by humans and wild animals. Even today it is where most Indian tigers are found.

Hunters also sought tigers in the Eastern and Western Ghats, mountains that run along the two coasts and the highlands that flank the border with Burma. These areas capture the full intensity of the monsoon, creating dense rain forests that are home to elephant, forest bison, wild boar, and numerous primates. They were some of the most difficult places to hunt tigers because of the tangled vegetation and wet conditions. And in Assam, the presence of hostile natives, some of whom were headhunters, made hunting a truly daunting experience.

Tiger hunting methods and rituals varied greatly, depending on topography and local custom. Tigers were hunted from howdahs perched on an elephant's back in open terrain, or from treetop platforms, or machans, in wooded areas. They were also tracked and killed from horseback and on foot. Early on, tigers were shot with muskets, although an intrepid few preferred ancient weapons such as lances, spears, and bows and arrows. In the nineteenth century bolt-action repeating rifles became widespread, and a range of calibers were used depending on personal preference and hunting conditions.

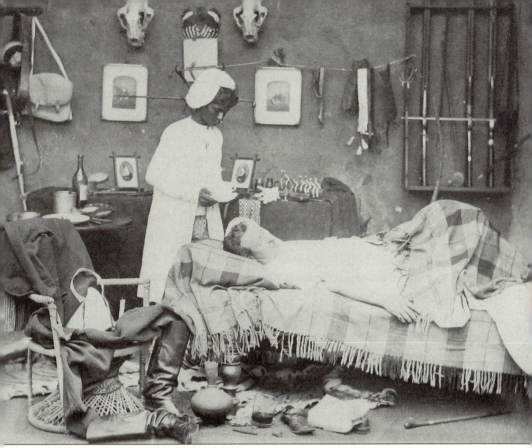

*An English hunter's quarters, mid-nineteenth century.*

The first Englishmen to hunt Indian tigers were soldiers, traders, and adventurers. Many were employed by the British East India Company, which had established trading posts across the land by 1700. Many were illiterate, so few wrote of their experiences. Those who did blended hunting accounts with military adventures or descriptions of scenery and encounters with natives. Such tales did not reach large audiences.

That changed, however, in the early nineteenth century as a result of more widespread printing, rising literacy, and the number of Indian adventure stories that started pouring into the mother country. Artists returning from India with paintings of scenery and architecture sparked a craze for the exotic, and hunting and nature enthusiasts followed suit, writing books in which the tiger often played a central role. That set a standard and tradition to be followed by writers for the next 150 years.

Tiger hunting changed rapidly after the Sepoy Rebellion of 1857, in which Indians rebelled against British rule. The British government replaced the British

East India Company as administrators of the subcontinent, and the period known as the British Raj began. As government and commerce expanded, British civilians and their families now accompanied traders and soldiers. Wilderness areas became more accessible with the introduction of modern rifles and trains in the following decades. Tigers became easier to shoot, and more were shot as the number of hunters increased.

The British established their own society and class system, one remarkably similar to Hinduism. At the top of Anglo-Indian society was the political or ruling class—namely, high-ranking administrators and civil servants. They were followed by military and police officers. Then came the commercial class, who were involved in banking, insurance, and industry. Finally there were the common soldiers, clerks, technicians, and tradesmen. Each class had its own social interests and rituals, which included different approaches and attitudes toward hunting. Naturally, the upper classes had the best opportunities and accounted for the majority of tigers shot.

The British elite readily adopted the ancient shikar rituals of the Moguls and maharajas. These massive displays comprised specially trained hunting elephants accompanied by dozens of retainers. "Beaters" fanned out in the forest and drove the bewildered tigers between stationary men, or "stops," and then toward waiting entourages where they were summarily shot. Although wounded tigers occasionally attacked elephants and their mounts or killed unarmed beaters, these massive tiger hunts were not much sport.

The real purpose of these rituals was to display the social and political power of the hunter. Tiger hunts brought together royals, dignitaries, and trophy hunters from around the world. Journalists and writers often accompanied them, to provide official accounts of these extravagant affairs. At the domestic level such rituals allowed the British to survey territory and rural populations, and to cement relations with Hindu and Mogul royalty, who were now their subjects. Apart from the value of their political support, native princes were also useful because they knew the terrain and introduced the many nuances of shikar to Europeans.

Maharajas, nawabs, and other royals often organized lavish tiger hunts themselves to impress their new rulers and to gain political favors. And some of the best hunting grounds in India lay in the regions ruled indirectly by the British, the so-called princely states, which lay outside the crowded Indo-Gangetic Plain, which was the heart of the Raj. Because they were remote and less developed, these states became favorite destinations for hunters.

*Skinning a tiger at camp, latter half of the nineteenth century.*

Native princes had always organized private hunts for their own entertainment, and tiger hunting became one of the last expressions of their dwindling power and prestige. And for many it became a lifelong passion. The Maharaja Scindia of Gwalior shot seven hundred tigers in his hunting career, and the Maharaja of Surguja supposedly killed seventeen hundred, probably more than any other person in history. Despite their love of hunting, many of these men were also keen naturalists and accomplished writers, artists, and historians who chronicled their many hunting adventures for English-speaking audiences.

Improved transportation and weaponry also made hunting more accessible to women. These memsahibs were usually the wives of prominent men. Some were devoted shikaris who braved the heat, insects, and discomfort along with their male counterparts. Female hunters remained rare, but the women who accompanied hunting entourages often brought European fashions and comforts with them, making the "Christmas camp," in particular, one of the most memorable social events of the Raj.

The majority of tiger hunters, however, were not political leaders, royalty, or international trophy hunters but soldiers and civil servants. Soldiers, in particular, rejected the social hunt for true adventure and sport. Those who had served long years in India were familiar with its geography and wildlife and became expert hunters because of their martial skills and because shooting was

*Prince of Wales (later King George V) and the Maharaja of Gwalior with their bag, 1905.*

one of the few indulgences available in the outback. As writers, they wrote the majority of tiger hunting books. These were the most comprehensive, incisive, and thrilling tiger tales because they drew from a lifetime of experiences that spanned the subcontinent.

Planters were another group of expert shikaris. They were ambitious men who often made fortunes in timber, coffee, indigo, and especially tea in the tropical forests of southern India or in the northeast. These men were socially ostracized from Anglo-Indian society because they were renegades who lived in the wilderness. Many spent their spare time shooting tigers, elephants, and other game. They were pioneers who wrote of frontier life and their frequent and often aggressive encounters with wild animals as plantations were carved out of the jungle.

Pursuing "problem tigers" became a specialty for certain hunters. Some were practical men who shot rogues that threatened villages and interrupted governmental economic development plans. For others hunting man-eaters was the ultimate sport, as those were the wariest and craftiest of cats. Tracking them could take months, during which time the roles of hunter and hunted frequently reversed. Some man-eaters took hundreds of lives before they were killed; others were never caught.

Hunters shot tigers for a variety of reasons. Some enjoyed the risk and physical exertion, others the camp life and camaraderie. Many simply relished killing for blood lust and status. Others came to India as adventurers and naturalists to escape the urbanization and industrialization that was engulfing Europe. But for all of them, tracking tigers and matching wits with the great beast was the pinnacle of the primordial relationship between hunter and hunted. And India, like Africa, was one of the last places where a man could still find that experience.

The end of the British Raj in 1947 brought an end to tiger hunting. The new class of bureaucrats who ruled India flaunted the old hunting laws and customs. As a result, tiger hunting became uncontrolled and excessive. Rapid population growth also led to widespread habitat destruction, putting the tiger in even greater jeopardy. The tiger population dropped from 30,000 on the eve of World War II to fewer than 2,000 by 1970.

Many hunters fought to protect the cat, which eventually led to the creation of Project Tiger in 1973, an extremely successful wildlife conservation endeavor. The writings of this last generation of tiger hunters were filled with nostalgia and lament, for they had witnessed the end of a relationship between tigers and men that had existed for millennia.

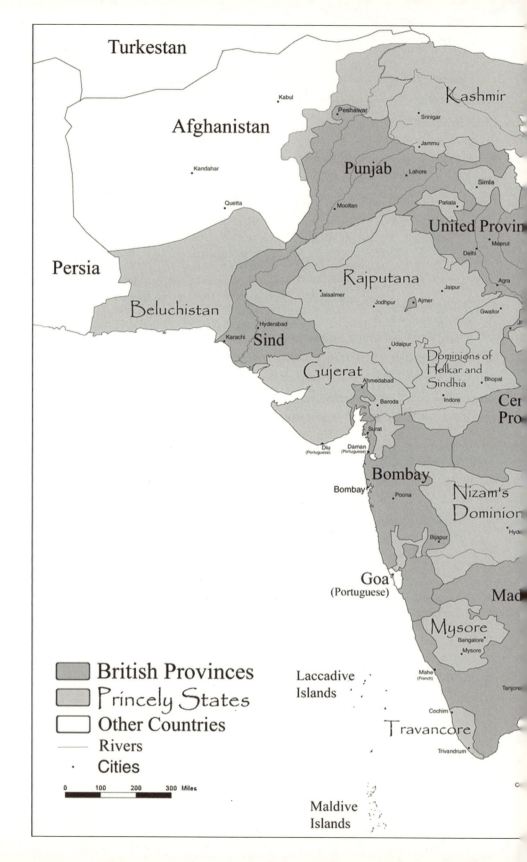

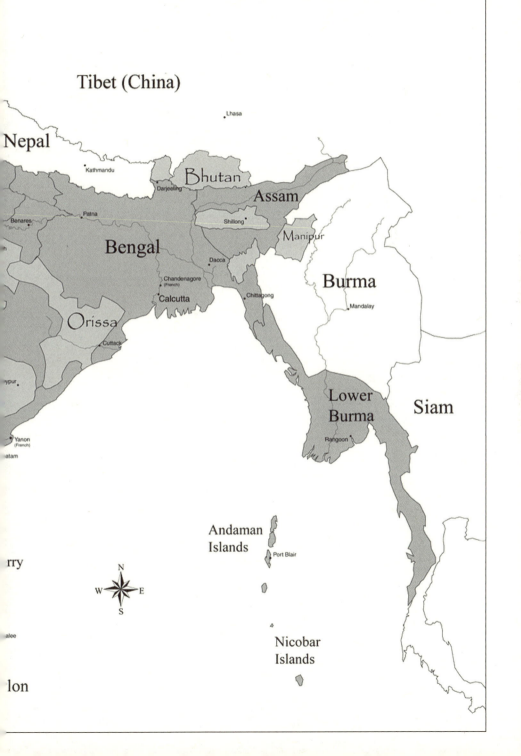

## Chapter One

# WILLIAM BLANE
### Cynegetica; or Essays on Sporting
### (1788)

William Blane was the author of Cynegetica, *the first book on Indian big-game hunting written in English. His account was based on his visit with Asoph ul Doulah, who was the nabob (governor) of Oudh, a province of the Mogul empire located in northern India.*

*Blane's account is brief but significant because it describes the Mogul hunt and a way of life that soon disappeared with the expansion of British power in the nineteenth century. The Mogul hunting expedition was more than just a sporting event. It was a massive social and cultural phenomenon in which tens of thousands of servants, merchants, soldiers, and nobles, along with almost as many animals, moved into the forests and set up camp for months. The normal hunting season was from December until March. The Mogul hunt also had military and political purposes—to train soldiers and survey the periphery of the empire.*

*This piece is an entire chapter from* Cynegetica or Essays on Sporting *published in 1788. It is the odd chapter in a work dedicated exclusively to hare hunting in Europe. Blane describes the many social and cultural aspects of hunting expeditions that took place in the Terai of the Himalayan foothills. He recounts adventures during the pursuit of tiger, elephant, buffalo, and rhinoceros, all of which were abundant at the time.*

### Asoph ul Doulah's Hunting Excursions

The vizier always gets out upon his annual hunting party as soon as the cold season is well set in—that is, about the beginning of December—and he stays out till the heat, about the beginning of March, forces him back again. During this time he generally makes a circuit of from four to six hundred miles, always bending his course toward the skirts of the northern mountains where the country, being wild and uncultivated, is the most proper for game.

When he marches, he takes with him not only his household and zenana but also all his court, and a great part of the inhabitants of his capital. Besides the immediate attendants about his person, in the various capacities of *rhidmitgars* [footmen], *frashes* [servants who pitch tents], *chobdars* [door/tent attendants], *harcaras* [messengers], *mewatics* [soldiers], etc., which may amount to about two thousand, he is attended in camp by five or six hundred horses, and several battalions of regular sepoys with their field pieces.

He takes with him about four or five hundred elephants; of these some are broken in for riding, some are used for fighting, some carry baggage, and the rest are reserved for clearing the jungles and forests of game. Of the first kind there are always twenty or thirty caparisoned with howdahs, and *amarys* [covered howdahs] attend close behind the one he rides upon himself so that he may change occasionally to any of them he likes, or he sometimes permits some of his attendants to ride upon them. He has with him about five or six hundred sumpter horses, a great many of which are always led ready saddled near him. Many of them are beautiful Persian horses, and some of them are of the Arabian breed, but he seldom rides any of them.

Of wheeled carriages there are a great many of the country fashion drawn by bullocks, principally for the accommodation of the women; besides which, he has with him a couple of English chaises, a buggy or two, and sometimes a chariot, but all of these, like the horses, are merely for show and never used. Indeed, he seldom uses any other conveyance but an elephant, or sometimes, when fatigued or indisposed, a palanquin, of which several attend him.

The arms he carries with him are a vast number of matchlocks (a great many English pieces of various kinds); pistols (of which he is very fond) in great number, perhaps forty or fifty pairs; bows and arrows; as well as swords, sabers, and daggers innumerable. One or more of all these different kinds of arms he generally has upon the elephant with him, and a great many more are carried in readiness by his attendants.

The animals he carries for sport are dogs, principally greyhounds, of which he has about three hundred; hawks of various kinds, at least two hundred; a few trained leopards, called cheetahs, for catching deer; and to this list I may add a great many marksmen whose profession is to shoot deer, and fowlers who provide game, for there are none of the natives of India who have any idea of shooting game with small shot, or of hunting with slow hounds. He is also furnished with nets of various kinds, some for quail and others very large for fishing, which are carried along with him upon elephants. He is

*A tiger hunt with Asoph ul Doulah.*

attended by fishermen so as to be always ready to be thrown into any river or lake he may meet on the march.

Besides this, he carries with him every article of luxury or pleasure; even ice is transported along with him to cool his water and make ices, and a great many carts are loaded with Ganges water, which is esteemed the best and lightest in India, for his drink. The fruits of the season and fresh vegetables are sent to him daily from his gardens to whatever distance he may go by bearers stationed upon the road at the distance of every ten miles, who in this manner convey whatever is sent to them at the rate of four miles an hour, night and day.

Besides the fighting elephants, which I have mentioned, he has with him fighting antelopes, fighting buffaloes, and fighting rams in great numbers. And lastly, of the feathered kind (besides hawks), he carries with him several hundred pigeons, some fighting cocks, and an endless variety of nightingales, parrots, mynahs, etc., all of which are carried along with his tents.

What I have hitherto enumerated are the appendages of the nabob personally. Besides this, there is a large public bazaar, or, in other words, a moving town attends his camp, consisting of shopkeepers and artificers of all kinds, money-changers, dancing women, etc., so that, upon the most moderate calculation, the number of souls in his camp cannot be reckoned at fewer than twenty thousand.

There are generally about twenty or thirty of the gentlemen of his court who attend him on his hunting parties and are the companions of his sports and pleasures. They are principally his own relations in different degrees of consanguinity. Those who are not related to him are of the old, respectable families of Hindostan, who either have *jaghirs* [villages] or are otherwise supported by the nabob. All of these are obliged to keep a small establishment of elephants—besides horses, a palanquin, etc.—for the purpose of attending the nabob.

The nabob and all the gentlemen of his camp are provided with double sets of tents and camp equipage, which are always sent on the day before to the place whither he intends going, which is generally about eight or ten miles in whatever direction he expects most game so that by the time he has finished his sport in the morning, he finds the whole camp ready pitched for his reception.

His Highness always rises before daybreak, and after using the hot bath, he eats an English breakfast of tea and toast, which is generally over by the time the day is well broke. He then mounts his elephant, attended by all his household and swary [soiree, social gathering], and is preceded by musicians on horseback, singing and playing on musical instruments. He proceeds forward and is presently joined, from the different quarters of the camp, by the gentlemen of his court, who, having paid their respects, fall in upon their elephants on each side of or behind the nabob's so as to form a regular moving court, or durbar. In this manner they march on, conversing together and looking out for game.

A great many dogs are led before the entourage and are constantly picking up hares, foxes, jackals, and sometimes deer. The hawks are also carried immediately before the elephants, and are let fly at whatever game is sprung for them, which generally consists of partridges in great numbers and varieties, quails, bustards, and different kinds of herons, which last give excellent sport with the falcons or sharp-winged hawks. The nabob takes great pains in ranging the elephants in a regular line, which is very extensive, and by proceeding in this manner no game can escape. The horses are generally at a little distance upon the wings, but small parties of three or four horsemen are placed at intervals, or before the elephants, in order to ride after the hawks and assist the dogs when loosed at deer. Very often the horsemen run down what we call the hog-deer, without any dogs. Wild boars are sometimes started and are either shot or run down by the dogs and horsemen.

When intelligence is brought of a tyger, it is matter of great joy, as that is considered as the principal sport, and all the rest only occasional to fill up the time. Preparations are instantly made for pursing him, which is done by assembling all the elephants with as many people as can conveniently go upon their backs and leaving all the rest, whether on foot or on horseback, behind. The elephants are then formed into a line and proceed forward regularly, the nabob and all his attendants having their firearms in readiness. The cover in which the tyger is most frequently found is long grass, or reeds so high as often to reach above the elephants, and it is very difficult to find him in such a place as he either endeavours to steal off or lies so close that he cannot be roused till the elephants are almost upon him. He then roars and skulks away, but is shot at as soon as he can be seen. It is generally contrived, in compliment to the nabob, that he shall have the first shot at him. If the tyger is not disabled, he continues skulking away, the line of elephants following him, and the nabob and others shooting at him as often as he can be seen till he falls. Sometimes, when he can be traced to a particular spot where he crouches, the elephants are formed so as to encircle him, and in that case, when he is roused, he generally attacks the elephant that is nearest to him by springing upon him with a dreadful roar and biting at or tearing him with his claws. But in that case, from his being obliged to show himself, he is soon dispatched by the number of shots aimed at him. The greatest difficulty is to rouse him and get a fair view of him.

The elephants all this time are dreadfully frightened, shrieking and roaring in a manner particularly expressive of their fear. This they begin as soon as they smell him or hear him growl, and they generally endeavour to turn back from the place where the tyger is. Some of them, however, but very few, are bold enough to be driven up to attack him, which they do by curling the trunk close up under the mouth and then charging the tyger with their tusks. Or they endeavour to press him to death by falling on him with their knees, or treading him under their feet. If one tyger is killed, it is considered as a good day's sport, but sometimes two or three or even more are killed in one day, if they meet with a female and her cubs.

The nabob then proceeds toward his tents upon the new ground so that every day is both a marching day and a day of sport, or sometimes he halts for a day or two upon a place that he likes, but not often. When he gets to his tents, which is generally about eleven or twelve o'clock, he dines, and goes to sleep for an hour or two. In the afternoon he mounts his elephant again and takes a circuit about the skirts of the camp with the dogs and hawks, or sometimes he amuses himself with an elephant fight, with shooting at a mark, or such-like amusements. This course he repeats every day infallibly during the whole of the party.

The other principal objects of the nabob's sport are wild elephants, buffaloes, and rhinoceros. I was present two years ago at the chase of a wild elephant of prodigious size and strength. The plan first followed was to endeavour to take him alive by the assistance of the tame elephants, which tried to surround him, whilst he was kept at bay by fireworks, such as crackers, porte-fires, etc. But he was always away from them, notwithstanding the drivers upon some of the tame elephants got so near as to throw nooses of very strong rope over his head and endeavoured to detain him by fastening them round trees. But he snapped them like packthread and held on his way toward the forest.

The nabob then ordered some of the strongest and most furious of his fighting elephants to be brought up to him. As soon as one of them came near him, he turned and charged with dreadful fury—so much so, that in the struggle with one of them he broke one of his tusks by the middle, and the broken piece (which was upward of two inches in diameter of solid ivory) flew up into the air several yards above their heads. Having repelled the attacks of the fighting elephants, he pursued his way with a slow and sullen pace toward his cover.

The nabob, then seeing no possibility of taking him alive, gave orders to kill him. An incessant fire from matchlocks was immediately commenced upon him from all quarters, but with little effect, for he twice turned round and charged the party. In one of these charges he struck obliquely upon the elephant that Prince Shah Zedah, son of the Mogul emperor Shah Alam, rode and threw him onto his side, fortunately passing on without offering further injury to him. The prince, by laying hold of the howdah, kept himself in his seat, but the servant he had behind, and everything he had with him on the howdah, were thrown off to a great distance. At last our grisly enemy was overpowered by the number of bullets showered upon him from all sides and he fell dead, after having received, as was computed, upward of one thousand balls in his body. He had carried us a chase of eight or ten miles after him, and afforded us sport from morning till twelve o'clock.

The following year the nabob took fifteen wild elephants at once. They had wandered up a narrow valley in the mountains that was terminated by inaccessible precipices, and when they had got to the end of it, the country people threw up a strong rampart of trees, stones, earth, etc., across the valley behind them, confining them in it. After having been much reduced by hunger, they were all taken alive, by letting the tame elephants amongst them.

The hunting of the wild buffalo is also performed by shooting from elephants, but a buffalo runs so fast that it is very difficult to get up with him, and as there are no dogs who will attack him, horsemen are sent after him to endeavour to stop or turn him. But they dare not venture near, for he runs at them and can easily toss a horse with his horns if one comes within reach. But when he can by any means be retarded, so as to let the elephants come up, he is soon dispatched by a matchlock. Some of the buffaloes are of prodigious size and strength and have an uncommonly wild and furious look, and they are so formidable in the jungles that it is said even the largest royal tyger never ventures to attack them.

I have never seen a rhinoceros hunted, although there are many of them on the route the nabob goes, but they generally keep to the thick forests, where it is impossible to follow them. When they can be got at, they are pursued upon elephants and shot, but it is both more difficult and dangerous than any other sport, for even the elephant is not safe against him. If he charges an elephant and rips him with his horn, he generally kills him on the spot, and except his eyes or temples and a small part of his breast before the shoulder, he is invulnerable to the largest musket ball in every part of his body.

When the prince is with the nabob upon the party, the etiquette observed in regard to him is this: As soon as the nabob is mounted, he goes in front of the prince's tent and there waits till the prince is ready. When his Royal Highness comes out of his tent, the vizier pays his obeisance by making his elephant kneel down, and then he makes three salaams to him. The prince is then mounted upon his elephant, which is made to advance about eight or ten paces in front of the nabob and the rest of the party, and in that station he marches on. When they arrive at the new camp, the nabob attends him to the door of his tent and then takes his leave, and this form he repeats regularly twice every day.

As you may be curious to know how I dispose of myself in the party, I shall briefly mention it. I generally have two or three elephant of my own well caparisoned and a double set of tents, one of which is always sent on with the nabob's so that I am entirely independent in respect to my equipage. And as both the Persian and Indostan languages are familiar to me, I mix a good deal in conversation with the nabob and the gentlemen about him, and conform myself as much as possible to their manners and customs. Although I am desirous of being considered entirely on an equal footing with the native gentlemen about the court, yet the vizier generally shows me particular marks of attention by making me ride close to him.

## Chapter Two

# Thomas Williamson
### Oriental Field Sports
### (1807)

Oriental Field Sports *was an instant sensation when it was published in 1807 as it was the first book to introduce Indian big-game hunting to England's general public. The thrilling tales of the chase mixed with lavish illustrations created images of India that tantalize the Western imagination even today.*

*Captain Williamson's book was part of a broader public exposure to Indian culture that began in earnest in 1795 when the artists Thomas and William Daniell first exhibited their paintings after years of travel on the subcontinent. Like the Daniells, Williamson's artist, Samuel Howett, created a vivid and romantic style—the "picturesque"—to convey life in the East. As such,* Oriental Field Sports *was as much an early guide to hunting and natural history as a work of art. Even today it remains a favorite of bibliophiles and is one of the rarest and most expensive books on Indian big-game hunting.*

*All the book's stories are set in eastern India, close to Calcutta, which was the capital of British India prior to the 1857 mutiny, after which time it shifted to New Delhi. This chapter and the corresponding pictures focus on hunting tigers with elephant, which was the preferred method in the tall grasses and dense jungles of eastern India.*

### Driving a Tiger out of the Jungle

There are few gentlemen in India who are partial to the ordinary field sports who do not eagerly embrace such opportunities as an offer of attacking tigers. So highly is this arduous amusement relished that many do not consider hog-hunting, which certainly is a very manly and somewhat dangerous species of the chase, as being worthy of notice. Hog-hunting has, however, a variety of inducements, and the great facility with which it may be practiced is one of the most important. Tiger hunting cannot be adopted in the same desultory manner, for without a competent number of well-trained and sizable elephants, nothing could possibly be effected. Nay, even then so material a point is established, much must not be expected if the party be not sufficiently numerous, and that those who compose it be not of an active turn, and, in some measure, accustomed to the sport. In this particular both diversions agree; in fact, throughout life, whatever be the pursuit, some previous understanding both of the matter engaged in as well as those with whom we are united will be found, not only to give facility but also to render success more certain.

It would be utterly impossible to define any limit as to the number, either of sportsmen or of elephants, necessary to kill a tiger. On the one hand, many instances might be adduced where great bodies of hunters with every requisite at command have failed, while at the same time the most surprising feats of individuals, but very feebly provided, might be quoted. Locality must ever decide as to the numbers required, the measures to be adopted, and the probability of a favourable result. In an open country where a tiger's course and conduct are easily watched and where an aim can be taken with tolerable precision, a single person on a good-size elephant and tolerably free in gait and disposition may often succeed; in a closer jungle, however, the tiger might bid defiance to thousands however well equipped.

Nothing is more common, in many parts of the country, than for a party intending an excursion with the view to hunt hogs only to come by surprise on a tiger. When this happens, provided the situation be considered at all favourable, every exertion is made for his destruction. The elephants are accoutred, and if there be camels at hand, they are added to the line since they are, in general, nearly as lofty as elephants and capable of giving great aid in observing the tiger's track.

Camels are also well calculated—and indeed in the armies of the native powers are used—for carrying rockets, ammunition, etc. As to any immediate utility with respect to tiger hunting, it is out of the question, for camels are incapable of defending themselves. They have, perhaps, the roughest paces of any domestic animal and, therefore, are ill calculated for enterprises like tiger hunting where mobility is indispensable.

Horses cannot be brought to follow the track of a tiger: They have such a nice sense of smelling and the tiger's scent is so very strong that, in lieu of

*The tiger is sighted.*

being useful, they would in all probability become restive, rear, and injure their riders as well as themselves, thereby creating confusion where order is absolutely necessary.

Tigers when satiated become perfectly lethargic and ill brook any disturbance. At this time they are easily found and, indeed, owing to the dullness that pervades them for the while, are often surprised in their nap. They are generally very unwilling to quit the spot that they have selected for their repose, nor are they much disposed to retire far from the remains of their spoils. If the animal be found in a grass jungle, too much caution cannot be used on account of his disposition to lie concealed and spring at whatever may approach.

On this account, as soon as the carcass of the beast he has killed may be found, the largest and best trained elephants should search the adjoining cover in which the tiger will assuredly be discovered. His immediate presence is generally made known by the elephants, which wind him from some distance. Commencing a peculiar kind of trumpeting and snorting, they become agitated and impart their feelings even to those that are not so near as to scent the concealed enemy. If the tiger rise and endeavour to sneak away, the whole of the cover becomes strongly impregnated with his rank smell. The elephants, uncertain how distant he may be, evince the most decided apprehension of a clandestine attack and often become perfectly ungovernable.

Some cannot be restrained from flight. Their trunks, as is usual with them whenever in a state of alarm, are thrown up into the air, and every pace seems to imply distrust. Their eyes display the utmost vivacity and serve as a faithful index to their inward sensations. Such is the case with at least nineteen in twenty: The few that may be excepted from such a general rule are highly valuable, and, if of adequate stature and free from blemish, never fail to bring good prices whenever offered for sale.

The stature of an elephant is of considerable moment in tiger hunting: both because a small one cannot make its way so well through the cover as a large one, and that the latter raises the rider to a good height, so as to give a more commanding view of the chase. Besides, it has happened that persons mounted on small elephants have at times had their legs in jeopardy because, in their dangling state, they are sufficiently low to be reached, without much exertion, by a moderate-size tiger. Suffice it for the present to observe that, owing to the many attempts I have known made by tigers to spring, or climb up, in every direction, I should ever make it a rule to select the largest male elephant offered to my choice. Further, I should take care not to accept one with a timid disposition, for he might turn as soon as he saw or smelled the game, and if he were to run at his fullest speed over broken ground, that might prove more dangerous than hunting on the smallest elephant in the field.

As a careful horseman never mounts his steed without examining his bridle, reins, etc., so should a person proceeding to hunt tigers pay due attention to the pads of the elephant that is to bear him. This precaution will, at the least save much inconvenience and delay, and may at times prove of consequence. It certainly is very unpleasant to ride an animal with the seat perpetually shifting and leaning to one side. In a howdah the inconvenience is yet more distressing and, if neglected for any distance, rapidly increases into danger. The weight of the machine and the elevation of its contents cause such a relaxation of the ropes by which the howdah is fastened to the back of the elephant as to produce a very disagreeable swinging and, if not rectified in time, may allow the whole to be upset by the least want of balance, or by the elephant's making a false step.

It may generally be taken as a rule that unless in cases of necessity an elephant should not be worked within an hour after being fed. A neglect of this precaution will be found to injure his health, and the ropes will to a certainty gradually become loose and produce the unpleasant defect above described. This will compel the parties to quit their seats while the cords are braced up afresh, which is a process not very agreeable in a hot climate. Moreover, some elephants are unwillingly to submit to this and, being perhaps of a morose, sulky disposition, oppose their mahouts on every occasion.

Bunds are jungles composed of underwood, perhaps mixed with grass, and have some large trees interspersed, and it is there that the action of the hunt takes place. There about a million little covered, quite concealed openings are found, which are inaccessible to such as are mounted on elephants; consequently, it is sometimes by no means easy to dislodge the game that sneaks through these bunds. In this species of hunting, footmen cannot, without extreme danger, be employed. In such situations nets are often used; though it is extremely difficult to drive a tiger into a toil, and not less dangerous to approach him when in one, unless he be so completely enveloped as to deprive him of all power to resist. Even when he may appear to be entangled beyond the possibility of self-extrication, it is not prudent to venture too close, for the nets are generally somewhat decayed, and have at times been known to give way.

In a grass jungle a net may be concealed, but in a bund it is difficult to find a right line that is a sufficient distance yet open enough to answer the purpose without having large gaps that allow the net to be seen. The tiger will never of himself enter the toil, but on seeing it will, in all probability, either crouch or steal back and take some incautious hunter by surprise. Whenever this retrograde movement occurs, the whole party must withdraw from the jungle and commence their labours anew. This must be done without loss of time so as to prevent the tiger from going so far back as to augment both the trouble and the uncertainty of again impelling him toward the nets.

The line of elephants must be formed anew, and double exertion must be used, for the tiger having once seen the net will not readily proceed toward it a second time. The chorus of discordant acclamation must increase as the line approaches the critical period of coercion when every possible means must be collected to force the tiger forward. However difficult this point may be to effect, it is nevertheless practicable, even though perhaps nearly the whole day may be spent in repeated disappointments. Hogs and deer are frequently taken on such occasions, but wolves, jackals, and bears are at least

*Pursuing the tiger across the river.*

as cautious as tigers; the former generally leap over, and the latter exhibit an obstinate determination not to approach something that instinct teaches them to mistrust.

Sometimes the whole reliance must be placed on fireworks, at which tigers, and indeed animals of every description, are greatly alarmed. The flower-pot and the *hurtaulbauzzee*, so called from its being made chiefly of orpiment [arsenic sulfate], are among the most powerful: the former causing a most brilliant and extensive display and the latter, by its hissing and incessant explosions similar to a volcano, producing great consternation. A small kind of *bhaun*, or rocket, is also used, and these are directed to fall between the tiger and the line of hunters. Their zigzag motion bewilders the already astonished tiger, but, after repeated efforts to avoid the fatal snare, at last in a moment of consternation and despair, the tiger will rush forward, conscious of the danger, but with a violent resolution to bear down all before him.

The *bhauns*, however, are not very safe engines, being apt to turn back toward those who use them. They are much employed among the native powers, who keep a large establishment of men and camels exclusively for this purpose. The contrivance is very simple, being nothing more than a hollow cylinder of iron of about ten inches or a foot long and from two to three inches in diameter. It is closed at the fore-end, and the other has only a small aperture left for the purpose of filling with a composition similar to what is used for making serpents, etc. These cylinders are tied very strongly to latties, or wild bamboo staves, of about six or seven feet long. They are firmly fixed parallel to the thickest end of the lattie, and when the fuse at the vent is lighted and a direction is given by the operator, as soon as the fire gains sufficient force, a slight cast of the hand commences its motion, and the dangerous missile, urged by its increasing powers, proceeds in the most furious manner to its destination! The panic it occasions among cavalry is wonderful! It would doubtless be the most formidable of all destructive inventions if its course and distance could be brought under tolerable regulation. When it does light where intended, its effect is inconceivable; all fly from the hissing, winding visitor, receiving perhaps some smart strokes from the lattie that gives direction to the tube, often causing it to make the most sudden and unexpected traverse. So delicate, indeed, is the management of this tremendous weapon, that, without great precaution, those who discharge them are not safe. It requires much practice not only to give them due elevation, whereby their distance is proportioned, but to ensure that they shall not, in the very act of discharging, receive any improper bias, which would infallibly produce mischief among their own party.

With respect to the number of elephants proper to be employed in driving tigers out of covers, that must, as in bog hunting, depend entirely on the nature of the cover, and especially on its breadth. It is evident that a narrow bund will require fewer elephants to form a sufficient line than a broad one. Whatever may be the expanse of cover to be searched, care should be taken that the line be sufficiently close and compact; else a party "may toil all day and catch no tigers." In bunds the elephants should not be more than ten yards asunder on any account, though in grass jungles not exceeding three or four feet in height, double that distance may be safely allowed as the elephant will soon wind the tiger, which in such a situation cannot easily escape. Although a number of elephants is certainly very desirable, yet as soon as the tiger is roused, it is best to collect all not immediately of service, that is to say, rejecting such as are not furnished with firearms, causing them to remain compact and out of the way of the hunters, whose shot might else do mischief among the party.

Ninety-nine in a hundred tigers are first discovered by elephants, and announced by their significant motions and noises. Whenever elephants display

*The tiger is surrounded.*

their usual tokens of uneasiness, the cover should be closely watched, and the slightest rustling of the grass, or bushes, be marked with the most scrupulous attention. If the motion of an animal through the grass be perceived, the nearest elephant should be halted and its left shoulder should be pointed toward the moving object. This is the most favourable position for taking a good aim, and the hunter should fire without hesitation, observing to proportion his level, as far within the space between himself and the tops of the yielding grass, as the height of the cover may dictate. By this precaution, which is equally necessary when shooting fish that are in any degree beneath the surface of the water, the ball will, in general, take effect. If the tiger is wounded, he will in all probability spring up with a hideous roar and, bounding through the cover, make toward the nearest elephant, his mouth open, his tail erect, or lashing his sides, and his whole fur erectly bristled!

When a tiger, as often happens, endeavours to steal away, in lieu of augmenting his apparent bulk by erecting his fur, he seems to draw in his breath, and to do everything in his power to appear as diminutive as possible; sneaking in the most subtile manner, and keeping as low to the ground as possible. This is often done with such success, as to enable the artful animal to effect an escape among ravines, where it would be the height of madness to attempt a pursuit. And such is the deception with respect to the size of a tiger, thus intent on evading his pursuers, that, if he be brought to bay, many of the party, and especially those of least experience, can scarcely believe that the fierce distended brute is the same that but awhile before appeared to be little more than a half-grown cub.

Nothing can appear more truly contemptible than a tiger when skulking before a line of elephants; such eagerness to hide behind every bush; such a cringing, sly, jealous, and cowardly demeanour; one really cannot, without some difficulty, believe him to possess such fire, and energy, as he displays when driven to extremities! A few, however, die, as it were, quite resigned; and absolutely disgust the hunters by a passive, tame, and imbecile demeanour, not only contrary to the nature of the animal in general, but rendering the chase quite insipid and uninteresting.

The native gentlemen are more disposed to hunt tigers than to ride after hogs. The former sport is more conformable to their pageantry, and to that *otium cum dignitate* [leisure with dignity] so particularly characteristic of Asiatics in general. However, it is rarely that the great man does much himself, the tigers being ordinarily roused, pursued, and killed by a few dashers, who fail not to relinquish, in the presence of their chief and of his host of followers, all claim to commendation; resigning to the all-powerful prowess of the proud chief the entire merit of the achievement; and, if peradventure his highness should have discharged his piece during the chase, appropriating the fatal wound to his unerring aim! Many of the mahouts, or elephant drivers, are wonderfully keen, and handle a spear with great dexterity. When confident in regard to their respective elephants, and of the spirit and skill of the gentlemen who compose the party, they display much energy and courage.

Mahouts are for the most part Mussulmans, and, in general, very dissipated characters. They drink freely and smoke *ganja* [cannabis], which is a stupefying herb, to great excess. They drink also of the *subjy*, which is a beverage made from the same plant, and, like the *ganja*, when prepared for smoking, generally renders those who partake of it in any quantity completely unfit for business. Those who once take to drinking or smoking the *ganja* may thenceforth be considered incorrigible debauchees.

As in all situations of life there are various degrees of promotion, so do the coolies, who commence as grass-cutters to the elephants, aspire to being ultimately mahouts themselves. Sometimes they are elevated by accident, but generally from some necessity, or from long service. As to merit, but few would rise who should rely on so slender a claim! After having a competent knowledge of the profession, which does not require any very tedious servitude, nor arduous application, they often leave their situations and, repairing to some distant camp, produce, as is very common in India, forged certificates of faithful service in the employ of some gentleman whom they apprehend to be in another quarter; when the strange mutilation of European names, so general among the natives, added to other circumstances, occasions at times very unexpected discoveries. As to the certificate, a few annas or a rupee will ordinarily suffice to bribe some mean European, a Portuguese writer, or some such person, to pen a famous good character.

A man, who was once a candidate for employment in my own service, very deliberately put into my hands a certificate stating that he had been in my employ for many years, and that he was quite a paragon in his way! The facility with which such errors may occur will be easily understood, when it is known that Colonel Ironside, who served thirty years in India, was invariably called Colonel Rung! This is only one of thousands equally

*The finale.*

miscalled. Nor can the natives remedy so strange a system of error, which must appear the more extraordinary since they do not want for ear, and in their own language pronounce very correctly!

To me, the avocation of mahout appears intolerable; and can, in my idea, be surpassed only by that of *surwan*, or camel keeper: The motion of an elephant, and particularly when seated on his neck, is extremely unpleasant, and must be injurious to health. That of the camel is tenfold worse, and no doubt tends much to that early senescence so remarkable in that profession. Indeed, I do not consider longevity to be at all the characteristic of India: Whether it proceed from the excessive heats, or from indolence of the superior classes, and from the drudgery of the lower orders, might be difficult to determine; but it is an undoubted fact that a man of sixty is very rarely to be found. Here and there, among the venerable Hindoos, we do occasionally meet with years in proportion to the symptoms of age; but those are very rare cases. Thousands who appear old are found, on examination, to be far less advanced in life than one, not aware of the truth, would imagine. The women, in particular, do not number many years; which may be attributed to their very early marriages, and it being by no means uncommon for a wife just entering her teens to have a child at the breast. It is singular that throughout India a girl's reputation would suffer were she to arrive at puberty in a state of celibacy!

I was never able to obtain any satisfactory information as to the origin or cause for so extraordinary a circumstance. All I could ever extract from the many to whom I applied for information was that some particular stigma must be with a family where the daughters were not all married at a proper age; namely, when from six to ten years old. The reader is to observe that, properly speaking, children are only betrothed at such times, and that the final ceremonies do not, in general, take place until some years after, when the bridegroom conducts his fair acquisition to his own residence.

## Chapter Three

# Daniel Johnson
### Sketches of Indian Field Sports
### (1822)

Doctor Daniel Johnson spent many decades in India as a surgeon for the East India Company. He was a contemporary of William Blane and Thomas Williamson, having served in India from the late 1800s to 1809, when he retired and returned to England.

When Johnson wrote Sketches of Indian Field Sports in 1822, he had two goals in mind. First was to provide an inexpensive book of English life in India for the general public back home, and second was to describe India's flora, fauna, and native life. He was especially interested in hunting and was the first Englishman to give detailed descriptions of native methods, a topic that few Europeans knew about or were interested in at this time. He provides a long chapter on the tiger and all the other big-game animals. He also dedicates separate chapters to less orthodox topics, such as catching poisonous snakes and dealing with rabid dogs, both common scourges across the land.

This excerpt is part of a chapter on native tiger hunting. Johnson describes how tigers are caught in nets and how they are killed with poisoned arrows. The author makes numerous critical references to Williamson's observations in this and other chapters in the book. Johnson's accounts are the more reliable of the two, as he spent more time in India and was keenly interested in native customs.

### TIGERS

Tigers are caught in nets. They are likewise caught in traps, but rarely, since they are extremely wary. Shecarries [shikaris] kill them with poisoned arrows. They also shoot them from platforms and pits. The villagers do the same, and they are killed by opulent natives from the backs of elephants.

One kind of trap for catching them is made of wood, and not unlike a common rat trap twelve or fourteen feet in length and about five in breadth. Both ends are open, and there are two doors, one at each end, that are elevated by levers on the top and kept suspended by an iron rod passing over the end of them; the rod communicates by a tongue with a board on the inside at the bottom of the box. A kid or goat is fastened in the middle of the box, and when the tiger seizes it and steps on the board and disengages the tongue from the iron rod, it flies up, allowing the doors to fall down through grooves so strongly made that he cannot force them open, so that he is caught.

The traps are sometimes made with only one door and an open grating at the other end. Another kind is made by driving stakes into the ground and fastening bamboos to the top of them, with doors similar to those already described, and which are let fall much in the same way. They are made considerably larger and are immovable; then they are covered all over with green bushes and so well hidden as not to be easily discovered from the natural cover. Whenever tigers are caught in these traps, they are driven into others prepared to receive them, in which they are carried off.

The following description of a tiger killed by poisoned arrows is taken from Captain Williamson's book, *Oriental Field Sports.*

> The construction of the apparatus for shooting tigers with arrow, whether poisoned or not, is extremely simple. There are various modes, but that in general use is as follows: The bow is fixed at the middle by two stakes, distant enough to allow the arrow to pass freely without touching, about eighteen inches or two feet from the ground, according to the size of the animal to be killed. The great nicety is, to fix the bow so that the arrow may fly quite horizontally, or, at least as much so as the principles of projectiles will admit. The cord should be parallel to the road frequented by the tiger. The string, drawn back so as to bend the bow sufficiently, is kept at its stretch by means of a stiff piece of stick, cut just the length so as to pinch a wedge against the inside of the bow. This wedge comes down six or eight inches, and at its lower end has a strong line fastened to it, which, being carried across the pathway for perhaps twenty or thirty yards, and strained moderately tight, is there fastened to a strong stake driven into the ground for the purpose, if no sufficient bush be at hand. This being done, the arrow is gently deposited in its proper place. To give it the requisite position before the cord was stretched

would be dangerous, for in setting the latter tight, the wedge might be drawn and the arrow be discharged at the operator.

The reader will, from this description, understand that the bow is firmly fixed and that the wedge introduced between the inside and the extended string of the bow operates as a lever, for when any power, such as the step of a tiger, presses against the string and causes it to depart from its right line, the wedge must necessarily give way to the force and turn the extending stick downward, thereby setting it at liberty and occasioning the bow to act instantaneously.

Such is the velocity of the arrow, and so more quickly does this simple contrivance act, that tigers are, for the most part, shot near the shoulder. But even were it less rapid, we might naturally conjecture that the tiger feeling his leg obstructed by the line would pause, thus affording ample time for the arrow to take effect before he could completely pass its range. Generally, tigers fall within two hundred yards from the fatal spot, they being most frequently struck through the lungs, and sometimes straight through the heart.

If the arrow be poisoned, as is most frequently the case, locality is no particular object. Without doubt, though, such wounds as would of themselves prove effectual, unaided by the venom, give the Shecarrie least trouble. The poison never fails to kill within an hour. It is not always necessary, but it is usual for one or more persons to be at hand, in the nearest trees, or in some secure situation, commanding a view of the spot to watch the event as well as to caution travelers who might inadvertently be proceeding toward the snare and be liable to its mischief.

The bows are, however, with little deviation, laid in places not much frequented, and mostly at a time when all the surrounding villagers, understanding that some tiger has committed ravages, expect the bows to be laid near his haunts, which, in consequence, are carefully avoided.

When bows are fixed in grass jungles, for which, indeed, they seem peculiarly calculated, the tops of the grass are cut away with a sickle so as to form a narrow vista for the passage of the arrow. The string that passes across the path, is, however, carefully concealed, and the grass is brought over to cover it from the tiger's observation. It is not that the force of the arrow would be sensibly diminished in so short a course but that some rather stiff reed or stick might touch and divert it from its proper direction. For the bow is ordinarily so very substantial as to require the whole force of a strong well-accustomed man to bend and draw it properly. The Pahariahs, or hill people, who may be said to be the only persons practicing this part of sporting, are, as already observed, quite a distinct race from the rest of the inhabitants of Bengal and, from every circumstance, may be with reason considered as the aborigines.

The arrows used for shooting tigers have generally but a moderate barb; I have seen some without any. The poison is for the most part a liquid, in which thread is steeped and wound round at the back of the barb. We are not acquainted with the real nature of the poisons in general use, but we are certain of their deleterious effects. Some pretend that only one kind is infallible; namely, litherage of lead, poured hot on some bruised herbs. This may probably be in part true. Litherage appears to be the basis of the poison, but, assuredly it is blended with some other stimulant, or active body, else it would fail of sufficient powers to operate so very suddenly as poisoned arrows often do.

The method of killing tigers with poisoned arrows is so curious and interesting that, wishing to give my reader as clear an idea of it as I possibly can, I have extracted the foregoing account from Capt. T. Williamson's book *Oriental Field Sports,* which, although detailed in a perspicuous manner, is in many points incorrect. That gentleman's book conveys an exceedingly good general idea of the different kinds of sporting, but it cannot be expected that he should be personally acquainted with them all. He must have gained a great part of his knowledge from the information of others, consequently not always to be depended on, which I think has been the case respecting tigers killed by poisoned arrows.

He observes that the mechanism of their bows is very simple. In this, I cannot agree with him, for, to me, it appears a complicated and ingenious apparatus: The different uses of the number of strings attached to a bow would puzzle anyone. Although I have seen them often set, I am certain that I could not set them myself. Of course, I cannot well describe how it is done, and I am confident that it would require a considerable time for any person to understand its principle sufficiently to be able to set them without instruction.

Captain Williamson says that the shecarries remain in trees, or somewhere near, so as to enable them to see the bow and string, where they can also apprise people going that way of their danger. This is not often, if ever, the

*The tiger in cover.*

case. The tigers are generally shot with poisoned arrows during the night, and in the midst of some thick cover, or in the dry beds of small rivers. They lay their bows and arrows before sunset and then go to some village where they sleep the night. Early the next morning, they visit the spot to examine their bows, and if an arrow has been discharged, they are certain that some animal, most probably a tiger, has been wounded and consequently is dead.

They then trace him by the blood, or, if they cannot follow it, they look about in all the thick covers nearby. Being well acquainted with their haunts, they know the direction he will most probably take, and seldom fail of finding him in a few hours. Some shecarries take a dog with them, which, being trained, hunts the animal out in a few minutes. They do not take the dog with them at the time of laying the bow for fear of disturbing the tiger or for fear of his smelling the scent of the dog, which might induce him to go another way, tigers having a great dislike of dogs. I do not think the shecarries would consider themselves safe in the trees, nor do I see of what use it would be. On the contrary, it might prevent so wary an animal as a tiger from approaching the line. Nor do I consider it probable that villagers would frequent such places in the night.

Whenever their bows are laid in the day or in the night across public roads, pathways, or any places where people often travel, they lay two other strings, passing them across the road or pathway, communicating with the tongue that lets the arrow fly, as the one already described by Captain Williamson. These strings cross the road or pathway, one on each side of the former, at six yards' distance, and are raised from the ground about four feet and a half, allowing a tiger to pass under them, but a man, or any large cattle, would run against them, and the arrow would be discharged before they arrived within its direction. The centre line is raised about two feet from the ground and strikes against the tiger's breast, so the arrow generally enters the shoulders. According to the account given to me by the shecarries, they seldom live half an hour after receiving the wound.

The captain observes that this method of shooting arrows is exclusively followed by Pahariahs, or hill people. In this, he has been misinformed. I believe the only people who practice it are a race of men who inhabit the district of Dinagepore, east of the river Ganges, and who travel all over Bengal wherever tigers are to be met with, for the sole purpose of killing them in order to obtain the reward, given by government, of ten rupees for every tiger.

Something more they receive as presents from the inhabitants, and gain a little by the sale of the teeth and claws, which are worn by the natives as charms.

I believe it frequently happens that they are paid twice by the government for killing the same animal, by producing the head of a tiger to a collector of one district and the skin to the collector of another. They travel about killing tigers nearly all the hot and cold seasons, and, if they are successful, they return to their families with a sufficiency to maintain them for a year or two. When it is nearly expended, they commence another excursion. They are extremely fond of spirits and of smoking intoxicating herbs, and they live a horrid life, independent of the danger they incur by searching for tigers and in setting their bows, in the act of which they are often taken away by the very animals whose destruction they are preparing.

With respect to the poison, Captain Williamson has also been misinformed. They use only one kind, which is extracted from the roots of a large tree, the bark of which is smooth like the ash, with very large leaves, and is known to the natives by the name of *boglear,* which signifies tiger's poison. An incision is made in the large roots, and a gummy liquid oozes out, which soon inspissates. They mix it with litherage and apply it whilst moist around the extremity of the iron of the arrow, at its insertion into the wood where a hollow is left for the purpose. It is then wound round with a few turns of fine silk to prevent it from cracking, and then exposed to the sun, by which, in a short time, it becomes as hard or harder than the wood. The iron point is very short, made with a small barb, and the arrow is discharged with sufficient force to bury the poison in the animal.

It is rather a strange circumstance that the same poisonous substance that they fix to their arrows is used by the native distillers to lute their stills. I had a young tree of the *boglear* transplanted into my garden, but I quitted that part of the country before the tree had attained a sufficient size to try any experiments with.

Whenever a bullock is killed by a tiger and the people of the village can find the dead carcass, they erect a machan in a tree, or on poles, or dig a pit in the ground near it. If there are no people in the village bold enough to remain in it to shoot at the tiger when he returns to feed at night, they send for some from the next village, or they employ shecarries. Neither have they occasion often to do, there being scarcely a village in Ramghur without people who are accustomed to shoot tigers in this way.

Whether shecarries or villagers undertake the business, they conduct it in the same manner. Villagers seldom remain alone, for a companion generally accompanies the marksman, and sometimes they are both marksmen. Shecarries, being more accustomed to it, are not afraid and often sit in machans alone with hopes of receiving the reward. They arm themselves with matchlock guns, swords, and spears. It is necessary that they should possess patience, a considerable degree of coolness, and be perfectly silent. The tiger, having glutted his appetite on the bullock not long before, cannot be very hungry; therefore, the least noise would prevent him from returning to it. If he should return, they generally wound him, and most times mortally, yet it seldom happens that he falls dead on the spot.

Captain Williamson says that when the shecarries have wounded a tiger, they frequently dismount from machans and follow him through the jungles. This I have never known to take place; however, it may have happened. Whenever it has occurred, I should think it must have been before dark, or after daylight in the morning. I cannot think that any man would be so foolhardy as to be searching about in the dark, through thick cover, for a wounded and enraged tiger, for even in moonlight the eye cannot penetrate the thickets on account of the shade. These animals are so tenacious of life that they often require many balls to enter them before they die. I knew an instance of a tiger's receiving eighteen balls before he fell. Like other animals of the feline species, their vision in the night is much more perfect than that of man, and if the shecarries or the villagers dismount from their machan and should be seen by the tiger, they would be attacked and could have no chance of escaping. I believe that they generally remain on the machan until daylight, when they descend, and if they have fired at a tiger during the night, they collect from the village or neighbouring villages a number of armed people. With these, and a few dogs, they search all the covers and if any blood is seen they follow it, and often succeed in finding the tiger wounded or dead. Although it may require more resolution to sit in the machan, the searching for the tiger is really the most dangerous part of the business; however, being a number together, they encourage one another, and are not apparently aware of their danger, though they are frequently carried off in the pursuit.

If a tiger kills and carries away a man or a woman and the body should be found not half devoured, none of the shecarries or villagers will ever sit up to kill the tiger when he returns to feed on the remainder. They are more afraid of the apparition of the dead person than of the living tiger. On several occasions I offered to sit up with them and to give them a present if we did not succeed in killing the tiger, but I could not prevail on any of them to accompany me.

I have often seen large tigers brought on poles by ten or twelve men from the most distant parts of the district to Chittrah in the Ramghur district, frequently a distance of 120 to 160 miles, to obtain the reward of ten rupees. Sometimes in the hot weather the carcasses, on their arrival, were so exceedingly putrid that it was almost impossible to approach them without being made ill by the stench. It may, in some measure, be conceived what joy their having killed them must have occasioned, to induce them to carry the animals such a distance, with such a horrid smell immediately under their noses when they might have obtained the reward just as well by carrying only the head or skin. No commander of an army ever felt more elated after a victory than these poor creatures experienced at the success of their prowess in destroying, perhaps, the pest of their neighbourhood. When any person praised them for their valour and dexterity, their countenances showed what pleasure they felt. It might also be plainly seen how gratifying it was to them to hear it said that it was a large tiger. On receiving the reward, they generally got gloriously drunk, and no doubt returned to their villages determined to risk their lives on a similar exploit the first opportunity that might offer.

Many of the natives of India believe in the doctrine of the metempsychosis, or transmigration of souls. As soon, therefore, as a tiger or leopard is killed, they light a fire and burn off the long whiskers that grow near the mouth; by doing this, they have a superstitious idea that they shall not be turned into tigers in another world.

A tailor at Chittrah went out with the gentlemen of the station and a number of natives to kill a tiger that had taken shelter in a plantation of sugarcanes near the town. He happened to be the fortunate man who shot the tiger, and in the excess of his joy, he vauntingly exclaimed that he would shoot a tiger at any time. Mr. Mathew Leslie, who was then the judge magistrate and collector of the district, promised to call on him for his assistance the first opportunity. Not long after, a tiger killed a bullock about a mile from the town, and the tailor was sent for, whose courage was considerably abated. However, he consented to sit up in a machan, which was soon erected, and he took with him a young man or rather a stout boy.

In the dead of the night, the tiger came to feed on the carcass. The gloominess of the place at such a time, with the fierce, horrid look of the tiger, had an instantaneous effect on poor Snip's nerves, and threw him into a fit. The noise it occasioned made the tiger carry off the bullock into thicker cover instead of feeding on it where it was. The boy, seeing the tiger go off with the bullock, tied his master to the machan, descended, and ran to the nearest village and gave the alarm that his master was dead. But when the people came to the machan, they found him perfectly recovered, protesting that he would never sit up again in the night to shoot a tiger—for he had seen the Devil. The truth of the whole story I will not vouch for, although I have often heard it related. It happened before I was stationed at Chittrah.

### Chapter Four

# Godfrey Mundy

#### Pen and Pencil Sketches, Being the Journal of a Tour of India (1832)

*Captain Mundy's generation of Englishmen were able to give even more detailed accounts of India than prior generations because of the rapid territorial consolidation of the British East India Company in the first decades of the nineteenth century. Europeans could now travel more freely, opening new areas for sport and adventure.*

*Mundy was among the first to write about the culture, scenery, and sport west of Bengal—along the Ganges River and the Himalayas. His travel opportunities were the result of his job as aide-de-camp to Lord Combermere, a famous British general and war hero. Combermere became a viscount after storming Bharatpur fort in western India in 1822, which previous British armies had failed to do. Mundy never discusses his military life, preferring to write about travel and hunting. What is amazing about Mundy's sporting tales is the number of tigers he encountered along the Ganges. The cats had already vanished from those locales just a generation later because of the spread of agriculture.*

*This story is part of a chapter from the first volume of* A Tour of India *(1832). Mundy's hunting party, which included Lord Combermere, is shooting tigers between the Ganges and Jumna Rivers, one of the most densely populated places in India today. The party had recently hunted antelope in Agra, where they used trained cheetahs, now long extinct in India.*

#### News of a Tiger

The 1st of March will always be a *dies notanda* [notable day] in my sporting annals, as the day on which I first witnessed the noble sport of tiger shooting. The Nimrods of our party had, ever since we entered upon the Dooab (a tract of country between the Ganges and the Jumna), been zealously employed in preparing firearms and casting bullets in anticipation of a chase in this favourite haunts of wild beasts.

Some of the more experienced sportsmen as soon as they saw the nature of the jungle in which we were encamped presaged that there were tigers in the neighbourhood. Accordingly, whilst we were at breakfast, the servant informed us that there were some *gongwalas* [villagers], waiting who had some *khubber* [news] about tigers to give us.

We all jumped up and rushed out, and found a group of five or six half-naked fellows, headed by a stout young man with a good sword by his side, who announced himself as a *jemadar*. As usual in like cases, all the natives began to speak at once, in a *veluti*-like tone and with vehement gesticulations. The young *jemadar*, however, soon silenced them with a *"Chup, teeree!"* and then gave us to understand that a young buffalo had been carried off the day before, about a mile from the spot, and that their herds had long suffered from the depredations of a party of three tigers, which had been often seen by the cowherds.

At 4:00 P.M. (so late an hour that few of us expected any sport), Lord Combermere and nine others of our party mounted elephants, and taking twenty pad elephants* to beat the covert and carry the guides and the game, proceeded toward the swamp pointed out as the lurking-place of the buffalo-devouring monsters.

Sancho, the *jemadar-hurkarah* [chief courier] of the quartermaster-general's department, insisted upon leading the cavalcade and mounted on his pony. This strange old character—who obtained his nom de guerre from the strong similitude he bears to his illustrious prototype, both in the short, round, bandy proportions of his person, and the quaint shrewdness of his remarks—served under Lord Lake in the Mahratta War, and has ever since distinguished himself as the most active and intelligent of the Intelligence Department. Almost the last act of Lord Combermere, before he left India, was to obtain for the faithful Sancho a snug Barataria [fictional island in Cervantes's *Don Quixote*] in the shape of a little *jaghite* [revenue collector], a possession which had long been the object of his ambition.

This noted individual now spurred on before our party, mounted on his piebald palfrey (or belfry, as his namesake would have called it), with his right arm bared and his scimitar flourishing in the air.

---

*Elephants with mattresses or pads placed on their backs.

*Starting off on a tiger hunt.*

The jungle was in no place very high, there being but few trees and a fine thick covert of grass and rushes. Everything was favourable for the sport. Since few of us expected to find a tiger, another man and myself dismounted from our elephants to get a shot at a florikan, a bird of the bustard tribe, which we killed. It afterward proved that there were two tigers within a hundred paces of the spot where we were walking.

We beat for half an hour steadily in line, and I was just beginning to yawn in despair when my elephant suddenly raised his trunk and trumpeted several times, which, my mahout informed me was a sure sign that there was a tiger somewhere "between the wind and our nobility." The formidable line of thirty elephants, therefore, brought up their left shoulders, and beat slowly on to windward.

We had gone about three hundred yards in this direction and had entered a swampy part of the jungle when suddenly the long wished for *tally-ho!* saluted our ears, and a shot from Captain M—confirmed the sporting Eureka! The tiger answered the shot with a loud roar, and boldly charged the line of elephants. Then occurred the most ridiculous but most provoking scene possible. Every elephant, except Lord Combermere's (which was a known staunch one) turned tail and went off at score, in spite of all the blows and imprecations heartily bestowed upon them by the mahouts. One, less expeditious in his retreat than the others, was overtaken by the tiger and severely torn in the hind leg; whilst another, even more alarmed than the rest, we could distinguish flying over the plain till he quite sank below the horizon, and, for all proof to the contrary, he may be going to this very moment!

The tiger, in the meanwhile, advanced to attack his Lordship's elephant, but, being wounded in the loins by Captain M.'s shot, failed in his spring and shrank back among the rushes. My elephant was one of the first of the runaways to return to action, and when I ran up alongside Lord Combermere (whose heroic animal had stood like a rock), he was quite hors du combat, having fired all his broadside. I handed him a gun, and we poured a volley of four barrels upon the tiger, who, attempting again to charge, fell from weakness. Several shots more were expended upon him before he dropped dead. We gave a good hearty "Whoo! whoop!" and stowed him upon a pad elephant. As Lord Combermere had, for some minutes, alone sustained the attack of the tiger—a three-quarters-grown male—the *spolia opima* [rich spoils] were duly awarded to him.

Having loaded and re-formed the line, we again advanced. After beating for half an hour, I saw the grass gently moved about one hundred yards in front of me, and soon after, a large tiger reared his head and shoulders above the jungle as if to reconnoitre us. I tally-ho'd! and the whole line rushed forward. On arriving at the spot, two tigers broke covert and cantered quietly across an open space of ground. Several shots were fired, one of which slightly touched the largest of them, who immediately turned round. Roaring furiously and lashing his sides with his tail, he came bounding toward us. Apparently alarmed by the formidable line of elephants, he suddenly stopped short and turned into the jungle again, followed by us at full speed.

At this pace the action of an elephant is so extremely rough that, though a volley of shots were fired, the tiger performed his attack and retreat without being again struck. Those who had the fastest elephants had now the best of the sport, and when he turned to fight (which he soon did), only three of us were up. As soon as he faced about, he attempted to spring on Captain M.'s elephant, but was stopped by a shot in the chest. Two or three more shots brought him to his knees, and the noble beast fell dead in a last attempt to charge. He was a full-grown male, and a very fine animal. Near the spot where we found him were discovered the well-picked remains of a buffalo.

One of the sportsmen had, in the meantime, kept the smaller tiger in view, and we soon followed to the spot to which he had been marked. It was a thick, marshy covert of broad flag reeds, called *hogla,* and we had beat through it twice and were beginning to think of giving it up as the light was waning when Captain P.'s elephant, which was lagging in the rear, suddenly uttered a shrill scream and came rushing out of the swamp with the tiger hanging by its teeth to the upper part of its tail! Captain P.'s situation was perplexing enough, his elephant making the most violent efforts to shake off his backbiting foe, and himself unable to use his gun for fear of shooting the unfortunate coolie, who, frightened out of his wits, was standing behind the howdah with his feet in the crupper and within six inches of the tiger's head.

We soon flew to his aid and quickly shot the tiger, who, however, did not quit his grip until he had received eight balls, whereupon he dropped off the poor elephant's mangled tail, quite dead. The elephant survived only ten days, but it was shrewdly suspected that his more mortal wounds were inflicted by some of the sportsmen who were overzealous to rid him of his troublesome hanger-on. Had the unlucky animal lived in those days "when use of speech was not confined merely to brutes of human kind," he would, no doubt, have exclaimed in his misery, "Heaven preserve me from my friends! I can defend myself from my enemies."

*Tiger attacking elephants.*

Thus, in about two hours, and within sight of camp, we found and slew three tigers, a piece of good fortune rarely to be met with in these modern times when the spread of cultivation and the zeal of English sportsmen have almost exterminated the breed of these animals.

During the chase the jungle was on fire in several places, and the wind being high, the flames at one time gained so fast upon us that the line was obliged to retreat. I saw here a confirmation of the fact that, in high grass jungles, fires run to windward, if there be a fresh breeze. This is easily accounted for: The wind bends the long, silky, dry grass over that which is already ignited, the flames catch the pendent tops, and thus, as long as there is material, the blaze spreads.

Four other sportsmen of our party returned to camp this evening having been out for four days in a different direction. They killed only one tiger, but he was an immense beast, and was shot on the head of Colonel F.'s elephant, which he wounded severely. This is considered the acme of tiger-shooting, so I know not how P.'s affair would rank in a comparative ratio!

When we returned to camp and had deposited our game in the main street, hundreds of spectators arrived and assembled round us. The claws and whiskers of tigers being looked upon as efficient charms by the natives, some of these desiderata were quickly snatched away before we could prevent the depredation.

March 2. Crossed the Ganges, and encamped near the village of Daranugger, in Rohilcund.

March 5. We reached Nujibabad, and the camp was pitched in a beautiful amphitheatre of mango groves, with a distant view of the Himalaya Mountains. Here we got information from some shikaris (native hunters) of two tigers having been seen in a forest about six miles from hence, in the direction of the hills. A party of seven will start from our camp tomorrow morning to beat up their quarters.

March 6. Whilst the camp marched thirteen miles to the hamlet of Asofghur, the seven sportsmen above mentioned galloped off early in the morning to a tent that had been sent forward, with some provisions, to the spot in the jungle where it was judged convenient to begin the chase. After breakfast we mounted our elephants and proceeded to the sporting ground. The features of the country were widely different from those of the scene of our last day's sport. We found ourselves in a luxuriant forest abounding in a species of tree which I had not seen before, namely, the *dhâg*. It bears a fine, wide, dark-coloured leaf and a beautiful tulip-shaped crimson flower. Occasionally we came upon wide open savannas of grass jungle or rushy swamps. Vast numbers of wild boars, hog-deer, and other

*Elephant charging tiger.*

small game started up before us, but we had determined beforehand not to fire at anything until we found a tiger, as these animals, when disturbed by a distant shot, are in a habit of sneaking away and escaping into the woods where it is impossible to follow them.

After diligently toiling for some hours and patiently abstaining from less noble game, I suddenly came directly upon a fine tiger in an almost impenetrable thicket of bushes. I shot him in the back, at the distance of half a dozen paces, but it only served to make him run faster. On breaking covert he directed his course right through a drove of buffaloes, which stood still and gazed at him, whilst the herdsman quietly smoked his *goorhee-goorhee* and sleepily pointed out the direction the tiger had taken. He took refuge in a thick rush swamp, and Captain Archer shot him, after he had severely torn the trunk of his elephant.

Later in the day we found another very fine tiger, but although he was viewed several times, he made good his retreat, favoured by the thickness of the covert and the numerous trees, which retarded the progress of the elephants. A hog-deer and a little wild pig fell to my gun. The former is a large and rather clumsy animal, with a bristly hide, and is supposed to constitute the chief food of the tiger.

During the day we several times approached within twelve miles of the lower range of mountains of Kumaon. Their bold and well-wooded heights, and the

*Shooting tiger from a platform.*

dim blue outline of the more distant Himalayas, were most refreshing to eyes that for so long a period had been accustomed to repose on the flat, unvaried plains of Hindostan.

After the chase we had a long and fatiguing march to camp at Asofghur. In the evening the jungle was on fire so near the camp that we were in some alarm lest it should spread to the tents of the servants and horses.

The next morning, refreshed by the "tired Nature's sweet restorer" from the fatigues of the preceding day, we sprung into our howdahs (as a novelist would say), and with twenty elephants repaired to the jungle. We had not far to go, for Asofghur, which must be the depot royale of malaria and jungle fever, is hemmed in on all sides by forest intersected by spacious, swampy plains covered with the rankest and most luxuriant grass and rushes. The appearance of the country and the very smell of the air were enough to give a fit of the ague to anyone but a truly ardent sportsman. The active employment of the attention, and the constant excitement of the spirits, must act as great preservatives of the constitution of an English sportsman in India, for, though I cannot myself boast of "a frame of adamant," I have been constantly on my elephant from "morn till dewy eve," in the hottest weather and the most pestiferous jungles, and never felt my health affected by it. There can be no doubt, however, that the constitution is eventually broken up by constant exposure to the sun in tropical climates.

This day we were not fated to carry home a tiger, the jungle being so thick and spacious that we could never bring them to bay, though we ascertained beyond doubt that there were several of these animals on foot. Just at the borders of a deep bog we discovered the carcasses of two oxen, which, from the liquid state of the blood, had evidently not been killed many hours. The impression of the tiger's claws on the haunches was deeply marked, and the gullets of both the animals were torn out. One of the bullocks was a very fine, powerful animal, and the ground was plowed up for many yards round the spot where the fatal struggle had taken place. The murderers had been most probably disturbed from their meal by the firing of our party, some of whom unfortunately could not resist the temptation held out by the hundreds of hogs, deer, etc., that fled before our line. We carried home to the camp, which we found on the right bank of the Ganges again, at the village of Baugpore, ten hog-deer, a brace of florikans, and about twenty brace of black partridge.

## Chapter Five

# Thomas Bacon
### First Impressions and Studies from Nature in Hindostan
### (1837)

Lieutenant Thomas Bacon, like Godfrey Mundy, was another soldier-adventurer who wrote a detailed book on his Indian experiences. And like Mundy's work, it is one of the few books that capture native and British life in pre-Raj India. Bacon was also an accomplished artist who sketched all the book's illustrations, in the "picturesque" style so popular at that time

Despite the title, most of Bacon's two-volume work focuses on Indian culture and architecture, rather than nature and field sports. He made a conscious effort to present Indian culture objectively, against the prevailing fixation on the "exotic" and bizarre. Nonetheless, he uses fictional characters throughout to describe these very real events. Bacon spent less time discussing hunting because most of his military tour was spent in the heartland of Indian civilization—the Ganges River and its many tributaries—far from tigers and other wild creatures. Bacon also did not seem to be a keen hunter, but, like most British soldiers in India, he was obligated at least to participate in field sports, hunting bear, elephant, and, of course, tigers.

The tiger hunt he recounts here is in the vicinity of Merat, northeast of Delhi. Although two tigers are bagged, Bacon laments that the number of tigers found there had been steadily decreasing on account of population pressure. And that was in the 1830s!

### Sporting Excursion in the Junguls

Having despatched servants into the junguls upon the banks of the Ganges to glean information on the haunts of the tigers, I applied for a month's leave of absence from my military duties—"upon urgent private affairs," as the form expresses it—and, in company with two of my brother officers, made immediate preparation for the excursion.

*The Himalayas near Musoori.*

The first object was to procure elephants, and these we obtained, six in number, from the company's commissariat. This indulgence is granted by the government to its officers, provided it can be done without infringing upon the demands of the service. While thus in private employment, both the elephant and his mahout (driver) receive daily from the person making use of them a small gratuity, which is known as extra *batta,* and they are placed upon a more generous diet than when idle. It is also customary for any person who may apply for elephants to indemnify the commissariat officer against loss, he being responsible to the government for their value, if injured or destroyed otherwise than in the immediate discharge of their duties.

Having laid in a stock of wines and other provisions necessary for our campaign, we sent them forward with our tents and camp-equipage upon camels to a village called Tiggeri, upon the east bank of the Ganges, about thirty-five miles northeast from Merat. Our elephants, servants, and extra horses were also despatched thither, so as to be in readiness for us upon our arrival.

We had selected May for our excursion because, though June gives better sport, we were disposed to avoid the extreme heat of the season, and though April would have been cooler, the sport would not have been so plentiful. On the first of May, then, a full hour before daybreak, we mounted our nags, and having each a couple of relays upon the road, we took to the open country in a direct line for our destination and in three hours' time were thirty miles distant from Merat. The last five miles, however, were not to be so easily run over. We had two channels of the river to cross, and lost much time in seeking the *ghát* [steps on riverbank], for the boat used in the transportation of passengers to and fro had been taken from its original situation. Our horses were becoming weary, for we had ridden hard the last stage, and every moment the sun was growing more and more powerful.

While we were discussing the expediency of swimming our horses over, one of my companions, who had incautiously approached too near the edge of the bank, was precipitated, horse and all, into the river by the loose, sandy soil giving way under him. The height of the bank was small, but it was sufficient to prevent either the rider or his horse from effecting a landing anywhere within five hundred yards of the place; consequently, they were fain to be carried down the current to a more convenient spot. Here we found the boat, under cover of a patch of jungul, which had screened it from us while under our very noses. We jumped in, keeping our horse in company with us, and in half an hour were upon the opposite bank. Then away we rode, helter-skelter, for our camp, distant at least four miles.

This unfortunate delay occupied as much time almost as the former part of the journey had done so that when we reached the village where we had ordered our camp, it was close upon eleven o'clock, and the sun's rays were beating upon our heads unmercifully. Nor was any tolerable shelter to be discovered, for, to the kindling of our utmost wrath, we found that our tents, through delay and carelessness on the part of our servants, had only that moment arrived upon the ground, leaving us with empty stomachs to seek cover from the sun where we might.

Not having broken fast, our tempers were less amiable than they should have been, so we avenged our grievances upon our slaves without compunction, and in retaliation of the discomfort that their negligence had inflicted upon us, we issued a decree that no man in the camp should taste food until the sun had set, and this act we unconscionably carried into effect. This was certainly some little alleviation of our miseries, and for the rest, we, in a measure, ameliorated our misfortune by taking refuge from the red-hot rays of the sun under the scanty tufts of a scraggy old banyan hard by. Here we lay upon the scorching earth, watching with thirsty mouths the preparations for our long-wished-for meal.

The whole company of cooks, scullions, and *khidmutgars* [waiters] were busily employed in grilling chickens, frying fish, frizzling ham and eggs, baking *chappatties* [thin cakes of unleavened bread], bubbling omelets, boiling curries, mixing seasonings, and in the thousand-and-one multifarious essentials of an Indian breakfast when suddenly an immense mass of thick, inky clouds spread itself over the western horizon and came sweeping up the heavens with a velocity which is never seen, I believe, in Old England. The scattered straw and the dried leaves lying upon the ground around us began to whirl about in fitful eddies, and, as it grew darker and darker, the cattle showed evident uneasiness at the impending storm. We, too, though somewhat tardily, became sensible of it, and with all the energy of hungry stomachs, started to our feet to save if possible our half-cooked meal.

The slaves were squatting round their roaring fires, far too intent upon their several duties, and too much enveloped in smoke, to notice what was coming. We shouted passionately to them to secure the breakfast, but, alas! before they comprehended our meaning, the weight of the hurricane fell upon us, hurling an overwhelming cloud of sand and dirt in our faces and carrying away our hats and every loose article about the camp. We were just recovering from the first surprise when a second blast, more violent than the first, struck us, rending the very cooking-pots from the fire and bowling them away across the plain, the savoury contents a prey to the multitude of canine beggars ever at hand. Helter-skelter away went the dogs after the good things, tumbling and rolling over one another and the pots and pans, howling with impetuous anticipation, and followed by an equally ravenous host of kites and vultures. The servants stood aghast at the havoc thus suddenly brought upon their handiwork, and at the moment they began to meditate some exertion for a rescue, another gust capsized the tent upon their heads and buried them under the folds of the canvas.

It was fortunate that the whole of the tent had not been pitched—the fly alone was raised to render us a temporary shelter while the larger tent was being prepared—for, in a few moments, before the canvas could be dragged from off the prostrate cooks, it had ignited over the fires, and the pole alone could be saved, besides some of the rope and a portion of the outer fly, which was cut away while the other side was burning. One man alone was injured in the fray; he had been deprived of his eyesight by a kick from one of his comrades while struggling for release from his thralldom.

The storm was short in proportion to its violence, and as soon as the confusion in a measure subsided, all hands were set to work in collecting the broken remnants of the feast and in pitching another tent for our reception. After all our troubles, a hearty meal was made upon the fragments, though certainly every mouthful of food added more than a due quantum of dirt to the peck that every man is said to devour before he dies.

None of our scouts had found our camp during the day, so we despatched messengers into the villages to collect information of tigers and to learn how the land lay. They returned, however, without any news, and in the cool of the evening we mounted our elephants to pursue smaller game. In this we did not consider ourselves successful, having no trophy to display beyond a wild boar, a couple of hog-deer, and a scanty bag of black partridge. Not that there was any dearth of game, but the truth was that we were three griffs [novices] at our work: We'd never been out shooting in the howdah before, and the shuffling gait of the elephant we found very perplexing to our aim. This inconvenience, which is felt by all beginners, is very quickly surmounted. A few days' practice will set aside the difficulty, and both hand and eye become so accustomed to the motion of the animal that men habituated to this kind of sport will generally be found to shoot much better from the howdah than on foot.

Though I believe the word howdah to be almost as well known to fireside travelers as the word "palanquin," yet I doubt if they have any more correct notion of the real fashion of the former, as used by sportsmen, than [Samuel] Johnson's *Dictionary [of the English Language,* 1755] supplies of the latter. Old prints of wild sports give specimens of state howdahs as fashion events, and modern writers seem to think that such errors have been long since corrected. There is neither tinsel, nor embossment, nor silk canopy, nor fringe, nor tassels, pertaining to the modern sporting howdah. It consists of two seats, placed like those of a phaeton, fenced around with a light but substantial framework of wood, with iron clamps, and paneled with open cane-work or with leather. The upper frame is surmounted by an iron rail like that upon a coach-box, to prevent the rider from being dismounted by any sudden evolution or unsteadiness of the elephant. The sportsman is seated in front with his battery on either side of him; this generally consists of four double-barrel guns and a rifle for long shots. In the rear seat, technically called the *káhause,* is a man carrying a large umbrella, or *chatta,* to screen his master from the sun, but he puts this aside when going into action with a tiger in order that he may be able to load his master's guns as fast as they are discharged. He also undertakes the care of the ammunition and whatever provision it is necessary to carry.

It should be mentioned that, in beating for tigers expressly, it is an understood thing among sportsmen that none of the party shall fire at any smaller game lest the nobler objects of the sport should be alarmed by the firing. Thus the deer, hog, hares, and birds are allowed to pass with impunity, however numerous, if tigers be suspected to be lurking in the neighbourhood, for they are very wild and take their departure from their common haunts the moment they fear an invasion.

Late at night, some of our scouts came in with information of a couple of tigers at a village called Shaerpore, several miles distant. The name, signifying the Place of Tigers, was sufficiently apropos, as much so as the name Tiggeri, famous for its abundance of wild hog. (I am not aware, by the by, that the word *tig* in Hindostani has any reference to the swine tribe.) Immediately upon receipt of this news, we caused tents to be sent on to the village overnight, and so despatched our elephants to within a mile of the spot, with the intention of riding to the ground on horseback at daybreak the next morning. I have said that we were all three griffs at tiger shooting, and never having beheld a tiger at large and in the majesty of his natural freedom, it may readily be believed that we were eager for the first encounter.

Before the dawn of the next morning, we roused the camp, and by the time that the first bright streak of light appeared in the east, we were marching quietly toward the scene of action, having fortified our stomachs with a cup of piping hot tea before we started. We were accompanied by the shikari, or native sportsman, who had given our servants intelligence of the game and who had followed them to camp for his reward, having placed men of his own to watch the movements of the beast in his absence. This man's name was Mirchi, a veteran in his calling, and well known to every sportsman in the neighbourhood of Merat, as one of the most daring and successful tiger scouts in India.

The old fellow is a man of great fame, and a character in his own sphere, and as such deserves notice. His age is possibly fifty years, though he himself can come no nearer to the mark than that he is an old man, having no idea of the date of his nativity beyond what is suggested by the evidence of his present strength and constitution. His figure is tall and straight and indicative of muscular power

*Scenes along the Ganges—Rajmahal.*

and energy far superior to what is enjoyed by the mass of his countrymen. His hair and beard are silvery white, and his deep-set, twinkling, inquisitive eyes are overhung with shaggy bushes of grizzled bristles doing duty as eyebrows.

His spare figure is usually clad in a most simple but becoming costume, the upper part of his person being covered simply with a purple scarf, thrown over his shoulders, and having on his head a bright crimson turban. His right hand is armed with a heavy bludgeon, formed of a male bamboo, about four feet in length, and about the thickness of a man's wrist, having six inches of one end shod with a spiral worm of iron—a weapon no man could affect to despise, having once felt the weight of it, particularly when wielded by so muscular an arm. In his cummerbund he carries a handsome dagger, which was given to him by Brigadier Brown, **CB**, who, as a keen sportsman and an admirer of true pluck, patronized the old shikari.

Mirchi says, and I fully believe him, that he has been present at the deaths of more than a thousand tigers, shot by officers and English gentlemen. Moreover, before he entered upon his present mode of life, he was an informer against them and had killed upward of two hundred with his own hand. After the hardships and adventures of his youth, the old man, finding his vigour of body failing, retired upon a less laborious branch of his profession. Now, instead of pursuing the game himself, he gains an honest livelihood by seeking the haunts of his former personal enemies, and betraying them to such members of the sporting community as are ready to afford him a fair remuneration for his trouble and risk.

The old man is full of anecdote and adventurous tales of the difficulties and encounters that he himself has undergone as well as some ultra-tragic disasters that have befallen others in his presence. He tells his story with a great deal of impassioned gesture and a seasoning of dry humour, and having never before found such a manner in one of his class, I strongly suspect that he has picked it up from the facetious sporting Englishmen with whom he has been conversant in matters of his calling.

We came up with our elephants about a mile from the belt of jungul where the tigers were supposed to lie. Here we mounted for action, loading and carefully re-examining our guns. The best elephants of the number had, of course, been selected for our howdahs; the others, being required only for beating up the spaces intervening between us, were of less consequence. Upon one of these we put Mirchi, and committing our course and manner of advance to his guidance, we formed a line upon the east side of the jungul, which, fortunately for us, was also the leeward side so that we had thus two great advantages: The sun was at our backs instead of in our faces, and the wind carried the noise of our advance from, instead of to, the game. I took the centre of the line, and each friend a flank, the beating elephants walking in the intervals. In this order of battle we moved forward, making our way through the high jungul grass in silence. Nothing could be more exciting than this slow and deliberate approach upon a powerful enemy.

The sagacious beasts on which we rode seemed aware that we were striking at the higher game, for, as the deer bounded almost from beneath their feet, they took no notice of them, nor did they stop, as is their habit, to allow their rider to take aim, but continued to advance step by step, with a slow and careful pace, as if designing to make as little noise as possible. Every step increased the excitement, and every head of game that was roused by our approach we thought must be the tiger, but we were green hands at the sport, as our friend Mirchi politely told us, for the timid deer are not apt to lie quite so close upon the quarters of their destroyer.

In this manner, we advanced at least half a mile through the jungul, without coming upon any signs of those we sought, and we were naturally beginning to fear that Mirchi had conducted us upon a false scent. But we still held on our march, and soon found the small game less abundant, as the jungul grew swampy and difficult to penetrate. I was about to express my disappointment and recommend our trying other ground when my elephant came suddenly upon the half-devoured carcass of a bullock, around which the ground was trodden down, and the jungul torn in fragments. The slaughter was evidently recent, and no doubt the tiger had made his banquet shortly before daybreak.

"Ha! ha!" I cried, "we have him now. Look here, Mahout, here are his footprints, each as large as a chappatti."

"Such *hi khodáwund,*" replied the obsequious driver, echoing each word of my exclamation, *"ab jeldi milega, oos-ki punja chuppatti ki muafik burra hi."*

Mirchi came up, and having made his comments upon the carcass, passed a hint to the two marksmen on the flanks to be upon the *qui vive* [on guard]. Presently, one of the elephants commenced trumpeting through his trunk, and the whole line advanced more warily. This is the most exciting stage of the pursuit: Every eye is fixed upon the long jungul grass, watching eagerly for the hidden monster; every waving blade is taken for the tiger; and every gun is raised to smite him. After passing the carcass, we found the jungul much higher than heretofore, it being in some places even with the tops of our howdah, but here the ground, though swampy, was not so adhesive as to impede the progress of our line.

My elephant now began to speak, uttering a long, low rumbling noise internally, accompanied with occasional nasal squeaks, the signals of alarm and caution. Then a loud shout of enthusiasm from old Mirchi proclaimed the sport in view, though we were greeted neither by roar nor charge, as is generally supposed to be the case. The only circumstance that attracted our notice was a slight waving of the grass in front of us.

*"Mar! Mar!"* screamed the old shikari, in the vehemence of his excitement: "Fire! Fire! He will get away."

A shot from the left howdah was the first fired, but without effect, for the grass in front of us continued to wave about as if moved by some bulky animal below it, slinking away ahead of us.

"Fire, again!" cried Mirchi. "Do you wish to let him escape?"

I fired, but with no better success than my friend before me, except that the grass began to move faster, as if the brute beneath was hastening his retreat. A double shot from the right did as little execution, and old Mirchi, with ardent interest in the pursuit, grew angry at our want of skill.

"Lower down, lower down," he cried. "What are the gentlemen doing that they fire at the grass and not at the tiger? Ah! if I had Judge Kummul Sahib, or Broon Sahib, or E-smit Sahib in the howdahs, it would not be so."

A simultaneous discharge from all three batteries was instantly followed by a roar, such as never was heard within the walls of the Tower or Exeter Change.

"Ha! that is bravely done," cried the old man, changing his note, and every feature of his aged countenance working with excitement. "Press on now, gentlemen, and give him chase. You are young hands at this sport, and shall make the most of it; press on now, mahouts."

And in obedience to his command, we urged our elephants forward at a long trot. They, it may be believed, shared in the general excitement, and exhibited their interest by a mixed concert of trumpeting and rumbling of their thunders within them.

The tiger, for a moment, made a pause, as if meditating vengeance of the injury he had received, but he again stole off, until he unexpectedly found himself in a circular patch of barren ground, quite free from cover. The spot was like a little amphitheatre in the centre of the jungul, which looked as if constructed purposely for the encounter. As he entered upon this bare spot, he turned for a moment and surveyed with terrible demonstrations of his wrath the formidable line advancing upon him. He was wounded in the hindquarter, whence the blood was slowly oozing. It was a glorious sight to see how proudly the mighty monster stood to reconnoitre us, displaying his tremendous tusks and grinders, as if to warn us off, and then making the heavens ring again, in echo to his awful voice.

By mutual consent our fire was reserved until we entered upon the open ground, and then a shot grazed his shoulder and brought him at once to the charge. Raising himself upon his hind legs, he uttered another yell of mingled agony and rage, and with a concentration of all his powers, he rushed at my elephant, evidently with the intention of fixing himself upon its head. Firmly and without wavering did old Eima (the elephant, a female) stand her ground, though not without preparing for the charge, if it should be made good. This, however, was not permitted, for when the tiger was within ten yards of me, having taken a careful aim, I put a ball into his chest, and then a volley was poured in on all sides, which quickly made him bite the dust.

Again he rose, again and again he endeavoured to effect a charge upon one or other of the elephants, but we were too strong for him, and a couple of shots through the skull brought him again to the earth, where, with all the tenacity of life attributed to the feline race, he lay, tearing the stumps of jungle in his now impotent wrath and glaring upon us with his flaming eyes a picture of vengeful antipathy even in the throes of death. I pushed my elephant close up to him and terminated his agonies—or so I thought—by putting a ball clean through his skull. His head sank upon the ground and his eyes closed.

I was about to dismount to examine the fallen monster when Mirchi cried out to me, "Wa! Wa! Sahib. Are we to lose the other tiger while you are eating this one? I saw him steal off to the other side of the jungul while you were despatching this fine fellow. Mirchi is an old sportsman, and has two keen eyes in his head, or you would have lost this second tiger. Come, gentlemen, will you be pleased to give the order for our advance? The business of this day is not yet finished. Let us do the work more cleverly next time."

We did as Mirchi advised, and he led us directly to the spot where the female had concealed herself. She was an animal of smaller growth, and did not show us such good sport as the former one, in consequence of an early shot from one of my companions having taken effect in her brain. This was unfortunate, as the female, generally speaking, exhibits even more courage and ferocity in the encounter than does the male. We packed her upon one of the *guddi* elephants (those not carrying a howdah) and returned to the scene of the first engagement, where to our astonishment we found our former enemy still breathing, though more than half an hour had elapsed since we had left him. Mirchi despatched him by burying his dagger up to the hilt in his chest, and he was then mounted upon the elephant and carried into camp side by side with his partner.

On our way back to camp, having ascertained that there were no more tigers in the neighbourhood, we beat the ground to the right and left of that which we had gone over in the morning, and within a couple of hours we bagged eight hog-deer and three of the swine tribe so that we looked upon our day's sport as a highly successful one.

In the cool of the evening, again we sallied forth on horseback with spear in hand, this time against the wild hogs. We were happy enough to slay a very fine one, though I cannot boast of any share in the glory of the chase, for my horse, putting his foot in a rat-hole, came to the ground with me and incapacitated himself from further work. Thereafter I was fain to bestride an ugly baggage camel and look on upon the dexterous deeds of my comrades without participating in the sport.

A firm seat, a delicate hand upon the bridle, a quick eye, a steady and skillful delivery of the spear, and good pluck are indispensable in this nice sport. The eye must be kept upon the hog, and the horse must be left to select his own footing through broken ground or other impediments, for if the attention be for an instant withdrawn from the chase, ten to one are the odds that the hog will run to cover unmarked and the game will be lost.

It is not only a more scientific, but it is also a more dangerous sport than tiger-shooting, for if the horse be borne to the earth in the charge, the rider will have little chance of escape, unless very expertly supported by his companions, who must make a diversion in his favour.

But we must away. Mirchi has more sport for us, and the old man loves not the mention of hog-hunting. He never engaged in it himself, and he declares it to be unsportsmanlike, inasmuch as it deprives the tigers of their lawful prey. If their food be not plentiful in the level country, it is pretty certain they will remain in the secret places of their native forests rather than expose themselves to the eye of the marksman. For the same very sufficient reason, he abominates the unrestricted wholesale destruction of the deer, so universally practiced by those who visit the junguls. His objection is undoubtedly valid: The number of tigers throughout the plains has very greatly diminished within the last few years, and in junguls where an expedition was formerly rewarded with seven or eight tigers daily, the sportsman may now think himself fortunate if he should come upon that number in the course of a month.

### Chapter Six

# Edward Napier
## Scenes and Sports in Foreign Lands
### (1840)

Maj. Edward Napier was a professional soldier, but like many Englishmen in India he also took writing seriously, stating: "In the wild and adventurous expeditions herein recorded, the pen and portfolio ranked second only to the rifle and boar spear."

His writings and hunting focus on the Deccan—the great land mass that makes up central and southern India—where Napier spent his military career. He begins with his days as a young griffin, or novice, when he first encountered exotic creatures like the vulture and adjutant stork, and forests filled with strange sights, sounds, and smells. Napier later focuses on hunting, much of it done on horseback with the use of spears and daggers. Many hunting camps were also set up in and around old ruins, something that added a sense of romance to these early nimrodic adventurers.

Scenes and Sports in Foreign Lands was published in two volumes in 1840. Napier, like many people of his generation, was also an amateur artist who drew all the sketches for his books. In this piece, the author gives an account of one of his first encounters with a tiger in the "deep jungles" of some unnamed Deccan forest. It was followed by a pursuit of a wild buffalo, which unfortunately escaped.

### Deep Jungle Shooting

Shooting in India may properly be classed under three distinct heads—wet, dry, and deep-jungle shooting. In the two former, excellent sport may be had by a good shot, and one who has a proper contempt for that great big bugbear "the sun." With these requisite qualifications, I have no hesitation in saying that a day in the paddy fields of the East will yield as

*Too close to be pleasant.*

good an account of "long-bills" as their brethren paddy fields in the Bog of Allan, or, for the dry'un, as decent a show of hares, partridges, etc. (barring pheasants) as a day's shooting might produce in Old England, provided always you have in your train suitable beaters.

But with all this for excitement—and what is life without it?—give me the "deep jungle" with all its dangers. When you load one barrel with large shot and drop a bullet into the other; when, bandit-like, you sally forth with the pistol and hunting-knife in your belt, not knowing if you are to stumble on a quail or a quadruped, a peafowl or a panther; when at the slightest rustling of the underwood, or crackling of the long dry grass under your footsteps, your heart leaps to your mouth and the ready-cocked piece to the shoulder; then, and not till then, can you appreciate the true delights of the chase. Then, if a real sportsman, although an exile in a burning clime, afar from friends, home, and kindred, you will not envy the old governor, or maybe an elder brother, who perhaps at the same moment, attended by John the gamekeeper, a couple of well-trained pointers, and all appliances and means to boot, is comfortably trudging through the stubble, or knocking down pheasants in the coverts like cocks and hens in a barn-yard.

But by the bright looks of Diana, ye sons of Cockaigne, imagine not this to constitute sport! Lay not, deluded wretches, the flattering unction to your souls! But after John has duly given the census of slaughter, after ye have swallowed, self-satisfied, your bottle of port, and having inserted your tender toes in slippers soft, and deposited your goodly person in snug arm-chair before a blazing fire, take up this volume, and I'll attempt to give you some faint idea of realms in which Nimrod himself might revel.

Like Othello, "rude am I in speech, and little blessed with the set phrase of peace"; therefore, without more preface, I shall say that in the month of January 183—, myself and another compañero left our snug little bungalow at Secunderabad, and by the "light of the moon" took our departure on our trusty nags in a northeasterly direction, in hopes of reaching the hill fort of Boanghir (where our tent awaited us) early in the morning. Our destination was a hitherto unexplored part of the country in the neighbourhood of the Perkhal Lake, a part of the extensive Cummermait Jungle, about a couple of hundred miles distant, where we were to join another party that had already been out several months engaged in the survey of that unknown region.

Boanghir was about thirty miles distant, and we therefore expected to reach it about breakfast-time, but, owing to our mistaking the track, we did not obtain the welcome sight of our tent till near twelve o'clock. We were too much fagged to attempt anything like shooting that day, but in the cool of the evening we scrambled up part of the dark mass of granite on which the fort is constructed, but were stopped midway by a party of Arab soldiers in the Nizam's pay, who composed the garrison of the place.

Next morning, and for the following four or five days, we pursued our journey amidst scenery common to this part of India—low jungle, occasionally broken by a few rice fields and date trees. In this neighbourhood was generally found a small hamlet, near which we always encamped. This gave us the double advantage of obtaining rice for our followers and buffalo milk for ourselves, our table being otherwise always well supplied with the produce of our guns. We thus journeyed on some eighty or ninety miles till we reached Hanamkonda; this appeared the extreme verge of civilization, in the sense of the word in India.

On leaving Hanamkonda, the "spirit of our dream" suddenly changed. We could no longer overlook the surrounding jungle, but entered at once into a forest land such as I had never before witnessed in India. The teak, the sylvan monarch of the East, now first made its appearance, and as our path wound under its deep foliage, it was no longer crossed by the bounding antelope or timid partridge. We would occasionally catch a glimpse of a spotted deer with its spreading antlers, hear the melancholy screech of the peafowl, or have a transient peep at the dazzling plumage of the jungle cock ere he rose and took his pheasant-like flight.

What a pity it is that this noble bird should not be introduced into our coverts at home—at least, I am not aware of any attempt having been made to do so—which, as it is a remarkably hardy bird, would probably succeed. The female differs little from the common barn-door fowl, but the plumage of the cock is brilliant beyond measure. The feathers on the back, a rich yellow-orange, are different from those of any other bird in one remarkable peculiarity: The end of each feather has the appearance and consistency of coloured and highly varnished card or pasteboard and, as they overlap each other, produce the most

*Sporting party in the ruins of Surroo Nuggur.*

splendid effect. It is a very shy bird and difficult to put up, but it runs along amidst the underwood with wonderful quickness and can carry away a good charge of shot.

As we proceeded, the forest scenery by degrees grew bolder whilst the track of larger animals often seen in the sand—amongst which we distinctly perceived that of the tiger—reminded us that we were entering domains where the sway of man was little known. These signs warned us to keep close together during the remainder of the day's march, which ended at a place called Gheezcondah, a hamlet composed of a few straggling huts by the side of a tank and occupied by wood-cutters.

Our first care on reaching our encamping ground was always (having first duly breakfasted) to send for the *potail,* or headman of the village, to inquire what game there was in the neighbourhood. On the present occasion, this important personage gave us wonderful accounts of the shikar (shooting) to be had in the vicinity. Amongst other things, he said that a wild buffalo sometimes came to the tank, and that on a neighbouring hill (which he pointed out from the door of the tent) there were no fewer than seven tigers.

We gave the old fellow full credit for laying it on rather too thick, but we resolved in the evening to reconnoitre the hill. On our way there, we banged two or three times at hares and spur fowl with our shot barrels, always taking the precaution of keeping one loaded with ball. We thus sauntered carelessly along, until, as we approached a rock, an object attracted our attention that put us on the *qui vive*: It was the carcass of a sheep nearly devoured, and that recently. This smelt rather tigerish, and as the underwood at the foot of the rock was extremely thick and tangled, it seemed a particularly likely covert for a beast of prey. We therefore proceeded cautiously.

Nothing, however, particularly fixed our attention until we had nearly reached the summit. There, on a ledge of granite overlooking a chasm many feet in depth, and in front of an aperture in the rock, we saw a quantity of tiger's hair, as if he had been in the habit of basking there in the sun. We resolved, therefore, to lie in ambush immediately above the fissure, which we supposed to be his den. There we would patiently await until he should emerge, hoping that our placement might allow us to get a shot at him within a few feet and before he could be aware of our presence.

But in this world the best concerted plans are liable to be frustrated. We had not been ten minutes in our position when, instead of coming, as we expected, from under our feet, and allowing us to take him in the rear, a slight rustling in the bushes immediately in front of us was followed by a noble royal tiger advancing most majestically along the ledge of rock. At first he did not perceive us, and we allowed him to approach a few paces. He then looked up, viewed us, and made a dead stop. Not a second was to be lost! He was within twelve yards and a single bound would have sent at least one of the party to eternity. We both fired instantaneously, and both with effect. He reared himself up on his hind legs as if to make a forward bound, fell back, and rolled headlong into the abyss below. My ball had hit him between the eyes; G—'s had struck him in the loins.

I know not how G— found himself, but I must confess that, although my hand was steady enough when I fired, after the business was over, and I was again proceeding to load, it felt uncommonly tremulous, much as if I had had a glass *de trop* [too much] overnight. As to the poor devil of a fellow who had accompanied us, he was a perfect chameleon, his polished black hair being transmogrified into an ashy blue.

By our log we now made ourselves to be somewhere about twenty miles from our surveying friends, so we stopped a day at Gheezcondah to await the arrival of a messenger we had despatched in search of them. We were much rejoiced to hear, on his return, that we were right in our calculations and that a couple of horses would be posted for us the next day midway between our position and Seevaporam, a small village where they had been some time expecting us.

Accordingly, "flaky darkness had scarce broken in the East" when we were mounted and chulling along at a rate our nags had latterly not been accustomed to, leaving our people to follow at their leisure. We found a couple of strong ponies at the appointed place, and having our own spurs and our friends' nags did not in the least tend to slacken the pace. About 9:00 A.M., we were brought in the presence of a very respectable encampment, in the midst of which was conspicuous the noble double-poled tent of my friend M—.

He and his assistant, D—, came out to give us an Indian welcome. They were both right good'uns, but at present rather rum'uns to look at.

D—, with a beard reaching down to his waist, reminded me so strongly of Robinson Crusoe that I could not help roaring outright, whilst M— only required a slight dash of Day and Martin to personate a very respectable Friday. We were ushered in to a capital breakfast whilst discussing their wild appearances, and then our wild men of the woods related to us all the adventures and hair-breadth 'scapes by field and flood they had encountered during the four months of their jungle exile.

### Chapter Seven

# WILLIAM RICE
## Tiger Shooting in India
### (1857)

Lieutenant William Rice served five years with the Bombay Regiment in Rajpootana (now Rajasthan) in western India. The region then, as now, was known for its fierce political independence, ornate culture, and a beautiful, arid landscape of stark mountains dotted by palms and acacia trees. Because of the rocky landscape tigers were usually hunted on foot, rather than from elephant or treetop machan. This made for thrilling and often dangerous hunting escapades.

During his tour, Rice and his accomplices shot sixty-eight tigers and much other game and had many narrow escapes. Rice was one of the first to comment on the use of repeating firearms, which he found inferior to his trusty Westley Richards No. 18 bore. Later he concedes that, with improvement, the new weapons would become the proper arm for the India hunter. Rice's detailed descriptions of landscape and hunting as well as the lavish lithographs made Tiger Shooting in India an instant classic when it was published in 1857. It remains one of the most sought-after books on hunting the Indian tiger.

The story presented here is about a hunt that takes place in the eastern edge of Rajpootana. It is interesting because Rice mentions finding a cheetah recently killed by a tiger. The animal, now extinct in India, was common in the open grasslands of Rajpootana in Rice's day.

### Tiger-Shooting in India

Even in the prolific jungle, large game does not everywhere abound. For the next seven days I sought diligently but found nothing except an old bear that I wounded when returning one evening wearied from the day's outing. In the end, even that bear escaped me.

*Tiger killed by a chance shot.*

    The tent had been moved on almost daily a few miles along the hills toward Kooakhera village to enable me to hunt over fresh ground each day, but no tiger could we see. Although, on one occasion, while following up some fresh prints of one in a dry riverbed, we constantly heard a *kole balloo,* or old jackal, calling just in front of us. Twice my men stopped short and pointed silently to what, at the time, we all thought must be the tiger lying up under some thick bushes though only a few yards off, but we were mistaken. These turned out to be nothing but large, red, rocky stones.

    It is very difficult sometimes to make out a tiger when thus concealed in grass or bushes, for they will often lie very close, and their skin is of the same colour as the dry grass and reeds around while the stripes even, if seen, are easily mistaken for shadows cast by the strong glare of the sun. It luckily happened for me that we were this time mistaken, for, on going home to my tent, I aimed at a very large alligator basking asleep on a bank by the riverside, but both my caps missed fire, having become damp from the continued wet weather. To prevent accidents of this sort occurring, we made it a rule always to change the gun caps for fresh ones every morning.

    One day, soon after this, while thus tracking a tiger as silently as possible, we found that the brute must have been moving off a long way just in front of us, for we came upon his fresh prints over the marks made by a flock of goats that had been driven along a road only a few minutes before. This proves how easily the large game moves about, even in the daytime, during such cool weather. On still further following this tiger's tracks, we came upon a dead hunting cheetah (or hunting leopard) that had just been killed by the tiger, he having, no doubt, surprised the cheetah asleep, for the marks of the tiger's claws, from which blood still was flowing, were quite plain on the body.

This animal (harmless enough except for deer) he must have killed in mere wantonness. On another occasion we found a hyena that had been thus murdered by a tiger, perhaps for heedlessly passing too close to him. The paw alone had been used to kill these victims, for there were no teeth marks. It struck me as rather odd to find a hunting cheetah in the hills, for these animals live mostly in the plains where they hunt deer or antelope in parties of four or five together in the same manner as the wolves do, secreting themselves in bushes at different points while one of their number chases the buck. On its passing the ambuscade, they pounce out upon the little gazelle, or take up the running in turn as it races past them.

On 9 April, I set out to beat the upper end of the Booj River, and seeing how quickly the game moved off at the least noise during this cool weather, I knew we would have a very long drive indeed. We went a mile, at least, ahead of the beaters. Presently I saw a very fine tiger coming slowly on, but as he seemed inclined to turn up a small branch of this big ravine, I was obliged to fire, though at 120 yards' distance. This shot luckily broke his forearm, whereupon he came roaring down toward me as fast as his disabled leg would allow. This gave me time for four more shots, the last of which rolled him over much crippled. He halted in some very thick patch of willow bushes about thirty yards off where I could hear him growling terribly but could not see him at all.

After waiting for the men to come up, we threw volleys of stones into this thick patch of jungle but could not turn out the tiger. I had fired nearly forty other shots into this place when suddenly the tiger was quiet. Then, very cautiously, we approached the place in a body and, luckily found the tiger dead. His body was much protected from my shots by two large rocks between which he was lying, but a chance bullet had struck his head and settled him. We skinned him on the spot, which job was not finished till dusk, so we did not get back to the tent till late, having six miles to walk. I pegged the skin down by candlelight, fearing it might shrink—it measured eleven feet eight inches long, and was very wide.

For the next five days, as the weather still continued so cool, I did not get a shot at any large game. At one cover a bear passed by me, but, expecting to find a tiger there I did not fire at him. At Ambah a cattle owner had lately poisoned two or three tigers by placing arsenic in the bodies of the bullocks the tigers had killed. This accounted for my finding no sport in any of the good covers about there.

By 15 April, my tent having been sent on to Bhynsrode Fort, I went across the River Chumbul to Amtee Amlee village where the people told me that a tiger had that day killed a bullock. Having collected some Bhil tribesmen, we went to his usual dwelling place. I was posted up a small tree to overlook the long grass and thick bushes when, soon after the beaters had commenced their work, a fine tiger appeared. He had nearly escaped me unseen, owing to the thick cover. As he was just going over a high bank on my left, I viewed him in time to fire one shot hastily at his shoulders. This brought him bounding down the steep bank in two long springs, close under the low tree in which I was stuck. Here he got another bullet, but was out of sight in the long grass beyond before another gun could be got ready.

Thinking he might be rolled over for good, for there was a great quantity of blood about, I waited for the Bhils [tribesmen] to come up before we began following up the blood in a compact body. Presently we heard some low growls about forty yards ahead but could see nothing, for the grass here was very thick and at least nine feet high. We now stopped, but the growling noise still continued. This tiger clearly had more life in him than we expected, so we slowly retreated, showing a front, however, for we half expected to be charged every minute.

There was no tree near on this open plain, so we had no means of finding out the exact spot where he was lying hid. The men did not wish the grass to be burnt as they intended cutting it for their cattle; besides, had we done so no one could have gone near such a fire, which would likely burn for days. It would also have the effect of driving every head of game clean out of the country, for it extended over the surrounding jungle. I was forced to let this tiger alone, and ride on reluctantly to my tent at Bhynsrode. His prints, on hard ground, measured six inches long by five wide, so he was a monster.

*Following a wounded tiger.*

On my way home, I saw a very large lynx, at least two feet high and very long but could not fire. He came close-by me without being aware of my presence, and was the largest animal of the kind I had yet met with in these parts.

On 17 April, I went with about twenty men to beat Paradur Ravine. The Bhils there saw an old bear lying outside his cave, but on their approach he retreated to his den. We could not drive him out, being afraid to apply lighted grass or sticks for fear of disturbing the bees, whose nests were very numerous on all the high rocks around. On beating the cover shortly afterward, a fine tiger came by my post. I dropped him with a single ball in the head, but was obliged to give him three more shots for trying to get up again a little while after he had fallen, having been only stunned at first. These shots killed him outright. He measured eleven feet, nine inches long. Being near the place, I much wished to have a look for the tiger wounded two days ago, but skinning this last killed one made it too late, for we had a long walk home.

The jungle all round here had been set on fire. This is done every year to cause fresh grass to spring up for the cattle to eat. But it spoils all chance of sport in the neighbourhood. At night the red line of fire of the burning grass looks very pretty as it appears in waving red lines over the distant hills. The jungle, when thus burnt, will continue on fire for days together, columns of black smoke by day pointing out the course of the fire, while at night there

71

seems to be a general illumination in the woods. The heat is very great from this burning grass. I have sometimes on meeting it had to run quickly through the long, thin line of fire, taking good care to first throw my powder horn over on the other side and a long way away. A person might walk for a mile or more before finding an opening in this wall of flames.

From Bhynsrode I moved on by easy stages to Mundulguhr, but without finding any tigers, for the country was very open. While I was bathing in a piece of water near where my tent was pitched, one of my servants, rather late in the evening, came to say that a bear had come down to drink on the opposite shore. I sent for the rifle and walked after him in the water until I was within about thirty yards. The shots told well, for with loud groans he bolted back into the jungle. It was too dark to look for him then, and by next morning he had managed to walk off.

There were a good many sambar about in this part of the country, but I did not fire at them.

On 22 April, after a long march with my camels across an open cultivated country—for I was anxious to get back to better ground—we arrived at a village where a man was reported to have been lately killed by a tiger in a very large ravine named Noorsinghur. I sent round to the different villages about for men, and sixty-five readily offered to help hunt for this tiger, so I set out for the cover. On arriving, I found it was far too wide to give me much chance of being able to guard even half of it. Choosing the narrowest part, I waited for the noise of the beaters to begin.

Almost directly afterward, double pistol shots, fired in rapid succession, gave me notice that the men had seen the tiger—for this was a signal agreed upon between us whenever a tiger or panther was known to be on foot so that we might look out and not spoil sport by firing at only a bear or even sambar. He was seen by the men placed above on either side of this big ravine on the lookout to be slowly creeping along just in front of the beaters. These men had brought him on from a long distance in beautiful style toward my post, which was on the top of a large rock where I was lying down with my battery by my side, expecting every moment to see the tiger. Suddenly a tremendous roaring was heard in the midst, it seemed to me, of the beaters. They, too, set up extra shouts and noise, rapidly firing six blank shots from the pistols with which they were provided. Then all was still. I feared some poor fellow had been hurt, perhaps killed, and waited in the greatest state of suspense while the men came silently up to my rock, having left off the noise of beating.

It appeared that two men had foolishly left the body of Bhils and gone down to a stream in the middle of the cover to drink. The tiger at once saw them and was observed by the men on the lookout above to crawl quietly toward these two fellows as if stalking them. They were quickly and just in time warned of their danger, for they both jumped down into the water just as the tiger, with awful roars, rushed toward them on the bank where they had been standing.

Being disappointed of his prey, he broke back over the very ground he had been so unwillingly driven, roaring terribly as he ran off to show his disgust at being so disturbed in the heat of the day. The men started to beat in two parties, keeping parallel with each other, and then joining when the cover got more narrow. Thus, through the stupidity of these two men, I lost an almost certain chance of killing this tiger, while they had a most wonderful escape from death. The footprints were enormous, and we found he had killed a large buffalo. It was too late in the day to again look for this tiger.

Next day I again tried with the same men to find this tiger, first going to a cover a little way off, where it was thought likely he had gone. But here the confounded bees turned out, so we had to leave the place at once, and some men were slightly stung.

Walking across to the big ravine we came upon the tiger's fresh prints. There was no mistaking their great size. Besides, the brute was well known and had been several times shot at by matchlock men, but with no effect. The beaters described this tiger as being very bold and fierce, killing buffaloes in broad daylight close to the walls of their villages. We followed the tracks silently for nearly four miles before finding that he had left this part of the country altogether. I sent back word for my tent to be brought on to Sawunt village, six miles off, while I continued following up the prints till dark. This pursuit compelled me to sleep out under a tree without any food till next morning, for the road was so bad and stony that the camels could not get on at all. Besides, the men left behind to assist in getting them up the *ghat*, or steep hill, took themselves off without warning. A few smashes among my baggage were the consequence of these bad roads, or mere paths rather. Rain unfortunately fell during the night, too, so we could not carry on and follow yesterday's prints any farther. The

*Bringing home a man-eater in triumph.*

villagers had lately found a dead tiger here by some water; most likely it had been poisoned. It's a dirty trick and the ruin of all sport, but they, of course, cannot view the matter in that light.

While looking over the ground here, on 24 April, I saw an old bear lying asleep at the mouth of a large cave, across a deep ravine and at least two hundred yards off. I fired three shots at her as she bolted downhill, on being woke up by my first bullet. Afterward went round and saw plenty of blood, but did not attempt to follow up this bear. She bolted, growling, and was accompanied by a half-grown cub, that also came out of the cave.

The weather still continued much too cool for sport, for though every likely cover was tried at the different places the tent was moved to, yet nothing was seen worth firing at.

After putting up a great many sambar at Gole Ambah, on the 28th, I was tempted to fire at one for the men to eat. As soon as I had fired, a bear turned out of a cave at my feet, only a few yards below. He quickly got the other barrel, which made him roar, but he rolled so fast down the steep rocks that formed the hillside that I could not get another shot at him before he disappeared in some very dense jungle in the plain below.

I had marched on as far as Buddana village by 2 May, with merely a few sambar shot. While beating a cover there, a tiger was seen slowly going over a stony open hill about five hundred yards off. The ground being quite cool this mild weather, I at once ran round sharp on the other side as fast as possible, telling the men to begin beating toward me in a few minutes' time. Just as I had got round the hill, the tiger came slowly on, about sixty yards off. When it saw me, it stopped still to take a good stare before passing on. This gave me a capital shot, which, to my delight, at once dropped the tiger, seemingly dead, for I had aimed at its head.

The beaters shortly afterward came up, and we were walking together toward the tiger when, at only twenty paces off, up the beast got, greatly to our surprise. Most of the men quickly sprang up trees while I fired two more shots, as sharp as possible, at this tiger. On forming a procession to follow up the blood, we soon came upon it dead. My first bullet had struck exactly between the brute's eyes, a little too low, so it was only stunned. I did not fire other shots at the time, for some of the Bhils declared there were two tigers known to live in this cover, so I hoped to see the other, but only this one appeared. It was a young tigress, a few inches over nine feet long and very prettily marked.

In consequence of the heavy shower, I had all the guns to clean on 4 May. A ravine named Ahmedghur, where there is a large ruined fort about four miles off, was said to be a likely place, so I went there with twenty-five men. On the road we saw two large snakes, called *dhamans,* at least ten feet long, and I shot them both. These reptiles have the most wonderful power of holding on by twisting the end of their tails round any substance presented to them.

The men, for fun, placed a stout stick on the extreme end of their tails when half dead; it was immediately seized and held so firmly that it was released with the greatest difficulty. In this manner the Bhils assured me these snakes caught and destroyed hares, young goats, etc. They did not think they were poisonous. Their colour was light brown, with a green tint above, and they have bright yellow bellies. The species does not seem common, for these were the first of the sort I had met.

On arriving at Ahmedghur, we heard a troop of monkeys swearing on the top of high trees, which told us what to expect. This ravine was so large that I was puzzled how to beat it, or where to post myself, and was unluckily persuaded to remain above on a precipice overlooking the cover. Almost immediately after the noise of the beaters began, out sprang a large tiger, but it was at least 120 yards off. I fired as he bounded down the steep hillside; the first shot missed, but my second bullet dropped him. He got up and crept into a small patch of very thick jungle just below me. There he remained for a long time, in spite of many shots fired at random into the thicket.

At last I caught a glimpse of him, slowly moving on to another patch of high grass and corinda bushes, and I made him roar loudly with another bullet. This last retreat, however, was even more dense than the first. After in vain trying to again make him show himself by firing away nearly all my ammunition at hazard into every corner of the cover, we went down in a body together to the first thicket. Here plenty of hair in tufts were found on the large, rough stones over which he had dragged himself. The men bravely enough much wished me to follow him into the other dense mass of bushes and high reeds where he had retreated, but this I feared to do, for there was not room even to use a gun if we had come upon him, and there would very probably have been an accident. We were thus obliged to leave him alone.

There were no trees over the cover from which a view could be obtained. This was one of those cases in which elephants are absolutely necessary to find a wounded tiger, for no one could have seen even one yard ahead in such thick vegetation. The tiger hunter on foot thus loses many a fine skin that would be secured easily enough if an elephant trained to the sport were at hand. Still, in the absence of elephants, it is better and more prudent to lose a tiger occasionally than to forgo the sport altogether for want of them.

It was very annoying to have to refuse accompanying the Bhils to look for a wounded beast in such dense bushes. If allowed, they would willingly have gone alone, having exaggerated notions from seeing other tigers killed of the effect of our bullets. Directly a drop of blood even was found, the wounded brute was sure to be pronounced dead, when perhaps it was only rendered more lively and vicious from the wound. Such caution on the part of the hunter then is sure to be considered merely another name for fear, which in fact it is.

Next day I again went over to this ravine, but I had the area beat first before looking for yesterday's tiger. Most unfortunately I took up another position below, for a tigress, quickly followed by her half-grown cub, at once turned out and, as ill luck would have it, sprang up the steep sides of the precipice

*The hunting camp.*

over which I had yesterday kept guard. I fired two shots but no doubt missed both since the distance was over a hundred yards. These tigers, in two leaps, managed to reach the top of the rocky level above the ravine, though the sides were as straight as a wall and at least twenty-five feet high. They rested, for a moment only, on a small ledge about halfway up and then bounded over. None of the men, or myself, had the slightest idea that they could so escape, but the schemes of these cunning animals seem endless. I never yet saw any two act alike. Hence, there is much to learn at this sport.

We next tried for the wounded tiger, and took his prints for some distance until they ceased on very stony ground. He had, therefore, far more life in him than we supposed. The ravine here requires at least three guns posted in different points to guard it, being so wide and steep.

Our next operations were in a beautiful cover named Earday, but we found no large game. This fact was accounted for by our meeting a party of men who were taking honey, of which there was a great quantity, because the sides of the rocks that formed this ravine were covered with bees' nests.

One or two Bhils, well protected with woolen clothes or coarse blankets, held up a pan of burning sulfur on the top of long bamboos, close to the bees' nests, and afterward knocked down the combs with the poles. They had several large earthen pots full of honey, and did not seem to mind the bees at all, although we gladly made our escape from the spot.

Going homeward, the men made a beat and put two tigers out of a cover. These brutes at once left the place and broke sideways over a steep bare hill, for it was raining at the time and quite cool. Had the weather only been hotter, they would have remained in the shade and no doubt have given me a fair shot as they passed by my post. For the next two days I saw no game, although we tried some very likely places a few miles farther on. At one the men did not seem to like the work, for, while hunting with a chief here lately for sambar only they were charged by a tigress with two young cubs, but no harm beyond the fright was done.

On 9 May, I sent on my baggage to Kunjaira village, and went to beat Bhogla Ravine, a fine cover that was full of tall willow trees. After a long drive, a fine tiger walked slowly out of the cover and coolly sat down under a shady tree about a hundred yards on one side, quite in an open space. Although the beaters were not far off, she did not seem to mind them at all. I was by a large tree about eighty yards off across the cover. I fired one shot as she was lying down. With a roar she jumped up and galloped across a rather open space for some high grass a short distance beyond. My second barrel missed. On going up to the spot with the beaters, my bullet was found about an inch deep in the stump of a tree. Of course we all thought it had missed, but, on cutting it carefully out with an ax, one or two men seemed to think it was too clean and bright. We began following up the tiger's prints and, after going about three hundred yards suddenly came upon this tiger, quite dead, in the high grass. There was not a single drop of blood to be found anywhere about. The ball had passed clean through her liver. This fine tigress was nine feet, four inches long, and very stout.

While following up this brute, most of the men seemed convinced she was hit in spite of there being no blood about. They believed she had been hit because, for a long distance, the ground was marked with her claws at each spring or leap she had made while bounding away. This, they declared, would not be the case if the beast were not wounded, for the action was very unnatural, and only caused by great rage and pain. A tiger may thus claw up the ground for a few yards only from fright on being shot at. If not hurt, however, he would instantly resume his usual pace. In this case his claws are always sheathed, for they are only ever protruded for the purpose of striking its prey or playfully tearing at tufts of long grass as they seem fond of doing, perhaps to clean their nails. At all other times the claws are completely hidden and protected. They would soon become blunt and worn down if used at all in walking. To alight on the hard, dry ground after each bound with the claws thus extended, the men declared, would greatly jar the tiger. We had cause two or three times afterward to notice this fact, and we became sure that a shot had told well even though no blood could be found if the ground was scratched for any great distance. It was proved in two cases when the tigers were both found dead, shot through the liver, after running about three hundred yards at most.

## Chapter Eight

# Walter Campbell
### My Indian Journal
### (1864)

When Colonel Walter Campbell wrote *The Old Forest Ranger* in 1840, it became one of England's most popular books on India. But, because it was fictional, Campbell felt obliged to appease his critics and describe the British experience in a more factual manner. The result was *My Indian Journal*, published in 1864.

Here Campbell gives a more nuanced account of Anglo-India, from the military routine to profiles of women and even ballroom dancing. But hunting is still a main theme, with stories on pig sticking and descriptions of bison, deer, and leopard hunts. Campbell describes many tiger hunts, including those that used nets by natives and spears from horseback. The author provides some of the first detailed accounts of the Nicobar and Andaman Islands, located off the east Indian coast. It was a land of inhospitable forests and equally inhospitable natives.

This story is part of a chapter on a "civilian camp." It is called so because Campbell, on military leave, spends it with his friend Elliot, a "civilian of high standards who travels with great comfort and luxury," something Campbell had never experienced. The campsite is in the plains below the malarial highlands where the party had been hunting until a colleague became ill, forcing them to the new location. Several tigers, including a man-eater, were shot by the party in their new camp.

### A Civilian Camp

April 22. While sitting at breakfast this morning, a messenger arrived with the welcome intelligence that the indefatigable Bussapa had marked down four tigers and two bears, and surrounded them in a ravine within six miles of our camp. We immediately mounted old Anak, placed a goodly supply of rockets and fireworks in the howdah, and proceeded to the place.

On reaching the ground we found the gorge closely guarded by some fifty well-armed Mahrattas. We learned that, just before our arrival, a fight had taken place between a tiger and one of the bears, which had taken off to the hills with a broken head. The others had not moved, and we immediately commenced beating.

The elephant was posted on a bank directly over the pass into one of the deep ravines that divide the hills. This was the tigers' path to and from their stronghold, and our position commanded it in every direction. After half an hour's tedious suspense, the cry of the beaters came shrilly echoing up the ravine, and signals were made that the tigers were afoot. Every rustle was now watched with breathless anxiety, and then the heavy tread of some animal was heard approaching.

The elephant trumpeted and the next moment, from under a tangled mass of creepers, appeared the grisly muzzle of an old bear, taking a precautionary peep before he ventured to expose his whole person. Fortunately for the poor bruin there was nobler game at hand, else he might not have met with so cool a reception. A hearty malediction, for intruding himself when not wanted, was his only greeting. Away he bundled, with most uncouth activity, down a precipitous bank, completely frightened out of his propriety by old Anak who had made a very loud sound.

Before the bear was out of sight, a tigress, in all the pride of her striped beauty, glided by with the stealthy pace of a cat. Two balls were into her before she passed, but she neither winced nor staggered, and without uttering a growl she disappeared among the bushes.

By this time the rockets were doing their work at the other end of the ravine. A short angry roar came hoarsely on the breeze that drove before it a sheet of flame from the ignited grass, and two tigers with their tails erect dashed past us at full speed. Each shot was answered by a savage growl, and a hind leg dangling after him showed that one of them was severely hit, as the bushes closed over his shrinking form. The other escaped untouched, Elliot and I having fired at the same tiger.

Signals were sent that the fourth tiger had broken away across country, so we ordered the beaters to retire to places of safety, and went in with the elephant to finish the wounded ones. Close to the bush where she had disappeared, we found the first tigress stretched on her side in a pool of blood and quite dead. She was shot through the heart and must have dropped just as we lost sight of her.

*The tiger in ambush.*

A little farther on the growling of the wounded tiger guided us to a dense thicket of creepers in which he was lying. Anak set to work in earnest, tearing away with his trunk the tangled mass till he came upon the tiger's lair. The crippled savage crawled out, grinning with rage but too weak to charge, and was rolled over by a volley of four barrels. He, however, recovered himself, and, while we reloaded, crawled away to another small clump of bushes where he lay watching us till we again went up to him. Game to the last, he rushed out to meet us and was shot dead directly under the elephant's trunk. As it was near sunset, we thought it too late to follow up the two tigers that had broken away, so we returned to the tents, well pleased with our day's sport.

In the evening a party of dancing girls from the neighbouring pagoda came to exhibit before us. They were pretty, graceful creatures, with antelope eyes and well-turned limbs, richly dressed in silken robes, with a profusion of silver bangles encircling their slender ankles, and wreaths of wild jasmine twined throughout their dark hair. Their dancing, too, or rather their motion—for the twining of their slender figures and the waving of their arms could hardly be called dancing—was rather graceful. The exhibition would have been pleasing enough were it not that they accompanied their movements with a song the shrill discordant notes of which were perfectly distracting and made us soon glad to dismiss them.

I have heard some shrill pipes enough among the lasses of my native land, but never have I heard a voice so shrill, so piercing, or so unmusical as that of an Indian *nautch* girl [dancer]. Yet the nobles of the East will sit for hours together, listening with delight to their discordant notes. So depraved is their taste that I never met with a single native who could appreciate European music. They acknowledge our superiority in most things, but declare that we are centuries behind them in the art of producing sweet sounds.

April 23. Elliot and I fell in with a "sounder" of hog this morning on our way back from a neighbouring village where he had been to transact some business. We fortunately had our hunters and spears with us, and soon collected a number of country people to drive them out of a field of grain in which they had taken refuge. We let the sounder get well away in hopes of a boar being left behind in the grain, but none appeared. We therefore laid into the largest sow at a pace that soon brought us alongside of her. Challenger went well on this his first trial, so it pleased me much. He shows great speed, is perfectly temperate, and turns well in a snaffle, which is a qualification of the utmost importance in a hog hunter. I ought to have taken the first spear easily, but being a novice in the use of the weapon, I missed my thrust, smashed my spear-head among the stones, nearly lost my seat, and was cut out by Elliot on a much slower horse.

We had hardly reached the tents when we were met by a peon with the welcome intelligence of a large boar wallowing in a small lake within half a mile of the tents. Spears and fresh horses were quickly produced, and we had just mounted when a horseman galloped up and announced a tiger had been marked in the opposite direction. We were now embarrassed with too much good news, but we speedily decided in favour of the tiger.

In less than an hour we were seated on the back of our trusty friend Anak and listening to the shouts of the beaters as they drove the tiger toward us. He came up boldly and was almost abreast of us when, unfortunately, the elephant trumpeted and spoilt all. The tiger instantly turned and galloped back at his best pace to some impenetrable covert. The flying shots we sent after him in his retreat only knocked up the gravel about his heels without doing him any harm. Every attempt to burn him out or force the elephant in was equally unavailing, for the bushes were green and the tangled thicket perfectly impenetrable. After expending all our fireworks, we were obliged to give in and leave him.

April 25. Fortune favoured us today with three tigers that were found by the merest chance when it appeared more than probable that we must return empty-handed. Elliot and I rode out at daylight to reconnoitre the country where our people had been sent the day before to look for tigers. We were holding a consultation with old Bussapa, who was quite in low spirits because he had failed in discovering any fresh tracks, and we had just decided on trying new ground when a tigress with two well-grown cubs, nearly as large as herself, came down from the hills and quietly walked into a ravine within a few hundred yards of us.

All was speedily arranged, the elephant posted in a good position, markers placed on every rising ground commanding the ravine, and the beaters drawn up, ready to act. The signal was given. In went a flight of rockets, accompanied by the true shikar yell, and the tigress was afoot, trotting toward us. We let her come up within ten yards, and then, as she stood hesitating whether to charge or turn back upon the beaters, we gave her a volley that sent her down upon her haunches. She instantly rallied and laid up in one of the strong coverts of the ravine.

The two cubs galloped past together, roaring so loudly that the elephant became alarmed and wheeled round at the moment we were about to fire. This disconcerted our aim, and they escaped, one untouched and the other slightly wounded in the hindquarter. The wounded cub crept, growling, into the first thick bush he reached and was marked down by one of the lookout men, and there we left him to his meditations while we disposed of the old tigress.

Little search was required to find her, for she came boldly forth to meet us, received our fire, and dashed at the elephant without flinching, although she was severely hit and was obliged to climb a high bank to reach him. A ball between the eyes dropped her just as she was in the act of springing on the elephant, and she rolled into the ravine dead.

A storm, which had been gathering for hours among the hills, now rolled in masses of cloud, black as night, and burst over our heads with a peal of thunder that seemed to shake the earth to its centre. The rain descended in a deluge, such as can only be witnessed in the tropics, and, in less than ten minutes, the dry channel of the nullah [gully] had become a foaming torrent, hurrying away the carcass of the dead tigress that, a few minutes before, had been trotting along its hot, sandy bed. The whole face of the country was soon a sheet of water, and there was nothing for it but to gallop home before the ravines became impassable. We reached our tents about sunset, more than half drowned, after a splitting gallop of eight miles across country, during which I thought myself fortunate in only taking one fall.

The tigress killed today was a savage devil and well known in this part of the country, for she had destroyed a number of people lately. One of her victims was the son of poor Bussapa. This man had fired at and missed her when she charged, and she had pulled him down from the tree on which he was seated and had carried him off. Her death has occasioned great joy among the country people, and no one glories in her fall more sincerely than old Bussapa.

April 29. We left the village with the unpronounceable name three days ago, and have done nothing on the road except frightening a bear, which escaped among the hills. This morning we found two bears asleep in one of the deep nullahs near the river, or rather they were found for us, just as we were on the point of marching. They were easily started, and came up abreast of each other along a ledge on the face of a steep rock. Elliot and I took one each, and they both dropped at the same moment. The largest, mortally

*The sambar, a creature of dense Indian forests.*

wounded, never moved from the spot but expired with a long yell that was returned by a hundred echoes.

The other looked at his fallen companion, rose slowly, and before we could snatch up our spare guns, threw himself over the scarped rock, and, putting his head between his hind legs, rolled like an avalanche into the dark ravine. He reached the bottom just as the beaters arrived at the spot and immediately charged one of them. But fortunately he was so much exhausted by his wounds and the rapid descent he had made that the man he attempted to seize was able with the assistance of his companions to beat him off without being bitten. Luckily he received no other injury than being spattered with blood.

In the midst of the melee a panther sprang up and broke cover at a racing pace. We gave chase, but he beat us, and reached the hills untouched. On our return we found that the wounded bear had fought his way through the beaters and escaped. We never found him again.

Gootul, April 30. A notorious old man-eating tigress, with four cubs, which has been the terror of the neighbourhood for some months back, was marked down this morning, and almost the whole population of the village turned out to assist in her destruction. As she had the character of extreme ferocity, unusual precautions were taken in the effort to destroy her, and volleys of blank cartridges with flights of rockets were thrown into every thick place, far in advance of the beaters.

The tigress was soon afoot, and our assistant mahout, who was posted on a tree as a lookout, held up five fingers to telegraph, while he shook with agitation on beholding the whole royal family passing close under him. On reaching the edge of the cover where we were posted, the tigress left her cubs behind, walked out into the plain, and boldly looked the elephant in the face, laying her ears back, growling savagely, and curling up her whiskered lips with a look of indescribable ferocity. Every hair on her back stood erect, her long tail switched from side to side like that of an enraged cat, and her glowing eyes were fixed upon us with a look of fiendish malignity. I never saw a more perfect representation of an incarnate devil. I remained for some seconds with my rifle poised, studying the magnificent picture that the scene presented and feeling a sort of reluctance to put an end to it by firing the first shot.

Every tree and rock was crowded with spectators watching with anxious looks and beating hearts the issue of our contest with their deadly foe. The wild yells of the beaters, the hissing of the rockets, and the rattle of firearms had given place to an ominous silence, like that which precedes the outbreak of a hurricane. No sound was heard, save an occasional low deep growl, which might well be compared to distant thunder that heralds an approaching tempest. The tigress, in the attitude I have described, and our noble elephant, with his trunk carefully coiled up between his tusks, stood face to face, like two combatants who have just entered the lists and scan each other with jealous looks before venturing to engage in mortal combat.

The elephant took one step forward, and the tigress, uttering a hoarse growl, drew herself together as if about to spring. It was now time to act, and the report of our rifles was answered by an exulting shout from the spectators as the tigress, hit in the point of the shoulder, rolled over, tearing up the earth with her claws in a fruitless effort to regain her footing. She at last succeeded in doing so and slunk back into cover, with one foreleg dangling from the shoulder. This shot decided her fate. To prevent any accident occurring to mar the sport we anticipated when she was brought to close quarters, we ordered the spectators and beaters to betake themselves to trees where they would be fairly out of reach.

Anak was now walked into the thicket, but we had hardly proceeded twenty yards when that harsh grating roar that makes the blood curdle, followed by a despairing shriek, gave us dread warning that some unfortunate beater had disregarded our caution and fallen a victim to his temerity. A wild cry of rage and execration arose from the assembled multitude, many of whom, from their elevated positions, were able to witness the tragedy. But so far from being awed by the fate of their companion, it was with some difficulty that we prevented them from rushing in, sword in hand, and hewing the tiger to pieces, although they well knew that in so doing many lives would have been sacrificed.

Every exertion was now made to hurry the elephant to the spot. The mahout plied his iron goad, and the sagacious brute crashed his way through the tangled brushwood to the scene of blood. The tigress, enraged by the pain of her wounds and roused to madness by the taste of blood, rushed out upon three legs and charged the elephant with determined bravery. Our large friend with the trunk did not like it, and, wheeling round with a scream of alarm, he shuffled off at his best trot. In consequence he jolted the howdah to such a degree that we found it impossible to fire, although the tigress was giving chase with open mouth and close on the elephant's haunches. The mahout at last succeeded in checking his pace to a certain degree, and just as the tigress was about to spring on his croup, I took a snapshot and hit her. This made the savage old devil rather faint, and she lay down to recover her breath. After some trouble, we succeeded in stopping the elephant and coaxed him into returning to stand another charge.

The tigress lay perfectly still till we were within ten yards, when she started up with a loud roar and made at us more savagely than ever. She had hardly got upon her legs, however, when she was knocked over by a volley from four barrels and completely doubled up. The elephant, whose nerves appeared to have been shaken by the first charge, again turned tail and ran. On returning after having reloaded, we found the tigress lying with her head between her paws, ready to receive us. We fired at her as she was in the act of springing on the elephant's trunk, and a lucky shot between the eyes rolled her over dead.

The fall of this noted tigress was hailed with shouts of triumph by the amateurs who had watched the whole proceeding from their perches. A poor little herd-boy, whose brother had been devoured a few days before by the tigress and her cubs, was the first to descend and exult over the prostrate man-eater.

As the cubs were described as not being larger than a pointer-dog, we commenced a hunt after them on foot, armed with swords, but the little brutes had concealed themselves so effectually that we could not find them.

The poor little herd-boy had twice before been attacked by this same tigress, but a herd of fine, large buffaloes that he tended, headed by a sagacious old bull, had come to his call and had driven her off. He was close to his brother that fateful day when she seized him, and he actually saw the tigress with her four cubs feeding off the body. Unfortunately, on that occasion the buffaloes were grazing at some distance. Had they heard the boy's cries or seen the tigress, they would probably have charged and beaten her back, for they had been seen to attack her in a body several times when she ventured into the open plain. The boy said he never feared a tiger as long as his cattle were near him.

The natives begged to be allowed to carry home the tigress after their own fashion, and she was accordingly handed over to them to be dealt with as they saw fit. They carefully singed off the whiskers and performed various superstitious ceremonies, and then they placed the body of the tigress, ornamented with garlands of flowers, upright on a cart. Drawn by eight bullocks, the cart in this state was dragged in procession through the village. It was preceded by a band of native musicians and followed by a crowd of men, women, and children, exulting over the remains of their deadly foe and invoking blessing on our heads for having rid them of her dreaded presence.

Killing a tiger is at all times a satisfactory exploit. But the death of a brute like this, such a terror while living and so game in her last moments, is indeed a glorious victory. Were it not for the melancholy fate of the unfortunate beater, I should say this was the most satisfactory day's sport I have yet seen in India. An accident of this sort is always a sad damper to one's feelings of triumph, but we have at least the satisfaction of thinking that it was occasioned entirely by the poor fellow's own imprudence and that by ridding the country of this dreadful scourge we have probably been the means of saving many human lives at the expense of one.

In a later part of my journal, I find the following remarks upon the foolhardy courage displayed by natives in tiger hunting, which, being apropos to the subject, may with propriety be introduced here.

Natives, in beating for a tiger, become excited in proportion to the increase of their danger, rushing wildly through the jungle as if running amok and frequently throwing themselves into the very jaws of the infuriated animal, in spite of the utmost exertions on the part of the European sportsmen to restrain them. This resolute manner of going to work generally ensures the death of the tiger. But too often, in the moment of victory, comes the heart-sickening intelligence that some unfortunate fellow is lying mangled beside the dead beast. Nothing can exceed the determined bravery of the natives on such an occasion, for death seems to have no terrors for them when a tiger is their game. Not even the sight of their companion's dreadful fate can daunt them, and they seem actuated by some inspired feeling that renders them unconscious of fear.

I never could account for this and have often in vain sought to trace the cause why the man who has for ages submitted to a foreign yoke, who trembles at the frown of a European, should possess courage enough, voluntarily, to face so fearful a death. There is something inexpressibly terrible in the charge of a tiger. Man appears so defenseless, so utterly helpless, opposed to the gigantic strength of the striped monster who springs upon him with a force that crushes him like a worm in the dust. I can say, from sad experience, it is a sight, once seen, of which time can never obliterate the remembrance. Yet the timid Hindoo, as he is called, opposes his feeble frame, armed only with a sword and shield, to this most formidable of all animals.

In the southern Mahratta country, I have known several instances of a body of men thus armed rushing in upon a tiger and cutting him to pieces, but I never knew one case unattended with a serious loss of human life. When firearms are used, it must be allowed by anyone who has ever seen an Indian matchlock that some determination is required to face a tiger, under any circumstances, with such a miserable weapon. A matchlock is, without exception, the most awkward, ill-constructed engine for throwing projectiles that ever was invented. The barrel is from six to seven feet long, seldom quite straight, and enormously top-heavy. The stock, disproportionately short, is furnished with a shallow pan to contain the priming, which is protected from wet by a sliding lid plastered with cow-dung. The rude trigger, connected with the cock—to which is attached a match of hempen-cord, dipped in saltpetre—completes this primitive weapon.

Thus armed, a European would be hopeless of doing execution. In the first place, the match must be lighted and the pan opened—and it is quite a matter of chance whether the match will even ignite the damp priming. If it does ignite, there is no certainty of its communicating with the charge in the barrel. The charge, consisting of a handful of gunpowder as coarse in the grain as bay-salt, is pounded into a cake by means of an iron ramrod, jammed down with a piece of damp cow-dung, and surmounted by one or more bullets—not cast but carved or hammered. Add to this that the weapon has probably been loaded for a month, and you will wonder, as I have often done, at anyone's hoping to make a successful shot with an Indian matchlock. A miss often proves fatal, but the Hindoo, strong in faith, mutters a prayer over his long barrel and fires at a tiger's head as coolly as if he were aiming at a target. I quote the following ludicrous instance of sangfroid on the part of a native hunter during a lion hunt in Guzerat, as related by one of the party:

> I was infinitely diverted with one of the village coolies who accompanied us, his matchlock over his shoulder, the pan carefully closed with a bit of cloth, and a lump of burning cow-dung in his hand, with which to ignite his match if necessary. This worthy, thus equipped, was literally poking his addled head into the very centre of the bush, said to contain the lion, and, moreover, pulling the grass aside to admit of a better view.
>
> "What, in the name of Heaven, are you doing?" exclaimed my companion.

"Doing!" replied the fellow, with evident surprise, and coolly blowing his fid of cow-dung. "Why, looking for the lion, to be sure! Are not you looking for him?"

One other anecdote of foolhardy daring on the part of a European, and I have done with tigers for this chapter. Some years ago a notorious tiger was marked in a thicket in Guzerat by the hunters of a young officer, who on that occasion was on foot. He proposed that they should beat out the tiger while he stood at one end of the jungle. In that way he could shoot the tiger as he broke cover. On this, his men tauntingly replied "that he dared not enter the jungle although he asked them to do so."

Fired at this, the young Englishman exclaimed, "I never bid another what I fear to do myself."

He then led the way into the dark thicket, followed by two natives. It was so interwoven with creepers that they were obliged to crawl on their hands and knees. In this awkward attitude they crept toward the tiger's lair in almost total darkness. Before there was time to raise a rifle, the monster was upon them with a roar of thunder. Both the natives were struck dead on the spot, and the gallant though imprudent young man fell, stunned by a blow that nearly fractured his skull. He was dragged out, severely lacerated, but he eventually recovered.

Never attack a tiger on foot if you can help it. There are cases in which you must do so. If so, then face him like a Briton, and kill him if you can, for if you fail to kill him, he will certainly kill you. But, unless you are ambitious of obtaining *la gloire* at any price, do not imitate the example of our Gallic friend Jules Gerard and challenge your feline to mortal combat when you have a chance of potting him from behind a stone. He did so . . . and by moonlight! But then, he was a Frenchman!

## Chapter Nine

# James Forsyth
## The Highlands of Central India
### (1871)

James Forsyth was the first Englishman to describe the natural history and cultures of India's central highlands, which form the northern rim of the immense Indian "triangle," or Deccan Plateau. Forsyth's job as a forester allowed him to travel widely throughout the highlands where he was able to see pristine forests and hunt many wild animals.

The highlands are a series of interconnected hill ranges—the Satpuras, Vindhyas, Maikals, and Mahadeos—covered with dense sal and teak forests. The mountainous terrain and location in the interior of the country made the highlands one of the last areas explored and developed by Europeans. That also made them a haven for wild animals and forest tribes, including the Gonds, Korkus, and Baigas. Forsyth's elegant writing style mixed with keen observations about plant, animal, and human life have made *The Highlands of Central India* a classic in Indian natural history, exploration, and hunting literature. It was Forsyth's only book, as he died a short time after its publication, in his early thirties.

Forsyth dedicates several chapters to wild animals. This chapter on the tiger describes the animal's habits and Forsyth's many experiences with the cat. This particular episode, which takes place in the Satpura hill range just south of the Narmada River, pits Forsyth against a local man-eater that had been wreaking havoc.

### The Tiger

In the end of April and May of 1862 I bagged six tigers and one panther in the Betul jungles, wounding two more tigers that escaped. I was unable regularly to devote myself to tiger shooting, having much forest work to do, and my shooting was also much interfered with by accidental circumstances.

A sprained tendon laid me up for fifteen days of the best weather (the hottest), and there was so much cholera about that many of the best places had to remain unvisited.

Another party was also shooting in the same district, and, though they arrived after me in the field, contrary to the well-understood rule in such circumstances, proceeded ahead and disturbed the whole country by indiscriminate firing at deer and peafowl. It is scarcely necessary to say that when after tigers nothing else should be fired at. The *lalla* [rural caste member] came out strong under these unfavourable circumstances, working ahead and securing a monopoly of information including the conduct of rival hunters who, he was told, harassed the people for provisions and thrashed them all round if a tiger was not found for them when they arrived.

On one occasion I reached their ground just as their last camel was moving off to a new camp. They had stayed here a week trying in vain to extort help in finding a couple of tigers whose tracks they had seen. The tigers were all the time within half a mile of their tents, and before ten o'clock that day I had them both padded. During a whole month I believe they succeeded in getting only one tiger, and that by potting it from a tree at night. Some years afterward, when I shot in the same country under much more favourable circumstances, the number of tigers had greatly diminished, owing to the high rewards and the steady attentions of the forest officers, and my bag was then just the same as in 1862. Five or six tigers may, in fact, be considered a very fair bag for one gun in a month's shooting, even in the best parts of the central provinces, but two or three guns, with a proportionate force of elephants, should, of course, do much better.

I spent nearly a week of this time in the destruction of a famous man-eater that had completely closed several roads and was estimated to have devoured more than a hundred human beings. One of these roads was the main outlet from the Betul teak forests toward the railway then under construction in the Narmada Valley. The work of the sleeper-contractors was completely at a standstill owing to the ravages of this brute. He occupied regularly a large triangle of country between the Rivers Moran and Narmada, occasionally making a tour of destruction much farther to the east and west, and striking terror into the inhabitants in a breadth of not less than thirty to forty miles. It was, therefore, supposed that the devastation was caused by more than one animal, and we thought we had disposed of one of these early in April when we

*The gaur or forest bison in its favored habitat.*

killed a very cunning old tiger of evil repute after several days' severe hunting. But I am now certain that the brute I destroyed subsequently was the real malefactor even there, as killing again commenced after we had left, and all loss to human life did not cease till the day I finally disposed of him.

He had not been heard of for a week or two when I came into his country and pitched my camp in a splendid mango grove near the large village of Lokartalae, on the Moran River. Here I was again laid up through over-using my sprained tendon, but a better place in which to pass the long, hot days of forced inactivity could not have been found. The bare, brown country outside was entirely shut out by the long, drooping branches of the huge mango trees. These were interlaced overhead in a graceful canopy and loaded with the half-ripe fruit pendent on their long, tendril-like stalks, while beneath them short glimpses were seen of the bright, clear waters of the Moran stealing over their pebbly bed. The green mangoes, cooked in a variety of ways, furnished a grateful and cooling addition to the table, and the whole grove was alive with a vast variety of bird and insect life, in the observation of which many an hour that would otherwise have flown slowly by was passed.

A colony of the lively chirping little gray-striped squirrel lived in every tree, and from morning to night permeated the whole grove with their incessant gambols. My dogs would have died of ennui, I believe, but for the unremitting sport they had in stalking and chasing these unattainable creatures, whose fashion of letting them get within two inches of them while they calmly sat up and ate a fallen mango, and then whisking up and sitting just half a foot out of reach, jerking their long tails and rapping out a long chirp of defiance, seemed to provoke them highly. Clouds of little, green ring-necked parakeets flew from tree to tree, clambering over and under and in every direction through the branches to get at the green mangoes. A great variety of bright-coloured bulbuls, several species of woodpecker, and the golden oriole or mango-bird flashed about in the higher foliage, while an incessant hum told of the unseen presence of multitudes of the insect world.

I was much amused by the result of my tent being pitched between two trees inhabited, respectively, by colonies of the common black and red ants so plentiful in all wooded parts of the province. Each side sent detachments down the ropes of the tent attached to their trees, and numerous were the skirmishes and reprisals I watched between them. At last, on coming in from a short stroll one morning, I found that the top of my tent had been the scene of a pitched battle between the entire forces of each party, multitudes on each side having been killed and wounded. Their telegrams to headquarters in the tops of the trees must have much resembled those of the French and Prussians, for both sides seemed to claim the victory, and each was busily engaged in carrying off the fallen of the other side, perhaps with a view to provender in case of a siege! There were far more of the black ones, however, killed than of the red.

The latter are most unflinching and venomous little devils, and prefer to have their heads and shoulders sticking where they have bitten rather than loose their hold. I shall never forget disturbing a nest of these red ants in an overhanging tree when hot on the fresh footprints of a tiger. In an instant the elephant, howdah, and myself were covered with a multitude of the creatures, rearing themselves on end and watching for a tender place in which to plunge their nippers. No philosophy—not even in the hot pursuit of a tiger—could stand this. Everything was forgotten in a wild rush to the nearest water where half an hour was lost in clearing ourselves and the half-maddened elephant of the tormentors, and in picking out the fangs they had left behind.

A few days of a lazy existence in this microcosm of a grove passed not unpleasantly after a spell of hard work in the pitiless hot blasts outside, but when the *lalla* brought in news of families of tigers waiting to be hunted in the surrounding riverbeds, I began to chafe. When I heard from a neighbouring police post that the man-eater had again appeared and had killed a man and a boy on the high road about ten miles from my camp, I could stand it no longer. I had been douching my leg with cold water, but now I resorted to stronger measures, giving it a coating of James's Horse Blister, which caused, of course, severe pain for a few days, but at the end resulted, to my great delight, in a complete and permanent cure.

In the meantime, while I was still raw and sore, I was regaled with stories of the man-eater: of his fearful size and appearance, with belly pendent to the ground, and white moon on the top of his forehead; his pork butcherlike method of detaining a party of travelers while he rolled himself in the sand and at last came up and inspected them all round, selecting the fattest; his power of transforming himself into an innocent-looking woodcutter, and calling or whistling through the woods till an unsuspecting victim approached; and how the spirits of all his victims rode with him on his head, warning him of every danger, and guiding him to the fatal ambush where a traveler would shortly pass. All the best shikaris of the countryside were collected in my camp, and the landholders and many of the people besieged my tent morning and evening. The infant of a woman who had been carried away while drawing water at a well was brought and held up before me, and every offer of assistance in destroying the monster was made.

No useful help was, however, to be expected from a terror-stricken population like this. They lived in barricaded houses and only stirred out when necessity compelled, and then in large bodies protected by armed men and people beating drums and shouting as they passed along the roads. Many villages had been utterly deserted, and the country was evidently being slowly depopulated by this single animal. So far as I could learn, he had been killing on his own for about a year. Another tiger who had formerly assisted him in his fell occupation was shot the previous hot weather.

Betul has always been unusually favoured with man-eaters, the cause apparently being the great numbers of cattle that come for a limited season to graze in that country and a scarcity of other prey at the time when they are absent, combined with the unusually convenient covert for tigers existing alongside most of the roads. The man-eaters of the central provinces rarely confine themselves solely to human food, though some have almost done so to my own knowledge.

Various circumstances may lead a tiger to prey on man—anything, in fact, that incapacitates him from killing other game more difficult to procure. A tiger who has got very fat and heavy, or very old, or who has been disabled by a wound, or a tigress who has had to bring up young cubs where other game is scarce—all these take naturally to man, who is the easiest animal of all to kill. As soon as failure with other prey brings on the pangs of hunger, a tiger will resort to eating man. And once a tiger has found out how easy it is to overcome the lord of creation and how good he is to eat, he is apt to stick to this diet, and, if it's a tigress, she will bring up her progeny in the same line of business. Great grazing districts, where the cattle come only for a limited season, are always the worst. Where the cattle remain all the year round, as in Nimar, the tigers rarely take to man-eating.

As soon as I could ride in the howdah, and long before I could do more than hobble on foot, I marched to a place called Charkhari, where the last kill had been reported. My usually straggling following was now compressed into a close body, preceded and followed by the baggage-elephants and protected by a guard of police with muskets, peons with my spare guns, and a whole posse of matchlocked shikaris. Two deserted villages were passed on the road, and heaps of stones at intervals showed where a traveler had been struck down. A better hunting ground for a man-eater certainly could not be found. Thick, scrubby teak jungle closed in the road on both sides, and alongside of it for a great part of the way wound a narrow, deep watercourse, overshadowed by thick *jamun* bushes, and with here and there a small pool of water still left.

I hunted along this nullah the whole way and found many old tracks of a very large male tiger, which the shikaris declared to be the man-eater. There were none more recent, however, than several days. Charkhari was also deserted on account of the tiger, and there was no shade to speak of, but it was the most central place within reach of the usual haunts of the brute, so I encamped and sent the baggage elephants back to fetch provisions.

In the evening I was startled by a messenger from a place called Le on the Moran River, nearly in the direction I had come from, who said that one of a party of pilgrims who had been traveling unsuspectingly by a jungle road had been carried off by the tiger close to that place. Early next morning I started off with two elephants and arrived at the spot about eight o'clock. The man had been struck down where a small ravine leading down to the Moran crosses a lonely pathway a few miles east of Le. The shoulder stick with its pendent baskets, in which the holy water from his place of pilgrimage had been carried by the hapless man, were lying on the ground in a dried-up pool of blood, and shreds of his clothes adhered to the bushes where he had been dragged down into the bed of the nullah.

We tracked the man-eater and his prey into a very thick grass covert, alive with spotted deer, where he had broken up and devoured the greater part of the body. Some bones and shreds of flesh along with the skull, hands, and feet were all that remained. This tiger never returns to his victim a second time, so it was useless to found any scheme for killing him on that expectation. We took up his tracks from the body and followed them patiently down through very dense jungle to the banks of the Moran. The trackers were fearful and trembling as they walked under the trunk of my elephant, even though covered by my rifle at full cock.

At the river the tracks went out to a long spit of sand that projected into the water. There the tiger had drunk and then returned to a great mass of piled-up rocks at the bottom of a precipitous bank, which was full of caverns and recesses. This we searched with stones and some fireworks I had in the

*The Korku, one of the main forest tribes of the Highlands.*

howdah, but nothing came out but a scraggy hyena, which was, of course, allowed to escape. We searched about all day there in vain, and it was not till nearly sunset that I turned and made for camp.

It was almost dusk when one of the men who was walking behind the elephant started and called a halt. He had seen the footprint of a tiger. At that point we were a few miles from home and passing along the road we had marched by the former day and the same by which we had come out in the morning. The elephant's tread had partly obliterated the track, but farther on, where we had not yet gone, it was found plain enough—the great square pug of the man-eater we had been looking for all day! He was on before us, and must have passed since we came out in the morning, for his track had covered those of the elephants.

It was too late to hope to find him that evening, and we could only proceed slowly along on the track, which held to the pathway, keeping a bright lookout. The *lalla* proposed that he should go a little ahead as a bait for the tiger, while I covered him from the elephant with a rifle! But he wound up by expressing a doubt whether his skinny corporation would be a sufficient attraction and suggested instead that a plump young policeman, who had taken advantage of our protection to make his official visit to the scene of the last kill, should be substituted, whereat there was a general but not very hearty grin. The subject was too sore a one in that neighbourhood just then.

About a mile from the camp the track turned off into the deep nullah that bordered the road. It was now almost dark, so we went on to the camp and fortified it by posting the three elephants on different sides and lighting roaring fires between. Once in the night an elephant started out of its deep sleep and trumpeted shrilly, but in the morning we could find no tracks of the tiger having come near us. I went out early next morning to beat up the nullah, for a man-eater is not like common tigers and must be sought for morning, noon, and night. But I found no tracks, save in the one place where he had crossed the nullah the evening before; he had then gone off into thick jungle.

After my return to camp and just as I was sitting down to breakfast, some Banjaras (Gypsies) from a place called Dekna—about a mile and a half from camp—came running in to say that one of their companions had been taken out of the middle of their drove of bullocks by the tiger, just as they were starting from their night's encampment. Since the elephant had not been unharnessed, I secured some food and a bottle of claret and was not two minutes in getting under way again.

The edge of a low savanna, covered with long grass and intersected by a nullah, was the scene of this last assassination. A broad trail of crushed-down grass showed where the body had been dragged down toward the nullah. No tracking was required. It was horribly plain. The trail did not lead quite into the nullah, which had steep sides, but turned and went alongside of it into some very long grass reaching nearly up to the howdah. Here Sarju Parshad (a large government *mukna* [tuskless male elephant] I was then riding) kicked violently at the ground and trumpeted, and immediately the long grass began to wave ahead. We pushed on at full speed, stepping as we went over the ghastly half-eaten body of the Banjara.

But the covert was dreadfully thick, and though I caught a glimpse of a yellow object as it jumped down into the nullah, it was not in time to fire. It was some little time before we could get the elephant down the bank and follow the broad, plain footprints of the monster, now evidently going at a swinging trot. He kept on in the nullah for about a mile and then took to the grass again, but it was not so long here, and we could still make out the trail from the howdah. Presently, however, it led into rough, stony ground, and the tracking became more difficult. He was evidently full of go, and would carry us far, so I sent back for some more trackers, and with orders to send a small tent across to a hamlet on the banks of the Ganjal, toward which he seemed to be making. All that day we followed the trail through an exceedingly difficult country, patiently working out print by print, but without being gratified by a sight of his brindled hide. Several of the local shikaris were admirable trackers, and we carried the line down within about a mile of the river, where a dense, thorny covert began, through which no one could follow a tiger.

We slept that night at the little village and early next morning made a long cast ahead, proceeding at once to the river where we soon hit upon the track leading straight down its sandy bed. There were some strong covers reported in the riverbeds a few miles ahead near the large village of Bhadugaon, so I sent back to order the tent over there. The track was crossed in this river by several others, but it was easily distinguishable from all by its superior size. It had also a peculiar drag of the toe of one hind foot, which the people knew and attributed to a wound he had received some months before from a shikari's matchlock. There was thus no doubt we were behind the man-eater, and I determined to follow him while I could hold out and we could keep the track. It led right into a very dense covert of jamun and tamarisk in the bed and on the banks of the river, a few miles above Bhadugaon. Having been hard pushed the previous day, we hoped he might lie up here, and, indeed, there was no other place he could well go to for water and shade. So we circled the outside of the covert and, finding no track leading out, considered him fairly ringed. We then went over to the village for breakfast, intending to return in the heat of the day.

There I was told by one of the mahouts a story that I afterward heard confirmed from the lips of one of the principal actors, regarding a notable encounter with tigers in the very covert where we had ringed the man-eater. It was in 1853 that the two brothers N. and Colonel G. beat the covert for a family of tigers said to be in it. Another brother was posted in a tree, while G. and N. beat through on an elephant. The man on the tree first shot two of the tigers right and left, and then Colonel G. saw a very large one lying in the shade of a dense bush and fired at it, on which it charged and mounted on the elephant's head.

It was a small female elephant, and she was terribly punished about the trunk and eyes in this encounter. The mahout, a bold fellow named Ramzan who was afterward in my own service, battered the tiger's head with his iron driving-hook so as to leave deep marks in the bones of his skull. At length the tiger was shaken off and retreated. When the sportsmen urged in the elephant again and the tiger charged as before, she turned round, and the tiger, catching her by the hind leg, fairly pulled her over on her side. My informant, who was in the howdah, said that for a time his arm was pinned between it and the body of the tiger, which was making efforts to pull his shikari out of the backseat.

They were all, of course, spilt on the ground with their guns, and Colonel G., getting hold of one, made the tiger retreat with a shot in the chest. The elephant had fled from the scene of action, and the two sportsmen then went after the beast on foot. It charged again, and when close to them was finally dropped by a lucky shot in the head. But the sport did not end there, for they found two more tigers in the same covert immediately afterward, and killed one of them—or four altogether in the day. The worrying she had received, however, was the death of the elephant, which was buried at Bhadugaon. This is one of the few instances on record of an elephant actually being killed by a tiger.

About eleven o'clock we again faced the scorching hot wind and made silently for the covert where lay the man-eater. I surrounded it with scouts in trees and posted a pad-elephant at the only point where he could easily get up the high bank and make off, and then pushed old Sarju slowly and carefully through the covert. Peafowl rose in numbers from every bush as we advanced, and a few hares and other small animals bolted out at the edges, such thick, green coverts being the midday resort for all life in the neighbourhood in hot weather. The centre of the jungle was extremely thick, and the bottom was cut up into a number of parallel water channels among the strong roots and overhanging branches of the tamarisk.

Here the elephant paused and began to kick the earth and utter the low, tremulous sound by which some elephants denote the close presence of a tiger. We peered all about with nervous beatings of the heart, and at last the mahout, who was lower down on the elephant's neck, said he saw him lying beneath a thick jamun bush. We had some stones in the howdah, and I made the *lalla*, who was behind me in the backseat, pitch one into the bush. Instantly the tiger started up with a short roar and galloped off through the bushes. I gave him a right and left at once, which told loudly, but he rushed away till he saw the pad-elephant blocking the road he meant to escape by, and then he turned and charged back at me with horrible roars.

It was very difficult to see him among the crashing bushes, and he was within twenty yards when I fired again. This dropped him into one of the channels, but he picked himself up and came on again as savagely, though more slowly than before. I was now in the act of covering him with the large-shell rifle when suddenly the elephant spun round, and I found myself looking the opposite way. At the same time there was a worrying sound behind me, and the frantic movements of the elephant told me I had a fellow-passenger on board I might well have dispensed with.

All I could do in the way of holding on barely sufficed to prevent myself and my guns from being pitched out, and it was some time before Sarju, finding he could not kick the tiger off, paused to think what he would do next. I seized that placid interval to lean over behind and put the muzzle of the rifle to the head of the tiger, blowing it into fifty pieces with the large shell. He dropped like a sack of potatoes, and then I saw the dastardly mahout urging the elephant to run out of the covert. An application of my gunstock to his head, however, reversed the engine, and Sarju, coming round with the utmost willingness, trumpeted a shrill note of defiance and rushed upon his prostrate foe. Thereupon he commenced a war-dance on the body that made it little less difficult to stay on the howdah than when the tiger was being kicked off. It consisted I believe of kicking up the carcass with a hind leg, catching it in the hollow of the fore, and tossing it backward and forward among his feet. He finished this dance by placing his huge forefoot on the body and crossing the other over it, so as to press it into the sand with his whole weight.

I found afterward that the elephant boy, whose business it is to stand behind the howdah and, if necessary, keep the elephant straight during a charge by applying a thick stick over his rump, had had a narrow escape in this adventure, having dropped off in his fright almost into the jaws of the tiger. The tiger made straight for the elephant, however, as is almost invariably the case, and the boy picked himself up and fled to the protection of the other elephant.

Sarju was not a perfect shikari elephant, but his fault was rather too much courage than the reverse, and it was only his miserable opium-eating villain of a mahout that made him turn at the critical moment. He was much cut about the quarters, but I took him out close to the tents two days after and killed two more tigers without his flinching in the least. The tiger we had thus killed was undoubtedly the man-eater. He was exactly ten feet long, in the prime of life, with the dull yellow coat of the adult male—not in the least mangy or toothless like the man-eater of story. He had no moon on his head, nor did his belly nearly touch the ground. I afterward found that these characteristics are attributed to all man-eaters by the credulous people.

## Chapter Ten

# Gordon Cumming
### Wild Men and Wild Beasts
### (1871)

*Wild Men and Wild Beasts is a hunting and adventure classic. The book's appeal lay in Gordon Cumming's masterful storytelling and his many adventures while stationed throughout India. The book was so popular that it remained in print for more than thirty years after its initial publication in 1871.*

*Cumming went to India in 1847 and was first stationed in Bombay but later served throughout western and central India. He was there when the mutiny broke out in 1857 and escaped to the jungles with the help of the local forest tribes. He later took part in the campaign that suppressed the mutiny. His military adventures were matched by thrilling hunting escapades, with plentiful game making possible many hunting opportunities. Cumming and various accomplices shot deer, antelope, bear, leopard, crocodile, wolf, birds, fish, and, by mistake, a (sacred) cow. He went pig sticking and witnessed a cheetah hunt with the nahob of Jowra. But his favorite was shooting tigers, four dozen of which were chronicled in this book.*

*This story is part of a longer chapter on pig sticking and tiger hunting in the Vindhya Mountains of central India. Cumming and his friend Captain Ward had already shot a bear and six tigers in a previous hunt, where one of their guides had been mauled to death by a tiger. They added five more tigers in this episode.*

### Wild Men and Wild Beasts

On the evening of 29 March 1862, Captain Ward met me at Dhurrempooree, a town in Nimar, situated on the north bank of the Narmada River. The stream at this place is about a quarter of a mile in breadth, swarming with *mahseer* and other fish, and moreover plentifully stocked with alligators.

The country to the north for some six or seven miles is partly cultivated, but the Vindhya range of mountains then rises with rugged slopes, covered with scrub

*Death of Foorsut, a native shikari.*

jungle and trees of moderate growth. To the south of the river, on the border of the Burwanee territory, the country, though apparently level when viewed from a distance, is cut up with innumerable ravines, all running down to the Narmada. These ravines, and indeed also the more level parts, are filled with long grass and dense thorny bushes, and though the district is fairly stocked with tigers, panthers, bears, and deer, I was never able to do much execution among them.

Our intended beat on this occasion lay at Kotra, about six or seven miles farther down the river where it is joined on the north side by the Maun and on the south by the Deb Rivers. Both of these streams almost cease flowing during the hot weather, but large, stagnant pools remain in parts. In many places along the beds of the rivers the bastard cypress grows freely, intermingled with willows and other green bushes that refresh the eye amid the general parched-up vegetation. These bushes are covered by the floods during the monsoon when the dried-up beds are swept by mighty torrents. But, though the water disappears in summer, the undersoil is moistened by the percolation through the sand, and the bushes retain their verdure. These form comparatively cool retreats for tigers, who, in addition to their ordinary prey of pigs, nilgai, and porcupines, are attracted by the herds of cattle brought down by their owners from the more dried-up districts.

We had received reliable information of the presence of game, and had sent on tents, servants, and shikaris, that all might be in readiness on our arrival. We had only one elephant, but he was a staunch one, though he could be dangerous at times. When employed with the troops on service in 1858, he had killed a soldier who had incautiously come within reach of his trunk. The elephant, together with our gunbearers and a native horseman, preceded us from Dhurrempooree before daybreak on the morning of 1 April, and it was still dark when my friend and I mounted our horses and followed them.

We had proceeded two or three miles along the track formed by village carts, which is all the apology for a road that the country affords, when the day broke. We then observed, in the very cart-rut in which one of us was riding, the fresh footprints of a tiger that had passed along in the early morning. They were not to be mistaken in the heavy dust, but were in parts obliterated by the tracks of the elephant and our gunbearers, who had evidently passed the spot in the dark. The prints, however, led in the direction in which we were going, and we quickened our pace, all the while keeping them in view.

*Tiger shooting at night from platforms.*

After proceeding about a mile, we came up with our men, who, on the day breaking, had at once perceived the tracks and had sent off the horseman to bring back the elephant, which had outpaced them. We dismounted and proceeded to load our things on the elephant, and then we again followed the track of the tiger. It continued for some distance farther along the same road and then turned north by a cross-path, for about a quarter of a mile, after which it struck into the jungle. There the ground being hard, we were at fault.

Leaving our men, we rode forward and carefully reconnoitred the country in the direction the beast had taken. It looked hopeless, stretching for miles in flat, thorny scrub, with small, open spaces here and there, and occasional thickets twenty or thirty yards in breadth. Half a mile in advance was a solitary tree, and we agreed that I should make a detour to climb this tree on the chance of seeing the tiger. Ward, who was to mount the elephant, would beat up the ground in my direction. We accordingly returned to the men, and, taking my two gunbearers with me, I set off for the tree. After I climbed the tree, I soon saw Ward advancing on the elephant and moving about among the thickets.

Presently I heard a couple of shots. The report was so small that I concluded Ward had only fired his revolver into some covert too dense for the elephant to penetrate, but soon after our horseman came up at a gallop, legs and arms flying in all directions, to inform me that the tiger was slain. I was not a little astonished, having been deceived by the report of the rifle, and, descending from my perch, I rejoined Ward, whom I found standing over the body of a fine tigress.

The beast had probably traveled a long way during the night in quest of food, and on the day breaking had lain up in the first quiet spot. Ward came suddenly upon her and finished her before she had time to rise. We were much pleased with this bit of unexpected sport, and making over our guns to our attendants, we remounted our horses and rode off merrily to breakfast, leaving the men to follow with the tigress, which we had bound on the elephant, after taking off the howdah, to prevent damage to the skin. The howdah was carried in by some villagers who had assembled at the spot.

On reaching the camp we were met by our shikaris, their countenances wearing a peculiar grin, which, from long experience, I knew meant business. They informed us that on their arrival they had found fresh tracks, so they had tied up sundry buffaloes on the previous evening in the most frequented spots. One of these had been killed during the night in the Maun River, half a mile above the junction, and the carcass had been dragged into a large patch of cypress in the bed of the stream. Markers had been posted on the trees along the bank, and only our presence was necessary to open the ball. Refreshed by this intelligence, we proceeded to breakfast, and soon after the guns and elephant came in.

Our followers, who had preceded us, had suffered a good deal from bees, several large swarms having been roused by the smoke of the campfires from the few trees at the place that afforded shade to our tents. The village cattle had, moreover, been in the habit of seeking shelter from the midday sun under these trees, and the ground was alive with ticks, by which our men had been grievously bitten. The bite of these insects is severe, and is followed by great itching and swelling, which lasts for two days or more. In such places we generally wore long riding boots all day, but the feet of the natives were unprotected, and they suffered accordingly.

At 11:00 A.M. we again set off, and at the end of a mile we arrived at the River Maun. The opposite bank was steep, and at its foot ran a long strip of cypress some ten yards in width, and two or three hundred in length. On this side, the bed of the river was covered with cypress to the extent of several

*Elephant charged by tiger.*

acres, and in the centre was a large pool of still water, in which the tigers (there were two) had repeatedly been seen by our markers to bathe themselves during the morning. The country on both sides was cut in all directions with small but deep ravines, very narrow at the bottom and filled with long grass and thorny bushes.

As we knew the tigers were gorged, we concluded that they would not leave the cypress, and we therefore both mounted the elephant and proceeded to beat them out, previously taking care that all our men were clear of the covert and safely perched on trees. The tigers were soon on the move, and, guided by the waving of the cypress, which was five and six feet high at this part, we pushed after them. Presently both beasts were wounded, but accurate shooting was impossible owing to the motion of the elephant and the density of the covert. The tigress was the first to succumb, which she did after one or two plucky charges, and soon after the tiger, a fine, heavy beast, dashed through the pool and disappeared in the strip of covert on the opposite side. We slowly followed, advancing cautiously, for the cypress was varied by rocks and bunches of long grass. Suddenly, with a terrific roar, the tiger rose and came on open-mouthed, but the shooting was good and the elephant steady. He was hurled back and again crossed the pool to the place where we had originally found him. We reloaded and followed, finding him very groggy, and we put an end to him without further trouble.

Thus ended our first day's work. Three tigers had been found and bagged. We bound the last two on the elephant and returned in triumph to our camp, where we found that, with the assistance of the village *chamars* [skinners], my servant had removed and pegged out the skin of the beast we had slain in the morning and was ready to turn his attention to the last comers. The skins of these were also pegged out before dinner. As we smoked our evening pipe and lay back in our comfortable arm-chairs, we discoursed the labours of the day and went to bed hopeful for the morrow, our men having told us that they believed other tigers were in the neighbourhood and that another lot of unhappy buffaloes had been tied up in the rivers and other likely places.

I forget whether one of these was killed during the night, but we went forth next morning (Wednesday) after a tigress that was said to have her cubs in the ravines near the river. A number of beaters was assembled and a line formed, while we took up positions ahead on foot. The tigress was soon started but got off without our having fired a shot. Making a note of the line she had taken, we mounted the elephant, and going round to the bed of the river, moved up along the bank and halted at the mouth of one of the small ravines. Our star was in the ascendant, for, as the beaters again came on, the tigress appeared on the bank above us, within thirty yards, and, firing together, we rolled her over into the ravine, where another shot finished her. Our men were anxious that we should not disturb the country more that day, as they supposed that other tigers were not far off, so we went quietly home with the main body of our forces, leaving our shikaris to make all needful arrangements for the following day.

On Thursday morning we were informed that a buffalo had been killed during the night close to the spot where we had slain the two tigers on Tuesday, and that the tracks led into the cypress. Thinking the beast would be too lazy to break cover, we placed additional markers on the banks on trees and other elevated places, and, mounting the elephant, we entered the jungle. The tiger was a cunning one, though, and on hearing us he sneaked down the covert for three or four hundred yards, and then, leaving the bed of the stream, went up among the ravines. Our men ran after and did their best to keep him in sight,

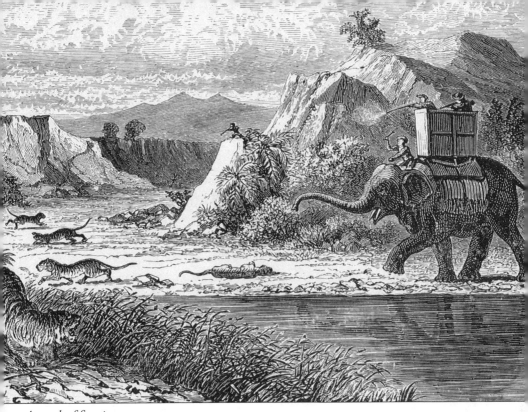

*A streak of five tigers.*

but to no purpose, and though we searched far and wide, we could not find him. So, leaving word for the buffaloes to be again tied up, we returned to camp.

The tiger came down to the river in the night, again killed a buffalo, and again lay up in the cypress. We went at him after breakfast on Friday. He had moved to the strip of cover on the far side. As we beat slowly down on the elephant, he again broke slyly and scrambled up a very steep part of the bank, where four or five small watercourses, meeting at one point, entered the river by an abrupt fall. We fired several long shots but failed to stop him. The elephant was unable to follow at this place, and we had to return and make a considerable circuit to ascend the bank. Then we found we had to turn the head of several ravines before we could arrive at that by which the tiger had left the river. We passed round the heads of all its tributaries, carefully examining the ground, but found no tracks, from which we gathered that we had succeeded in heading our game. The heat at this time was great, and Ward, who was not very well, began to be knocked up, so, getting off the elephant, he took shelter under a tree while I went to hunt up each small watercourse closely by passing up one side and down the other.

I had carefully examined them all and had turned away in despair from the last when I happened to cast my eye back, and there, within twenty yards, lying in the bottom of a small channel some eight or ten feet deep, was my friend, looking pleasantly at me. I quietly called to the driver to stop, and kneeling on the seat of the howdah I gave him two through the shoulder. He spoke at once, and scrambled along the bottom of the watercourse toward the spot where I had left Ward sitting. He did not go far, however, and, following him up, I gave him a final shot.

The feet and claws of this tiger were badly blistered and damaged. The blisters were probably occasioned by his walk in the hot ravines on the previous day, and his claws were no doubt broken as he scrambled up the steep bank this morning. But for this we might possibly not have got him, for on both days he seemed to think discretion to be the better part of valour.

A tiger of this description is apt to mislead an inexperienced sportsman as to the dangerous character of these beasts. Having seen a huge brute flee ignominiously before the hunters, the inexperienced hunter rashly concludes that all tigers will do the same, and, conducting his subsequent operations in accordance with that erroneous theory, sometimes pays the forfeit with his life.

Descending to the water's edge, we cracked a bottle of Moselle, and, after the inevitable pipe, moved homeward. The following day being Saturday, we determined not to shift our camp, though, having already killed four beasts close to the same spot, we were not very sanguine about finding more. Buffaloes were, however, again tied up in the evening, and next morning one of our men came in greatly excited and said that a calf had been killed in the night and that four fresh tigers were in a patch of cypress in the Narmada, close to the junction where our markers had seen them.

We were not long in turning out, and on reaching the place proceeded to examine the ground. The tigers were in a covert some two hundred yards in length and one hundred fifty broad, thick in parts, but broken into ridges by the action of heavy floods, and between these ridges were open spaces of sand and shingle. On the bank at the angle of the junction was a point from which a good bird's-eye view could be obtained of the bed of the river, and round the corner, in the Maun, was the cypress covert, in and about which we had hunted on the four previous days.

We arranged that I should stand at the angle, while Ward beat up the tigers with the elephant. As he approached the covert the scene became very interesting, and the tigers moved rapidly from one ridge to the other. I had a perfect view of the whole proceeding, and as the beasts showed we fired with various effects. Several, I knew, were hard hit, but so many were running about the covert that it was impossible to say which were wounded.

Presently, with her tail standing out behind her like a kitchen-poker, the old tigress charged past my post, growling savagely. I had a good shot in the open but very disgracefully missed her, and she went at full speed round the corner into the Maun River. Meanwhile, Ward was not idle, and as I watched his movements I observed a tiger enter a ridge of cypress on the far side of the covert and close to the stream of the Narmada.

Soon after, Ward moved up toward me and said they were all dead, with the exception of the tigress I had let go.

I asked, "How many were dead?"

He replied, "Three."

"Then," said I, "there is still a fourth in the covert."

Ward was incredulous, so I came down and, mounting the elephant beside him, directed the mahout to move toward the ridge near the water. We beat it down very carefully with no result, but I knew the beast was not far off.

The side of the bank next to the river sloped sharply down some eight or ten feet to the water and was heavily fringed with a thick green shrub. I directed the mahout to take the elephant round and enter the water. This he did, and as we moved along in front of the bank, in water about five feet deep, we spied the tiger lying almost hidden by the bushes. Being anxious to save the skin, only one shot was fired, with the best aim allowed by the imperfect view. On receiving the shot the tiger roared and sprang clean out from the bank toward us and was shot in the water swimming at the elephant's head. He was a young tiger, but a most determined beast.

When we towed him ashore, he was found to be riddled with bullets. We thus had four lying together on the sand. They were all young tigers and tigresses, but as large as the mother, and only to be distinguished at a distance by their imperfect stripes. After a slight refreshment we followed the old lady into the Maun River and soon came on her in the cypress. She died game, but the shooting was too good for her this time, and she had no chance.

On the death of the four, we had sent off to the camp for two light carts. These had arrived by this time. Two tigers were placed in each, and with the fifth bound on the elephant, the procession moved on the tents. We had within the week killed ten large tigers, the result of five days' work. Of these, nine were killed within a circle half a mile in diameter. The villagers turned out in considerable numbers and rejoiced in their own apathetic way. Had we not come, many of their cows would no doubt have suffered. They seemed to think it strange that so many beasts should have been disposed of without loss of human life or accident of any sort.

The five tigers made a goodly show as they lay in front of our tent. Loud and noisy was the discussion over the slain, and many and varied were the accounts given by our men of the week's work, while the principal actors, again ensconced in their arm-chairs, quietly smoked the fragrant pipe and quaffed the beatific beverage of Bass, weakened with water, sweetened with sugar, flashed with ginger, and vulgarly known as "mug."

### Chapter Eleven

# George Sanderson
## Thirteen Years among the Wild Beasts of India
### (1882)

George P. Sanderson's first claim to fame was elephant catching. The practice involved herding wild elephants into large enclosures, or khedahs, where they were slowly pacified and eventually marched across the country to be sold at the giant elephant market at Dacca [Bangladesh]. But he was also an avid naturalist and tiger hunter.

He worked for the Irrigation Department in southern India for thirteen years and shot tigers and other large game during his spare time. Tigers were so common in his department that they were considered vermin by the British administration and were summarily shot and even poisoned. Sanderson took part in some of these campaigns. But despite the less-than-sporting methods used to rid the countryside of tigers, he still had a keen interest in the animal and a respect for it as a worthy game animal. Much of his book describes hunting episodes, as well as descriptions of the tiger's habit and those of other wild animals.

The author of Thirteen Years among the Wild Beasts of India spent his career in the princely state of Mysore, located near the wet and warm, Western Ghats mountain range. This story is part of a longer chapter on tiger shooting near the village of Morlay, where Sanderson eventually established his camp. He pursues a man-eater that had been creating havoc for the local villagers.

#### Tiger-Shooting in Southern India

When I pitched camp at Morlay in September 1873, to commence the elephant *khedahs,* the countryside was in a state of considerable alarm from the attacks of a man-eating tigress. This tigress's fits of man-eating seemed to be intermittent since, after killing three or four persons some months before, she had not been heard of till about the time of my arrival at Morlay when she killed

*A man-eater strikes.*

two boys attending goats. I anticipated some trouble from her in our *khedah* work, for her presence made it unsafe for one or two men to go alone through the jungles, but whether it was from the disturbance caused by seven or eight hundred work-people or other reasons, we heard nothing of her for some time.

 On 30 November when the work-people had dispersed, news was brought in that a man, returning to the village of Nagwully (about six miles from Morlay) with cattle, had been carried off the evening before. From an account of the place where the mishap had occurred I knew it was useless to look for the tigress. It had been a lapse of eighteen hours, and she would have retired to impracticable jungle. I urged the people to bring news of further losses at the earliest possible moment.

 On 19 December another man was carried off close to the village of Iyenpoor, five miles from Morlay, but I did not hear of this till two days afterward.

 On Christmas Day I thought I would look up the jungles in the Iyenpoor direction, so I took an elephant and some trackers in hopes of learning something of the tigress's habits. The unfortunate man's wife, with her three small children, were brought to me as I entered the village. The woman, with the strange apathy of a Hindoo, related what she knew of her husband's death without a tear. She would have to expend a small sum in accordance with caste usage to rid her of the devil by which she was supposed to be attended on account of her husband's having been killed by a tiger, so I gave her some money so that she would be admitted into her caste's villages. Then, accompanied by the headman and others, I went to the scene of the last disaster.

A solitary tamarind tree grew on some rocks close to the village, but otherwise there was no jungle within three hundred yards, only a few bushes in the crevices of the rocks and close-by was the broad cattle track into the village. The unfortunate man had been following the cattle home in the evening and must have stopped to knock down some tamarinds with his stick, which with his black blanket and a skin skull cap still lay where he was seized. The tigress had been hidden in the rocks and in one bound had seized him and dragged him to the edge of a small plateau of rock, from which she had jumped down into a field below, and there killed him. The place was still marked by a pool of dried blood. She had then dragged her victim half a mile to a spot where we found his leg bones.

After walking for two hours with the trackers in the hopes of seeing recent marks of the tigress, but without success, the village cattle were sent for and herded into the jungles in the hope of attracting her. The poor beasts were, however, so frightened by the constant attacks of tigers that we could scarcely get them to face the jungle, and a partridge rising suddenly was too much for their nerves and sent them, tails up, to the village before they had been out half an hour. After some time they were got back.

About 1:00 P.M., as they were feeding near a hollow encircled on three sides by low hills covered with bamboo, and a very pretty spot for a tiger, a wild scurry took place as a large tiger rushed amongst the foremost of them. Strange to say they all escaped, with only two being slightly wounded. A few plucky buffaloes had been in advance and had interfered considerably with the tiger's attack, as those animals never hesitate to do.

Up to this time I had been walking, rifle in hand, amongst the cattle, but the heat was considerable, and at this unlucky moment I was some little distance behind getting a drink, or I might have had a shot. The herdsmen were not certain whether the tiger had secured something in his rush, so we went in force to look through the covert. We found only footprints, however, and knew they were not those of the man-eater but of a large male who was a well-known cattle killer. We shortly heard a spotted deer bark over the saddle of the hill to our left; the tiger had moved off in that direction upon his discomfiture. We saw nothing more of him that day, or of the man-eater, and I returned to camp by moonlight. It was so cold that I was glad of an overcoat. A good camp Christmas dinner was awaiting me, and had I only been lucky enough to bag the man-eater, I should have been able to enter this amongst my red-letter days.

After this nothing was heard of the tigress for a week; however, when the trackers and I were going to look after some wild elephants at the ford in the river below the Koombappan temple, we found a tiger's pugs that were immediately pronounced to be hers. I sent back two men on my riding elephant to warn the people of Morlay that the tigress was in our jungles, as her usual hunting grounds were to the east of the river, and the people on our side were liable to be off their guard. We tried to follow her, but she had crossed open dry country, in which tracking was impossible, and we had to give her up. During the day I made arrangements for hunting her systematically the next day, should she still be in our jungles.

Whilst at dinner that evening, I heard voices and saw torches hurriedly approaching my tent and could distinguish the words *naie* and *nurri* [dog and jackal], pronounced excitedly. The Canarese people frequently speak of a tiger by these names, partly in assumed contempt, partly from superstitious fear. The word *huli* [tiger] is not often used amongst jungle men, in the same way that, from dread, natives usually refer to cholera by the general terms of *roga* or *járdya* [sickness]. The people were from Hurdenhully, a village a mile and a half away, and had come to tell me that their cattle had galloped back in confusion into the village at dusk, without their herdsman. Only one man had been with them that day, as there was some festival in the village. We suspected he had fallen a victim to the tigress, but it was useless to attempt a search that night. The cattle had been two or three miles into the jungles, and we had no indications where to look for the unfortunate herdsman, who was, moreover, probably now half devoured. So, ordering some rice for the men, I sent them to Morlay to tell the trackers, and to sleep there and return with them in the morning.

At dawn we started on the backtrail of the cattle from Hurdenhully till we found the point where they had begun to gallop, just below the embankment of a small channel drawn from the river near Atticulpoor and supplying the Hurdenhully tank with water. The ground was hard and much trodden by cattle, and we looked for some time for the tigress's tracks in vain, and it wasn't till the distant caw of a crow attracted that we found the man's remains. Only the soles of his feet, the palms of his hands, his head, and a few bones were left. We lost no time in taking up the tigress's track and used every endeavour to run her down, as we had over a hundred men ready at camp to beat her out, could we but mark her into some practicable cover. But though she had eaten so much, she had recrossed the river as usual and had gone into the jungles toward the hills where there was no chance of finding her.

About a week after this the priest of a small temple ten miles due west from Morlay was jogging along on his riding bullock one morning. He was on his way to sweep out and garnish the small jungle temple in which he officiated and to present to Yennay Hollay Koombappa the offerings of the simple villagers whose faith was placed in that deity. He was in comparatively open country where a tiger had not been heard of for years, yet suddenly a tigress with her cub stepped into the path. The terrified bullock kicked off his rider and galloped back to the village, whilst the tigress seized the hapless *poojáree* [priest]. The dreaded Iyenpoor maneater, far out of her ordinary haunts, carried the poor man off to the bed of a deep ravine nearby.

Upon hearing next day of this, my men and I thought it must be some other tiger. At that point this fiend had managed with such cunning that we did not then know that she had a cub, and it was not till we found this out subsequently that we traced this death to her also. Up to this time she must have left her cub in the thick jungles along the hills, making her rapid hunting forays alone. The cub had never been with her before, and this accounted for her invariably crossing the river and making for the hills after a raid. The absence of the tigress from the vicinity of Morlay during September and October was probably caused partly by her keeping out of the way when this cub was very young.

The next death was of a horrible description. Several villagers of Ramasamoodrum were grazing their cattle in a swampy hollow in the jungle near the temple when the tigress pounced upon one man who was separated from the others. She in some way missed her aim at his throat, seized the shoulder, and then, either in jerking him, or by a blow, threw him up onto a thicket several feet from the ground. Here the wounded and bleeding wretch was caught by thorny creepers, whilst the tigress, as generally happens when any contretemps takes place, relinquished the attack and made off. The other men and the cattle had fled at the first alarm. The village was some distance away, and there was not time before nightfall for a party to search for the man, whose being still alive was not known.

Next morning the lacerated wretch was found. In his mangled state he had been unable to release himself. He was moaning and hanging almost head down amongst the creepers, and he died soon after he was taken down.

Before long the tigress visited my camp, but fortunately without doing any mischief. Close to my tent (my bungalow was not built then) was a large banyan tree. Every night a fire was kindled near it, and here I sat and discussed plans for work or sport with my men. One morning when the trackers came to wake me early, they found the man-eater's tracks leading down a path close to the banyan tree in question. As we thought she might still be on our side of the river, I accompanied the men to examine its vicinity and ascertain if she had recrossed it toward the hills. If not, we intended to hunt the different coverts on its banks during the day.

Upon reaching the river, we walked down the sandy bed overshadowed by drooping *homgay,* Indian beech trees *(Pongamia glabra).* The scene at early morning was very pleasant. Gaudy kingfishers fluttered and poised over the pools and shallow runs of clear water into which the river—a considerable stream in the rains—had now shrunk. At a bend we came upon a troop of langur monkeys *(Semnopithecus hypoleucos)* feeding upon some fallen fruit; they ran nimbly across the sand to the sanctuary of the large trees when we appeared. In one stretch a spotted stag and several graceful hinds were drinking at the cool stream, perchance admiring their shapely forms in nature's mirror, but for the nonce they passed unheeded. The soothing cooing of doves, the scream of the toucan, the cheery game cry of the jungle cock *(Gallus sonnerati)* perched aloft, whilst his ladies ruffled themselves in the sand below, combined to make one of those tranquil phases of beauty in nature that are such a contrast to the wildness and grandeur of other scenes.

The trackers moved quickly and silently along. We passed two or three pugs, but these elicited no notice, except one into which Dad Sidda drove the butt end of his spear without a word; this was the night's track of the tigress to

*A tiger closes in on tied bait.*

our side of the river. We had nearly got to the temple, below which it was not likely she would have crossed, and were in hopes of not finding her outgoing trail when a single track across an unblemished stretch of sand caused an exclamation of disappointment: One glance showed it to be the unmistakable small oval pug of the man-eater.

We felt our chances of finding her that day were very small, but there was nothing like trying, so, sending for an elephant to come to the temple and there await my return, we cast ahead toward the hills and again hit off the trail. After several hours' work of finding tracks now and then in the sandy beds of ravines but all leading to a country where the cover was continuous, we were obliged to give it up as useless, for we could neither keep the trail nor have done anything toward driving in such extensive cover had we even found where the tigress lay hidden. We were forced reluctantly to return, consoling ourselves with the hope of finding her in more favourable country soon, and vowing to leave no stone unturned till we bagged her. It had become quite a point of honour with the trackers; we had never been played such successful tricks before by any animal, and they said the tigress was "throwing dirt into their mouths."

We got back to the temple late in the afternoon. There I found the elephant and several of my people, and a man with a note from Captain C., of the Revenue Survey, who was in camp a few miles from Morlay. I started the messenger back with a reply, and though we were pretty certain the man-eater was miles away, it was a nervous job for him to get through the jungle till he reached open country on the far side. He left us, already casting furtive glances around him, to the great amusement of my men, who had not the job to do themselves! Before he had got far, one of them, who was a bit of a humorist, called him back.

The man came, when the wag, assuming a concerned air, said: "You know, keep a good lookout ahead of you—never mind the rear. If a tiger seizes a man from behind, what could any of us do? But, you know, you can see her if she is coming for you from in front, and you might try a run for it. Good-bye! Koombappa be with you! Don't delay; it's rather late as it is!"

The poor villager grinned painfully at the joke, which the rest enjoyed immensely. Nevertheless, I saw he was in such a fright that I sent half a dozen men (the joker amongst them) to see him safely into the cultivated country on the other side, for I reflected that the tigress might as likely be near as far away.

Shortly after this, work took me to Gundulpet, twenty-five miles from Morlay, on the Neilgherry road, and I returned on 14 January 1874. As I rode into camp about midday, the trackers were waiting for me. They informed me that they had heard the "death-cry" raised at a small village called Bussavanpoor below Ramasamoodrum Lake, and some two miles from Morlay, that morning. On inquiry they found that a woman had been carried off by the man-eater from the village during the night, but they had not followed the tracks as I was not with them. Bussavanpoor was a small hamlet situated in the middle of open rice-fields, then bare, as the crop had been cut. There was no jungle to cover the man-eater's advance, and a tiger had never hitherto been heard of near the village. This attack was therefore the more unlooked for and terrifying to the villagers.

Immediately breakfast was over and an elephant made ready, I started and soon reached Bussavanpoor. The attack had been most daring. At one end of the single street of the village stood a shady tree, round the base of which a raised terrace of stones and earth had been built as a public seat; within ten yards of this tree the houses began. From the marks we saw that the tigress had crouched upon this raised terrace, from which she commanded a view of the street. The nearest house on one side was occupied by an old woman, the one opposite by her married daughter. The old woman, it appeared, sometimes slept in her own house, sometimes at her daughter's. The night before she had been going to her daughter's, and as she crossed the street, only a few feet wide, the tigress with one silent bound seized and carried her off. No one heard any noise, and the poor old creature was not missed till morning.

When I arrived, the son-in-law came forward, and with the other villagers gave an account of the mishap. The son-in-law's grief was really painful to witness, and when he told me how all his efforts to find any trace of his mother-in-law had been unsuccessful, he gave way to the most poignant outbursts. Now, knowing pretty well how little store is placed upon an old woman in India, I could not but regard this display of feeling by the fat, young son-in-law as rather strange. A mother-in-law is not usually so highly esteemed (amongst natives) that her loss is deemed an irreparable calamity. When I further noted that the afflicted youth could only give a shaky account of his exertions in looking for the body, I thought something was wrong, and had him taken along with us.

The tigress had gone toward the river, and though cattle and people had been over the fields and it was now afternoon, the sun hot, and a strong wind was blowing clouds of dust about, the trackers carried on the trail very cleverly. They pointed out that several footmarks had followed it before us, for which the prostrated son-in-law found some difficulty in accounting. After passing through a field of standing rice in which the broad trail was very distinct and where in the soft mud we got a fair impression of the tigress's pugs, we saw some bushes where strips of the woman's blue cotton cloth were hanging. We then came to a cocoa-nut garden near the river, and there, amongst some aloe bushes, we missed the drag. There was a place that looked as if the tigress had lain down, probably to eat, as there were marks of blood, but there were no remains, and her trail continued across the river, whither we followed.

The trackers soon thought something was amiss since no trace could be found where the body had been dragged. One of them remarked that the tigress would hardly eat the whole at once, whilst, had she carried off the remainder in her jaws, she must have laid it down at the pool in the sandy bed where she had drunk. There was no trace of her having done this. We returned to the aloe bushes.

After examining these for some time, one of the men looked inside a thicket, and with an exclamation turned upon the son-in-law and gave him a sound box on the ear. He then asked the son-in-law "what he meant by it." The tracker pointed at the ashes of a fire inside the thicket, explaining what he thought had happened and what we subsequently learned: The villagers had followed the track with horns and tom-toms in the morning and had burnt the remains to avoid police inquiry, the dejected son-in-law acting as chief mourner. The woman was of good caste. Had her death been reported, the remains would have been handled by outcastes, and the death would have formed the subject of a sort of inquest by the police at Chamrajnagar. To avoid this, the relatives had burnt the remainder of the body as soon as they found it.

What could be done when the foolish villagers either brought us news too late or acted in this way? We sent the now truly smitten son-in-law back to the village, bewailing his mother-in-law more sincerely probably than before. Finding that the tigress had gone east, we returned to Morlay, it being useless to follow her in that direction.

This death caused great consternation. The villagers concluded that they would now not be safe in their houses at night and that some of the outlying hamlets would have to be temporarily abandoned. But this was to be her last victim. Though our chances of killing her seemed still as remote as ever, a few more hours were to end her bloody career.

Next day, 15 January, I determined upon a more organized plan of hunting her. I arranged that Bommay Gouda and three trackers should go to Iyenpoor, at one end of her usual range, whilst I remained at Morlay. In case of anyone being killed near Iyenpoor the men were to let me know immediately. I supplied them with strychnine and a gun charged with powder, as a safeguard in their jungle wanderings. The four men started early in the afternoon. About an hour afterward one of them came running back, pouring with perspiration and covered with dust. I feared some accident had happened until he found breath to say that the party had met the tigress, and that she was then at Karraypoor Guddah, a small hill two miles from camp.

This hill rose to a height of about two hundred feet out of a level, cultivated plain. On three sides it was almost bare granite, a few bushes and boulders being the only cover, and the country was open all round. On the east face there was a little more cover, and the main jungle was five hundred yards distant, but between it and the hill was open ground, so that the tigress was in an isolated position.

I ordered a pad-elephant at once, whilst I thought over the best plan for hunting her. Such a chance as getting her into a detached hill could hardly be hoped for again, and the present situation offered a fine opportunity of extinguishing her. The only plans were to drive her out, or to watch for her return to the carcass. The first I saw would not do, as all the Morlay men—the only ones amongst the villagers who would have been useful for this service, the others being too terrified—were at their fields, and time would be lost in collecting them. And though that might possibly have been effected, and the tigress have been driven out, as there was no doubt she would flee readily from a hunting-party, it would be impossible for one rifle to command the entire east side of the hill, at any point of which she might break. I therefore decided to watch for her return to the carcass, and, hastily securing a bottle of water and some bread, and an overcoat in case of night-watching, I started.

On the way the tracker told me how the party had met the tigress. They were going across open fields and saw an object moving over the bare ground. At first they could not make it out, but presently they discovered it to be a tiger on the far side of, and partly hidden by, a bullock, which it was half dragging, half carrying toward the hill. They immediately divined it to be the man-eater, and ran shouting toward her, obliging her to drop the bullock at the foot of the hill, up which she sullenly trotted. One tracker then hastened to camp; the others remained to prevent her returning to the bullock before I arrived.

I need here hardly say, except for the information of those who have had no experience with man-eating tigers, that they never refuse a bullock or other prey if such offers, and that when opposed by man they give way at once. Their tactics in attacking man may be described in one word—surprise—and if discovered in their attempt, they generally abandon it. The most confirmed man-eaters never lose the innate fear with which all inferior animals regard human beings, and unless they can stalk and catch an unwary cow-herd or

*Tiger netting in the Ghats.*

wood-cutter in their own fashion, they are not to be dreaded. When the tables are turned on them, they flee as readily as other tigers.

When we got near the hill, we left the elephant and joined the trackers. The only covert near the carcass was a large rock, but the wind was wrong for watching from that quarter. About seventy yards away in the plain was one solitary bush, not sufficiently large to hide a man, but there was neither trees nor other covert within a couple of hundred yards. The situation certainly presented difficulties, and it was not easy to decide what to do. At last I hit upon a plan: I sent the men to bring leafy branches and creepers and when these came, we walked past the bush in a body, and the branches were thrown on to make it larger. At the same time Bommay Gouda and I hid behind it, the others going on in full view from the hill. By this manoeuvre, should the tigress be watching, she would not perceive that we had concealed ourselves.

We sat till evening. The sinking sun threw a strong light from behind us upon the granite hill, whilst in the distance the Billiga-runguns were bathed in purple light, deepening to blue in the gorges. The smoke of evening fires began to ascend from the small hamlet of Hebsoor, away to our left, and a thick, white cloud of dust moving slowly along the riverbank toward the village marked the return homeward of the village herds. There would only be sufficient light to shoot, at a range as seventy yards, for half an hour or more, and I was beginning to fear the tigress might not return during daylight. The afternoon had been hot, and I had drunk all the water in the bottle, whilst patient Bommay Gouda, who being of good caste could not drink from my bottle, had sat with his bare back exposed to the grilling sun, watching without a movement.

At this time of the year—January—the change in temperature in Mysore, and, in fact, the whole of India, between day and night is very considerable, sometimes upward of thirty degrees, and as the sun neared the horizon the evening quickly became chilly, but this disturbed Bommay Gouda no more than the heat in his imperturbable watch. A couple of hares appeared from somewhere and gamboled in the space between us and the hill, and a peacock perched himself upon a rock, and with his spreading fan of purple and gold opened to the full, turned slowly round and round, courting the admiration of a group of hens who pecked about, more intent upon their evening meal than the admiration of their vain swain. Satisfaction with himself, however, rendered him oblivious to the want of homage in his harem.

We had been whispering quietly, as we were out of earshot of the covert, and Bommay Gouda had just said, after a glance at the sinking sun, that it was the time, par excellence, for a tiger's return to its prey when a peahen that had been hidden amongst boulders on the hillside to our right rose with a startling clamour. This signal, as well known as unmistakable, made us glance through the leafy screen, and there we saw the man-eater, a handsome but small tigress, her colour doubly rich in the light of the sinking sun, walk from behind a rock across the side of the hill, here a bare sheet of blue granite, and come downward toward the carcass. She halted now and again to look far out into the plain behind us. Was the beast dreaded by thousands, hunted by us so long, and which we had never even seen before, the guilty midnight murderess, really before us? Could nothing but some untoward failure now avert her fate?

I followed her with my rifle so eagerly that Bommay Gouda whispered to me to let her get to the carcass before I fired. When she reached the bullock she stooped, and at the same instant I fired at her shoulder, broadside on, with my Express. Bommay Gouda could contain himself no longer and jumped up before I could stop him. I did so also, but I could see no tigress! It was extraordinary, certainly; we looked up the hillside, but she was not there. Was she really a devil as all believed, and had she vanished in air?

Just then up went a tail on the far side of the bullock in a convulsive quiver, and we saw that she had fallen exactly behind the carcass. I ran along the hillside to intercept her should she gain her feet, but it was all right. She was only opening her mouth in spasmodic gasps, and I settled her. The trackers came up in great glee. They had seen from their perch in a large tamarind tree away in the plain the tigress come over the summit of the hill and enter the rocks on our side half an hour before we saw her. On examining her we found that she was in milk, which was the first intimation we had that she had a cub. She was in the prime of life and condition and had no lameness or apparent injury to account for her having taken to man-killing.

I may here say that we never killed her cub. It was heard calling to its mother for several nights around Iyenpoor, but we could not find it in the daytime, and it must have died of starvation, as had it lived we should certainly have encountered it.

We soon had the tigress padded (after the trackers had beaten her with their slippers and abused her in dreadful terms). As our way to Morlay lay through Hebsoor, a messenger started off in advance with the news. Before we had gone far, we were met by almost the whole community of Hebsoor, with torches and tom-toms, who begged to parade the tigress through the village. The women and children were delighted, though half-terrified, at the sight of her. They had never seen a tiger before, there being no zoological gardens handy in India except those of nature, and the creature was only known as a fearful beast that had eaten papa or mamma or sons or daughters. Soondargowry, the elephant, was fed with cakes, balls of sugar and rice, and plantains by the pleased housewives, and seemed to enjoy herself, though at first the torches and shouts made her rather nervous, especially as this was the first tiger she had carried, for she had been a wild animal herself not long before.

On the way to Morlay beyond Hebsoor we entered an extensive stretch of rice fields, the rice then dry and the crops cut but yet on the ground, below Ramasamoodrum Lake. Ordinarily fires were kept up at the threshing-floors, and much merriment went on all night, but the dread of the tigress latterly had been so great that all was quiet and apparently deserted. Not a fire was to be seen nor a voice heard. Dotted about the plain were large trees that we knew sheltered the anxious watchers of the threshing-floors below. We had brought torches and men from Hebsoor, and after much calling that the tigress had been shot, voices were at last heard from different trees, lights began to appear, and watchers came from all directions, some shouting to us from the distance to let them come up and see the "dog." We humoured them and they were delighted, all remarking what a huge tiger it was. (Was there ever a small tiger to the native mind?)

# Chapter Twelve

# Arthur Pollock
## Sporting Days in Southern India
## (1894)

*L*t. Col. Arthur John Osborne Pollock was stationed in the Madras Presidency, which encompassed all of southern India. The favorite hunting grounds in the south were the Western Ghats, mountains that run along the entire coast and include many smaller ranges such as the Wynaad and Nilgiri hills.

The area is known for its dense forests, which harbored many wild animals including deer, gaur, bear, leopard, elephant, Nilgiri tahr (in the higher elevations), and tiger. Pollock hunted all of these animals and wrote about it in Sporting Days in Southern India (1894), in what became the consummate guide to hunting in southern India. He dedicates individual chapters to the natural history of various game animals as well as to personal hunting experiences and proper hunting methods. He also provides tips on traveling, camping, and even preparing for the monsoon, which unleashes a deluge in the region every summer. Pollock hunted elephants in his early days in India before elephant hunting was banned in 1871. He is one of the last hunters to describe that endeavor, to which he was introduced by Gordon Cumming.

Naturally, tigers are a major theme in his book. He describes several hunting expeditions in the Western Ghats and other parts of the Presidency. This story is part of a chapter in which he recounts, among others, his first tiger.

### My First Tiger

After many days' unsuccessful beating in various jungles in the Deccan and Mysore (forty-seven days without even seeing a tiger), my first tiger was shot near Santawerry, on the Baba Booden Hills, in Mysore in 1870. The previous fortnight had been devoted to a solitary and unsuccessful excursion so far as tigers were concerned, down to the plains, and on the morning of

13 May I had ridden twenty miles from Kadur to join my friend Patterson on the hills.

On arrival there, I found that all six sahibs were beating for a tiger on a hill opposite the bungalow. My rifles had not yet arrived, but, taking a spare one of Patterson's, I went off to join them. They had been beating some time before my arrival, but without seeing anything. An hour later on, the tiger, startled by the beaters, passed between the gun on my left and me. We never saw the brute, although we were only sixty yards apart and in fairly open ground—nor would we believe it, until the pugs were pointed out. A few small patches of yellow grass, barely enough covert for a hare, were dotted about in the glade we were watching, so how the tiger passed through these without being seen is still a mystery, for we were both on the lookout, hearing the beaters shout *huli* (tiger).

The next beat was about half over when a spur-fowl started up with a note of alarm, some fifty yards in my front. This was soon followed by a slight rustling noise, as if some large animal were walking with measured tread on the dead leaves in the undergrowth in front. Whatever it was seemed to be moving from side to side, as if hesitating to emerge from the thicker covert.

As the beaters approached, the crinkle-crinkle on the dead leaves became more distinct, and soon a handsome tiger appeared about thirty yards off, coming slowly down the thinly wooded slope straight toward my tree, an *Ailanthus*. Its head was swinging from side to side as it advanced, panting from the heat, and it presented such an enticing mark that I was obliged to avert my eyes to avoid the temptation to fire.

It approached thus to within fifteen yards and then stopped to listen to the beaters. This was the long-wished-for opportunity, and, aiming a little in front of the near shoulder and rather high (as I was twelve feet above the ground), I fired. The tiger gave a grunt, sprang into the air, and was then obscured for a few seconds by the smoke. When it cleared away, I saw revealed a striped mass writhing and tearing up the ground. During this performance, I missed handsomely with the left barrel, and the tiger, retiring slowly up the slope, soon disappeared in the bushes, while I shouted to the beaters to climb the trees. Descending from my tree, I went over to the gun on the left, an old hand at the game, and asked him to cover me with his rifle while I pugged up the tiger, assuring him it was probably dead.

He replied, "Not a step shall I stir out of this tree until something is known about the tiger."

*Stalking the tiger.*

After some interval all the guns came up, and wisely declined to follow the wounded brute into heavy jungle—whereupon, like the headstrong young fool that I was, I proceeded to do so alone. I had not gone a few yards on the track when Edward Hall pluckily came forward and volunteered to help me. The tracks were plain enough, being marked by much blood, and in several places the claws had been driven into the ground with force, a sure sign of a severe wound.

It was ticklish work owing to the dense jungle, and the dogs would not stir from our heels, although generally very game. At length they went forward a few yards—every hair bristling—over the slope, some twenty yards ahead, but had hardly disappeared when back they came all of a heap, barking and in a terrible state of mind. Some four or five natives had followed us, and this was the signal for a general stampede, most laughable only for the dangerous state of affairs. Everybody thought the tiger was on us; the natives were up the trees in a twinkling; and we who were in front jumped behind the trunk of a large forest tree within a yard of us, remaining at the "ready" for fully half a minute, but the foe did not appear.

With much difficulty I then ascended an adjacent tree, in order to "crane" over the top of the slope, and saw the tiger lying on the ground, apparently dead, about fifteen yards off. A shot having no effect, I descended, and, preceded by volleys of stones, we advanced and found the brute quite dead. The spherical bullet had entered exactly at the spot aimed at, and, traversing the lungs, had come out just behind the off shoulder.

It was a handsomely marked tigress, but, thinking the orthodox measurement too small (it was probably about seven feet, nine inches), it was not recorded in the diary. The skin is entered as being nine feet, five inches, and no doubt it was well stretched to give this, but then it was my first tiger. She had two old bullet wounds in the neck, which had passed clean through but missed the spine.

One day a Brinjarry tribesman (called Lombani in Mysore) brought in news of three kills near a place named Attagherry, some three miles lower down the hills. We collected five guns and some beaters with dogs, and found the tiger had killed at the upper end of a long, shady nullah. Patterson was posted at the lower end in the nullah, the remaining four rifles being placed at intervals on both banks toward the *gara* [kill].

Edward Hall, who was posted at the upper end, near the kill, fired at and wounded the tiger at the commencement of the beat; it then, without speaking to the shot, charged down the nullah, and mysteriously disappeared. I was posted at the lower end in a sandalwood tree within fifty yards of Patterson, and when the beaters arrived I got down out of my tree and was crossing through the nullah when some of the dogs with me began to bark at a small clump of bushes between me and Patterson, who at once shouted, "Get out of the nullah. The tiger is within a yard of you."

I lost no time in climbing up the bank, the dogs continuing to bark in the harsh way they always do when on a tiger or panther. The covert was very sparse, but we could see nothing although we beat every foot of it. Patterson then joined us and pointed out the spot where he had seen the tiger, but it had disappeared again and our subsequent beats were blank. There was but one spot where it could have got away unseen—namely, between my post, which was vacated, and Patterson's tree, as it was open ground elsewhere.

In this instance there was every accessory favourable for an accident: a wounded tiger in a nullah among a lot of beaters. But why should I have remained in my post after the beaters had passed it? Such a thing is never done without special orders. It may be said that the beat ought to have been stopped when the tiger was wounded, but that was uncertain, as blood was not discovered till the beaters had arrived within fifty yards of the end of the beat. They were preceded by dogs, and the covert was thin. It is wonderful how a large animal like a tiger can conceal itself on ground where there is barely cover for a hare. As a rule, you will seldom see his outline when he is attempting to hide or escape unseen. There appears to be a movement in the general colour of the herbage or scrub jungle, but no outline is visible—merely an undefined mass of vitality, which vanishes when motion ceases. And the same thing occurs with every wild animal, great or small, from an elephant down to a woodcock.

One evening at Yemadody, a famous place for spotted deer, about six miles from Santawerry, I had strolled out with a rifle into some scrub jungle near a tank fringed with forest trees and was passing a clump of karoonda bushes close to a large peepal when a low growl reached my ears. I peered through the bushes and saw a tiger about twenty-five yards off, moving slowly through the trees toward the camp, not three hundred yards distant. Knowing he must turn to the left to reach the scrub jungle, I watched a small glade toward which he was heading and where he would give a clear broadside shot when crossing.

Just at that moment another growl emanated from a spot a few yards to my right, and there, within ten yards, was another tiger, slowly heading in the same direction as its comrade, but, owing to the bushes and its being tail-on to me, I could not get a fair shot, so resumed watching the glade. As neither appeared after some seconds, I followed as noiselessly as possible till the confines of the camp were reached, but I never saw them again.

They undoubtedly crossed into the scrub jungle when I was following them up, as the tank barred the way on the right. I then told Patterson what had occurred, offering to go halves in any damage done if he would tie up his pony. This he declined to do with a good deal of warmth. We had no baits available, and my horse was too big a bait, so the incident closed.

We beat for them throughout the following day, but without result. In those days the forests from Shimoga, by Luckwalli on to the Baba Boodens, were prolific in big game of all kinds, except buffaloes, which are not as a rule found south of the Narmada River. Although tigers were numerous, a man-eater was very seldom heard of, owing, no doubt, to the abundance of pigs and deer throughout that district.

A few years before an exception had existed in the famous Bankipore man-eater, a tigress credited with having killed more than 250 human beings. Her favourite stronghold was the Kargeehully ravine, a heavily wooded nullah of large extent, three miles distant from the travelers' bungalow at Bankipore. My *haylas* [young buffaloes] were tied up there, and after two days there was a kill, followed by a beat. The tracks showed it was a tigress with two cubs, but the jungle was very dense. It was full of karoonda and jamun bushes and over one hundred yards broad in places, so it would have required 150 beaters at least to work it properly, whereas but sixty could be obtained. Moreover, although the man-eater had been killed, her memory was still green, and they kept too close together, leaving strips of jungle unbeaten.

I once lost a fine tiger in the Hyderabad country owing to the beaters grouping themselves in this way. We were beating a broad and dry nullah, which was said to be the favourite lurking place of a local cattle-lifter. Early in the beat a hyena was started, and somebody mistaking it for a tiger, raised the cry *"Pedda huli."* This unsteadied the beaters a good deal, and they commenced to gather into groups, in spite of the shikaris' efforts to preserve an unbroken line.

It was a fearfully hot day in the month of May. The shikari wanted me to climb a tree, but it was not the weather for that sort of amusement, and I took up a position on a sloping sheet of rock, close to a cave on a small island in the nullah, having placed some palas-kino leaves on the burning rock to sit upon and poured water from the *chagal* [a leather water bag] over my head to keep me cool. Presently a fine tiger came slowly down the nullah toward me.

At that time I had a stupid and fallacious theory that, in addition to other catlike attributes, a tiger's sight was bad in bright sunshine, and I accordingly made no attempt to conceal myself (which might have been done, as he was more than two hundred yards distant and frequently hidden by bushes). Instead, I merely remained perfectly still in the belief that he would not discover me. My second rifle lay on the rock beside me, as the gun-carrier had been sent away to lessen the chance of being seen. When about eighty yards off, he stopped and had a good stare at me. I remained perfectly still, but he had evidently spotted me.

He then moved a yard or two to his right and quietly lay down under the tree I was to have been posted in. The foresight was "swimming" owing to the

*The tigress attacks.*

intense heat, and as the distance was too great for a certain shot, I tried to stalk him, but he was too much on the alert and kept raising his head from time to time to watch me. The beaters came on in an irregular line of groups, and the tiger, watching his opportunity, doubled back through the line between two groups, passing them within a few yards without being seen. One cannot blame the poor natives for acting thus, unarmed as they are. Considering everything, they work well and pluckily as a rule when properly handled by a sufficient number of armed shikaris distributed among them, which gives them greater confidence.

The Bankipore folk had also been shaken by an amusing incident that had occurred shortly before my visit. The village shikari, who was my informant, stated that about two miles up the River Boodra, which flows past the travelers' bungalow, there was a very large tiger, the largest he ever saw—like a horse in size!—and that a certain sahib went out one day to beat for him over a kill. They beat right up to the bank of the river where he was posted in a large tree, but they saw no trace of the tiger. So the sahib descended, and he and the beaters were walking along the bank toward a fresh beat when suddenly the tiger jumped up from some long grass in the bed of the river and, entering the water, which was about thirty yards broad, swam toward the opposite bank. When he was almost across, the sahib opened fire, whereupon the brute turned about and commenced swimming back again. More shots were fired without result, and the tiger was soon near terra firma again. As the jungle was low scrub, containing no suitable trees for climbing, a stampede ensued, the tiger remaining master of the situation!

My last regular trip after tigers was in the Singareni district, in the nizam's dominions, in the hot weather of 1881. The party consisted of my colonel, Colonel Russell, commanding the 12th Lancers, and myself. Colonel Russell, being detained by duty, did not join us until we had been a week in the jungle, and we were only able to devote some five weeks to the jungles that remained untried. Previous to the arrival of Colonel Russell, we had got a tigress at Komalapully, a well-known tiger haunt near the Warangal road, some ninety miles distant from Secunderabad. We had employed Kistiah, a famous shikari who lived in that district, which was a good one for tigers, as large herds of cattle grazed there during the hot weather, and it was well provided with water and shady jungle. He was assisted by three shikaris of lesser note, but all were plucky, reliable, and hardworking men.

We arrived in camp about nine o'clock one morning in the month of March, and while at breakfast news of a kill was brought in. About one mile distant was a very remarkable conical hill of basaltic rock, at the foot of which a network of shady nullahs radiated throughout a tract of scrub jungle, which, stretching away for some miles, joined another hilly area, also a noted tiger haunt. The *gara* was close to a small pond at the edge of the jungle near the base of the hill, and we were posted so as to intercept the tiger if it attempted to break away through this wooded zone.

The beat commenced close to the foot of the hill, toward which we faced. The colonel was posted in a tree about seventy yards to my left, I being on a small rock commanding a nullah about twenty yards to my right. I soon heard the coughing roar of a tiger, which had been disturbed by the colonel and his gunbearers on their way to their post, but nothing appeared for some minutes. Then the beat commenced with the usual preliminary burst of tom-toms, horns, shouting, rockets, and blank cartridges—a delicious, if discordant, overture, that always sends a thrill of pleasure through a sportsman.

The tiger roared in response and immediately afterward appeared on the edge of the jungle about forty yards to my left. It then galloped over a slope of sheet rock in front and, crossing the nullah, halted broadside toward me under a tree forty yards off on the opposite bank. I raised my rifle to aim, and the slight movement caught her eye, and she turned her head to stare at me. A second later I pressed the trigger, and up she went on her hind legs before charging me straight as an arrow and roaring as she came. She then fell stone dead into the nullah within twenty yards of my post, the Express bullet having taken her clean through the heart—a prettily marked tigress exactly seven feet, ten inches between uprights.

The shikaris reported that two of her cubs, about the size of big monkeys, had taken refuge in a cave at the base of the hill, but as they could not be bolted, they recommended us to wait for them after sunset, which we accordingly did. This proved ineffectual, nor was a beat next day more successful. We heard afterward that they had been found half starved in the jungle and killed by some native shikaris. That was the most luxurious day's tiger shooting I ever enjoyed—the whole thing took place within a mile of camp and we were only one hour absent.

Four days later we were joined by Colonel Russell on our march to Rajavole, where we arrived on 29 March after an uneventful fortnight, during which we had high winds and comparatively cool weather. The second day after our arrival a *gara* was reported, and the tiger marked down in a small rocky hill about two miles from camp. This we proceeded to beat, and very shortly afterward three bears were driven out and passed to my left toward the colonel's posts. Then a tiger made his appearance, heading in the same direction, so I did not fire, but, much to my surprise, neither did they. I therefore came to the conclusion that he had doubled back before reaching their posts. The beat ended without a shot being fired, and it then transpired that the tiger had passed within twenty yards of my colonel, who being in an awkward position in his tree, could not fire.

Three days afterward we were beating over another kill, at a small isolated cluster of boulders about three miles from camp. We were certainly posted too near the tiger's lair, and he must have detected us. He lay till the beaters were almost on the top of him, being evidently most reluctant to emerge from his retreat, which he eventually did at full gallop, straight under the colonel, who was posted in a leafy tree, which prevented his seeing the tiger. I got two snap-shots at him as he galloped through the jungle about seventy yards off. He spoke to the left barrel, but went on.

We then tracked him for some distance—dangerous work, which should seldom be resorted to without an elephant—but there were no signs of blood, and to this day I don't know where he was hit, for we never saw him again. This tiger undoubtedly winded us, for we were posted upwind and within seventy yards of the cairn where he was hiding. Although we were all at least ten feet above the ground, it gradually rose in front toward the cairn, so that, as a matter of fact, we were actually on the same level as the tiger himself. He very nearly succeeded in getting away on the left flank without being fired at.

The only fault of the Secunderabad shikaris is their neglect to credit the tiger with the fine sense of smell he undoubtedly possesses. When the covert is of ordinary thickness and extent, a tiger, as a rule, appears noiselessly and suddenly, perhaps within ten yards of one's post. But it not infrequently happens in jungles where the withered leaves abound and are large—like those of the bastard teak, for instance—that his approach is heralded by their rustling under his tread. However, from small isolated hills or piles of rock where he has to cross the open ground, he bolts like a rabbit at full gallop, and usually gives a pretty difficult shot. In such spots, however, the space available for his escape is limited, and can generally be commanded by two rifles, so any extra ones should be utilized as "long stops" in case he gets through the first line.

A few days after the occurrence just recorded, news of two *garas* was brought in, and that the tiger was "ringed" into the small hill, the scene of our first day's defeat. The monkeys had discovered and were swearing at him, and as this annoyance might induce him to shift his quarters, we pushed on quickly to the ground. On the way we examined the carcasses of the two *haylas*, which were within a few hundred yards of each other and had been dragged into the shade of some bushes near at hand to protect them from the vultures, in accordance with the tiger's invariable custom. Very little remained of either, but one had been killed by a tigress and cubs that had gone away to some thick jungle which lay two *koss* [a *koss* is equal to two miles] toward the east, and was beyond our sphere of operations that day.

The second tiger was lying up close at hand in the small hill already described. Orders were issued to post the guns at a greater distance from the hill than heretofore, and the beaters were to commence farther off from its base. The two colonels were in trees about fifty yards behind their former positions, and I acted as a "long stop" about seventy yards in the rear.

The tiger soon appeared, coming slowly down the face of the hill to within fifty yards of Colonel Russell, but a stop that had been placed in my original post caused him to turn to the left. He presently emerged at a gallop between the two colonels, who fired simultaneously, and he rolled over and expired in a few seconds.

He was a good, average specimen of a short-tailed tiger, measuring as follows: round forearm, 17¾ inches; length from nose to tail between uprights, 8 feet, 2 inches; length of tail, 31½ inches. With the length of an ordinary tail, he would have been more than nine feet.

We stayed two days longer at Rajavole without a kill before marching to Mankote. We had a scuffle with bears on the way, which we found already in possession of a rocky hill we had intended to ambuscade at break of day. We camped in a mango grove full of interesting birds, including several orioles and specimens of white and chestnut paradise fly catchers.

## Chapter Thirteen

# Alexander Glasfurd
### Rifle and Romance in an Indian Jungle
### (1905)

Capt. Alexander Inglis Robertson Glasfurd set out to write a book on shikar that would "update" an already well-worn topic in 1905. His approach, one adopted by many later writers, was to incorporate many details of his hunts—vegetation, scenery, weather—rather than simply the thrill of the chase. The result was Rifle and Romance in an Indian Jungle.

The author embellishes even further by including fictional accounts of an antelope's and tiger's life in the beginning of the book. The remainder is devoted to actual encounters with tigers and other jungle creatures. He also includes many of his own drawings to further highlight his tales. This synthesis of fiction, fact, and art made Glasfurd's book one of the most popular on Indian wildlife and hunting in the early decades of the twentieth century. It went through several printings between 1905 and 1921.

Glasfurd spent most of his time in central and south-central India. This story takes place in the jungles of the Melghat, a mountainous region that today is home to the largest tiger reserve in the state of Maharashtra. He hunts down an aggressive tiger that has threatened the precious water pool of a local Korku tribe. The piece also extols the natural beauty of the pool at night and describes the many wild creatures, hidden by day, that come there after the sun has set.

### A Night by a Jungle Pool

Evening shadows were lengthening apace, and the last mellow shafts of the declining sun bathed the jungly hillside in a warm glow and threw into relief the heavy heads of the scattered mango trees under which we passed—a silent party of four—as we wound in file down the little woodcutter's path, through the long yellow spear-grass, leading to the already hazy bed of the stream some hundreds of feet below.

It was past seven o'clock, and an hour since I had left camp with the intention of passing the night of the full moon at a solitary pool, deep in the heart of a great ravine, several miles from any other water. In this parching Indian hot weather it is the last resource as a drinking place for all the game within a long distance.

The ravine into which we were descending forms the headwaters of a large tributary of the Tapti River, and is a deep and fiercely raging torrent in the rainy weather. Like most of its neighbours, it has a short course over more or less flat-topped plateaux, from whose edge it plunges over a precipice of black basalt into a deep glen winding a couple of thousand feet below in a tangle of miasmatic vegetation. Shrinking up quickly through the cold-season months, the commencement of the hot weather sees but a few scattered pools in all its mountain course, and a couple of months more of fierce sun exhausts all moisture, save a solitary puddle or two in such spots as are favoured by peculiar geological conditions for the retention of water.

The general appearance of these jungles is that of English woods in October—thin on the steep, exposed slopes of now parched and beaten-down spear-grass, dense and thickety in the ravines seaming their sides. Along the dry, boulder-strewn bed of the stream rises a fringe of larger, taller trees, opening into little occasional bays or natural clearings, and the entire forest is carpeted, often knee deep, with the great dried and fallen leaves of the teak and other trees. In such ground not a step may be taken in silence. On the other hand, game that might otherwise have escaped notice betrays itself here by its movement through the loud-crackling leaves.

In those parts game is scarce and wary, and to anyone who would condemn me as a poacher I would recommend a few days in the dense and hard-to-work jungles of which I speak. If you cannot come to your game, why not let it come to you—which is, after all, the raison d'être of beating or driving? Besides this, there is a certain great charm in a night vigil, such as I hope to describe. It is understood that under these conditions you don't smoke heavily or open sodas with a noisy gurgling every half-hour and then go to sleep condemning it all as a fraud.

We had taken the precaution of "stopping" this pool for the past two nights, by the simple expedient of placing a couple of jungle men and a smouldering

*The author with shikari and attendants.*

cow dung fire a hundred yards or so up the glen. My Korkus reported that on the second night they spent most of their time in a tree, as a tiger had shown extreme impatience at being balked of his water, and had prowled round and round within a short distance of the pool, giving vent to his disappointment in low growls. I thought I knew this tiger: a shy, wily game-killer, who had evaded many a carefully devised beat, and who had been the cause of much bad language and disappointment for the past two years at least.

But here we are! An abrupt descent over large piled-up boulders, and we are soon at the water's edge, which lies below a flat outcropping ledge of black, trap-rock sand along the north side, and the steep fall of a precipitous bank lining the far shore. Here, some fifteen feet up, is our hide, on the summit of a jumble of great rocks, and hedged around with jamun bushes—unnoticeable and natural to a degree.

My orderly called my attention to the fact that a herd of sambar had been down during the day since the Korkus had left in the morning. The sambar had not been able to withstand further the claims of a fierce thirst, although they are able to let a couple of days at least elapse between drinks. They are very partial to water, however, especially for the sake of a good wallow in the mire. There were also traces of other animals, pigs, and, strangely enough, a bear. He must have been hard up to stir after the hot sun had risen. Then, of course, there were numerous marks of the little four-horned antelope and barking deer. These nearly always choose noontide to slake their thirst, tripping with daintily picked and fearful footsteps to the cool damp sand that fringes the forest pool. We examined the ground carefully for the tiger's tracks, so as to try to obtain a hint from which direction to expect him, but the hard withered grass and fallen leaves afforded no information.

As the last glow of dying day fades from the peaks above us, the night chorus of goatsuckers strike up their refrain of *chuckoo-chuckoo-chuckoo,* and many small birds come to sip and to flit about, rejoicing that the torrid fervor of the day is past. Abbas Khan and I mount to our hiding place, and the Korkus, having deposited their burdens, and bearing their little gourd water-bottles, disappear uphill, where we long hear their feet crackling the great dry teak leaves in the warm, still air.

The rug is spread, haversack and water *chagal* put ready to hand, rifles and binoculars disposed handily, a few extra cartridges laid in that little niche in the black rock, and we are ready. What charm is in this delicious quiet, this heavy-scented air, and the curious cries of the jungle breaking the profound silence! The little barbet has changed his day *coppersmith!* note for the no less monotonous and everlasting nocturnal one of *ouic-kur-kur!* As the shadows deepen, a large, fluffy mass sails noiselessly overhead and settles on the gaunt arm of a dead tree, answering a distant call by a deep *whoo!*

I was lost in a reverie, watching the orange disk of the full moon lift over a shoulder of the hills when the extreme right-hand corner of my eye caught a gray shadow hesitatingly approaching among some rocks in the dry bed of the stream, and the glasses revealed a hyena nosing about near the place where we had come down off the hill. He then stood, cocking his strange pointed ears in our direction for some time, but finally limped up right under our rock—a fine, big fellow with a good coat. By leaning over we might have almost touched him with a stick. After drinking, he went off downstream.

Later, a little barking deer came rustling in the teak leaves on the far side of the nullah on its way down to the edge of the water; another, farther off, moving here and there, kept up his funny little yap of *aow! aow!* Higher rose the moon in a perfectly cloudless sky, and the gentle breaths of air died away until every stick and blade of grass stood out sharp and clear in the brilliant light. Small bats wheeled and circled with soft whirring wings over the dark pool, ever and anon kissing the glassy surface in a downward swoop. Why is it that moonlight should throw such mystery over the woods? The slightest sound appears to be a loud and startling uproar, and the occasional scratching indulged in by Abbas Khan as if it would be sufficient warning to all animals for miles. Curious small noises come and go in the dry leaves, and two tiny owls cause quite a stir as they softly alight on a slender teak pole, which has a few huge dried leaves attached to its topmost twigs.

The mind, too, is gently influenced by the quiet scene and wonders how there can be such things as rage and strife. Why should life not glide thus peacefully on, without jar, in calm beatitude! The ear catches a far-distant, gentle stirring in the carpeting of dry teak leaves, now dying away, and then again increasing, coming nearer, stopping, recommencing. The sounds come from the lower portion of that long, steep spur that runs from the little level vale of yellow grass right up to the soft, indistinct distance of crag-encircled plateaux far above us.

*Tiger coming to drink after dark at the jungle pool.*

The colours of the sleeping landscape, though restricted to blues, grays, and palest yellow, are still marvelously diverse in tone: there the rich, soft, blue-black of some deep ravine, here the sharp, dark branches of a gnarled tiwas tree in high relief against a pale background of long, withered grass.

The crackling of leaves is more pronounced now, and the binoculars are raised to the dark line of forest where it touches the grassland. Nothing shows for many long minutes. At length a tall, black object is spied moving slowly forward, and after a while it steps into a patch of moonlight that falls through the twisted boughs, and appears to view—a fine, old sambar stag, with newly sprouted horns in velvet. A tall salai tree is before him, and here he pauses and raises his muzzle; then, leaning sidewise, he scrapes his rough hide luxuriously against the bark.

Tiring of this exercise, the stately, measured walk is recommenced, and he feeds slowly off over a little glade, and gradually disappears in the labyrinth of ghostly yellow trunks. He is probably one of those who drank at our pool today, and so is indifferent to water for the next forty-eight hours or thereabouts, though he may turn up in the hour before dawn for a roll and mud-bath. The sound of his wandering steps in the leaves dies gradually away, and all is again still, save for the eternal *chuckoo-chuckoo!* of the nightjars, and their prolonged cry of *hoo-hoo-hoo!* as they flit and sail from tree to tree and rock to rock.

One of the most exciting bits of this night work is the waiting to see what it is that for the last half-hour has been moving toward the pool through the telltale leaves, and now emerges and halts—a dark, shapeless mass—on the edge of the jungle.

Perhaps it were hardly interesting to record how several sounders of hog—boar, sows, and many little squeakers—approached, wallowed, drank, and finally trotted off, grunting satisfaction, to where their favourite roots were to be had for the grubbing. Or how a pair of jackals arrived, and while one danced a remarkably fantastic fandango in a sand hole, how its mate discovered some brooding danger, and, the signal given, how the pair disappeared, with many a suspicious halt and backward stare—all this in the effulgence of a full tropic moon.

I took out my notebook and penciled little notes. I smoked gently, for I hold that, except under certain circumstances of position and wind, when tobacco smoke can be detected, the natural perfume of he who smokes not would be no less noticeable. Many a night had I passed in this al fresco manner, but never a one when all so combined to please, and when I had such chances of observing unsuspicious wild creatures.

I was lying back on the bed of boughs, grass, comfortable rug, and cushion when a long, cold, trailing thing passed over my hand, and away from under my hips, leaving the hairs of my head in a state of electric separation. When the slight rustling had receded well into some rocks, I again drew breath, and quickly removed my haversack of cold roast fowl and other delicacies to another spot. Whether of a deadly species or not, I object to snakes hunting for *murghi* [chicken/fowl] in my pockets!

It was now well past 2:00 A.M., and I felt drowsy, especially as the tuneful breathing of my faithless disciple sounded like a lullaby in my ears. Perhaps an hour or so had passed in this borderland of dreams when a sound struck on my ears that instantly roused us both. It was the sudden, sharp, rending, trumpet sound of a sambar's bell: *dhank!* There it came again from up the glen and continued at intervals, apparently retreating slowly for some minutes when all was again quiet. Then came another bark, louder and much nearer, and the crashing of leaves and jungle as the sambar apparently moved rapidly uphill.

Pulses beat more quickly now in keen anticipation, for this kind of thing has but one meaning. Two figures, dark and stiff, peered over the lip of the

*A fatal pause before the tiger was shot.*

rock, the glint of moonlight on a double-barrel .577. There came the deepest of guttural sighs from the big, black boulder under a far clump of bamboo.

The moon shone on, and the watch ticked loudly in my pocket, and we waited—weary work, with all senses at highest pressure. Five minutes must have passed thus. Ah!—a stone turned then—and now the moon's rays fall on the white face and chest of a tiger as he moves out of the blackness and comes gently forward. This one was a rather small and lightly made brute, but with twice the grace and elegance of the beef-eater of the plains.

He came to a sudden halt, moving his head slowly from side to side. Perhaps a slight human taint reached him, but it apparently escaped notice, for, pausing but a little while, he passed straight to the water. The powerful shoulder-blades worked under his glossy coat as he crouched like a great cat, and down went his head to lap. Gently, ever so gently, the rifle came to the shoulder, and the white card sight on the muzzle stood out well in the moonlight.

A sudden star of bright sparked, a struggling and a rolling, and then a *woof!* as *bang!* went the left barrel at a vanishing streak of faint gray that flashed up over the dark rocks and was gone. Caution and quiet were now unnecessary, and as we discussed the pros and cons of a hit or miss, I treated myself to a well-merited whiskey and soda and turned in for a snooze. I slept till awakened by words repeated in Hindustani:

"*Hazur* [sir], the fate of the tiger has come to pass!"

My orderly being, as befits a pious Moslem, is a firm believer in kismet. On sitting up with the fresh breeze of dawn fanning my cheek, I felt rather grubby after the long, warm hours of night in this close ravine. The men were washing their mouths, noisy native fashion, in the far pool, and gray jungle-cocks called defiance from every side. Little parties of them and of the sombre spur-fowl pattered in the leaves round the head of the pool.

Sitting thus, a movement in the limbs of a tall tree beyond the nullah attracted my attention, and shortly two dark. Lithe objects appeared, chasing each other up and down the long branches, against the beautiful green flush of the young day. At length they scurried up to the topmost twig, whence one, detaching itself, sailed with a steady downward flight straight over my head, and, curving upward again like a hawk, alighted softly on the gnarled trunk of a kowa tree. Its mate, answering its curiously harsh cry, followed suit, and, as they disappeared in the gray twilight, it struck me that I had lost a chance of adding a flying squirrel to my collection. Their flight was wonderfully easy and graceful, and they must have covered about fifty yards clear from tree to tree.

A sluice in the clear water and a bite of food were followed by the matutinal cigarette, and thereafter we examined the hair and splashes of blood on the boulders before we started. The tracks led uphill into an extremely thickly jungled little *khora* [place]. We passed a spot where the tiger had rolled in agony, and we followed his erratic course from the bits of white hair on his chest that we found on any stumps or rocks in his way. As the men picked up the easily read trail, I kept a sharp lookout ahead, rifle at the ready And so we crept along, under some bushes, round a rock here, through a tangle of small bamboos there, until at last there he lay on his side, thirty yards away, apparently quite dead.

Turning silently to the men, I motioned the Korkus back, tipped a wink to Abbas Khan, and took the little white patch under the forearm. Over the smoke a huge, tawny form rose up, glared in our direction, and then all was a chaos of gleaming teeth, viciously laid back ears, and flying leaves, as we darted behind a thick tree. Round he came— nullah rolling, falling, rising, doing his best to get at us, when another bullet caught him in the back, and all was over.

When the shivering Korkus had come off their trees, we turned the tiger over and saw that last night's bullet had struck full in the chest, but, owing to my raised position, had merely run along not far below the skin. It was subsequently found lodged below the stomach. To my surprise, he measured nine feet as he lay.

An hour later, as I passed slowly up the precipitous spur leading to the plateau and camp, and took a breather ere climbing the little mural precipice that skirts the flat tops of these hills, my eye fell with grateful recollections on the glint of the little pool, now a thousand feet below in the yet dark glen, which had afforded me one of the pleasantest nights of my life.

## Chapter Fourteen

# Alfred Watson
### King Edward VII as Sportsman
### (1911)

*E*dward Albert (Later King Edward VII) was heir apparent to the throne longer than anyone in British history. This is because he was the son of Queen Victoria, the longest reigning queen in British history. During his long wait (during which time he held the title Prince of Wales, like all male heirs apparent), he led the classic life of aristocratic leisure.

Edward was a passionate hunter and the last of Britain's great sportsman-aristocrats. Although after his time royalty continued to hunt, he considered field sports integral to aristocratic life and his own identity. One of his greatest hunting adventures was his 1875 India tour. He and his entourage spent eight months visiting Indian princes, which involved a good bit of hunting. Edward's trip was the first by a member of the royal family to India. It was also the first time hunting was publicly criticized, a trend that intensified in the twentieth century.

This selection is from writer Alfred Watson's book *King Edward VII as Sportsman (1911)*. It is based on the account of the famous war correspondent Sir William Howard Russell, who was the king's personal secretary on the journey. The tiger hunt described here took place in the Nepalese Terai. The term "royal Bengal tiger" had just been coined after the Prince shot a large tiger in neighboring Purnea.

### Sport Abroad: The Indian Tour

Sport was a prominent feature of the then Prince of Wales' famous tour in India, and, indeed, had he not been devoted to the gun and rifle, the expedition would in many respects have been carried out on widely different lines. There can be no doubt, moreover, that the skill and adroitness with which His Royal Highness adapted himself to entirely new surroundings, particularly in the

*The Prince of Wales hunting tigers with Sir Jung Bahadoor.*

Terai, and the success that happily attended his efforts, had their effect on all classes of the Indian community. More than once, it is no exaggeration to say, the Prince was in danger of his life, as will be made clear from some of the incidents that have to be recorded, notably in one elephant hunt, details of which will follow.

It has happened of late years that some leading English politicians and prominent personalities have had no sympathy with the sports that used to be pursued by English gentlemen, almost as a rule. The socialistic disposition to abuse sport has, however, only sprung up in comparatively recent times, nor is it to be supposed that the Prince would have been in any way affected by it. In any case, as regards his Indian journey, it is certain that affectionate reverence would have marked his reception, but it is equally certain that the manner in which His Royal Highness comported himself in the jungle largely increased the admiration with which the natives regarded him.

The full description of the journey, written by the late Sir William Howard Russell, the great Crimean correspondent—on which graphic narrative I am drawing largely for the material utilized in the following pages—shows in what fashion His Royal Highness was welcomed, and we may be sure that the impression was vastly strengthened by the courage and address which he consistently displayed, because, in fact, they were characteristic of him. Not long after the publication of this book, His Majesty King George is to visit the empire, in which memories of his father remain, and it is fervently to be hoped that in all respects the journey will be equally successful.

It was in the winter of 1874 that the project of a tour in India was first mooted. On the 16th of the following March the Marques of Salisbury officially announced to the Council of India that the Prince intended to visit the country, and on the 22nd of the month a paragraph appeared in *The Times* confirming the rumor which had become current and stating that if no unforeseen obstacle arose His Royal Highness would leave England the following November. The announcement was warmly acclaimed in England, for, as a writer in *The Times* remarked: "An immense respect is due from the conquerors of India to the venerable kingdoms, institutions, and traditions, of which they have become the political heirs, and an adequate manifestation of this feeling has always been one of the great wants of our Indian administration."

The utmost enthusiasm reigned throughout what was to become the Indian Empire at the prospect of the royal visit. Some debate followed as to the precise capacity in which it should be paid, and Mr. Disraeli, as he then was, carefully pointed out that the Prince did not go to India as "the representative of the Queen" but as "the Heir Apparent to the Crown," a distinction, however, that does not seem to have been of primary importance, though it arose from questions asked and pressed in the House of Commons.

On the 16th of October, His Royal Highness, with his suite and attendants, boarded the *Serapis*. The late Duke of Sutherland had been graciously commanded to make one of the party; Lord Suffield, then head of the Prince's household; Colonel Ellis, Equerry to the Prince; Major-General, now Sir Dighton Probyn; and Mr. Francis, now Lord Knollys, the Prince's private secretary, completed the list of selections from members of the royal household; Lord Alfred Paget, clerk-marshal; Lords Aylesford and Carrington; Lieutenant, now Admiral, Lord Charles Beresford; the Rev. Canon Duckworth, chaplain to the Prince; Lieutenant, now Colonel, Sir Augustus FitzGeorge of the Rifle Brigade; Sir Bartle Frere and his private secretary, Mr. Albert Grey; General Owen Williams; and Sir William Russell, temporarily attached as the Hon. Private Secretary to the Prince, made up the suite.

The royal party, after visiting Egypt, reached Bombay on 8 November, and soon grew somewhat perturbed by rumours that cholera was rife in various places that had been included in the itinerary, fear of the dire disease more than once afterward causing alterations in the routes that had been planned. It is with the sport that the Prince enjoyed that we are here concerned, however, and much that is of great interest must necessarily be omitted, though it is impossible not to say a word in recognition of the grateful homage that was done to His Royal Highness.

Rich gifts were humbly offered for acceptance, the Raja of Kolhapur being singularly happy in his choice of the manner in which the honour bestowed on him should be signalized, for, besides the ancient jeweled sword and dagger, of which he begged the Prince's acceptance, he assigned a sum of £20,000 for the purpose of founding a hospital, to be called after His Royal Highness, as a memorial of his presence in the dependency. The account of the reception by the Gaekwar of Baroda reads more like a dream of the East than a record of an actual event. A clang of drums, trumpets, and clarions announced the arrival of the royal party, and then Sir William Russell continues:

> The Prince took the little Maharaja by the hand, sat down, and talked with him for a short time. He then passed outside to the steps leading from the entrance to the station, before which towered an elephant of extraordinary size; on his back was a howdah of surpassing splendour that shone like burnished gold in the morning sun, and lay dead, a full-grown tigress, eight and a half feet long.

On the 8th of the month the party moved to the shooting camp at Bareilly, on the outskirts of the Terai, a term that the chronicler of the expedition explains. "As a 'forest' in Scotland means a mountain on which there are no trees, so the word 'Terai,' often applied to the wooded belts of the base of the Himalayas, is really the prairie that lies outside it for hundreds of miles."

Many tiger stories were naturally told. One was of a village where the people were terribly troubled by one of these creatures, and sent for a wise man to charm it away by his magic arts, but the tiger came out and ate the wise man, after which the villagers migrated. "For," they said, "now that the tiger has eaten our sage, he will know all our secrets, and we shall have no chance of evading him."

There is no royal road to success in tiger shooting, and the first day was a blank. It was believed that a tiger was hiding in a patch of deep grass and leaves, and elephants were sent in to beat. Just prior to this His Royal Highness had been advised to move to another place a little distance away, and soon after his departure a splendid tiger rushed out within twenty yards of where the Prince had been only a few minutes before. He was still sufficiently near to see the beast and, indeed, fired but was unable to obtain a clear view of it, the grass being so high, so the animal escaped. A leopard was, however, put up and shot, and the bag included many head of deer and small game.

On the 11$^{th}$ the party visited Peepal Perao, thirteen miles to the eastward of the camp, a wonderful district for jungle life. Sir William speaks of "duck, teal, kingfishers, reed warblers, painted and common snipe, rails, dappers, butcher birds, partridge, and quail; parrots, many sorts of thrush or grackles, woodpeckers, fly-catchers, owls; jungle cock in the thick stuff, black partridge on the outskirts, and porcupines rattling over the dry watercourses; hares near the cultivated patches; by the edges of the woods little burrowing creatures like marmosets. Above all career eagles, falcons, hawks, buzzards, and kites." But these were left unmolested, the quarry being tiger, and the sound of shooting, had guns been fired at insignificant game, would probably have driven away any of these beasts that might be in the immediate neighbourhood.

The camp must have resembled a species of town. It contained 2,500 persons, exclusive of General Ramsay's separate establishment; there were 119 elephants, 550 camels, 100 horses, 60 carts drawn by oxen, many goats and milch cows, 600 coolies [laborers], 60 tent-pitchers, 20 water-carriers, 40 messengers and attendants, 75 noncommissioned officers and men of the 3$^{rd}$ Gurkhas and their band, troopers of the Bengal Cavalry and Native Infantry, together with mahouts, camel-men, and the Europeans. The Prince's person was guarded exclusively by natives.

"Certainly," Sir William says, "I should feel rather proud of myself if I were a wild beast and knew all this."

The going was dreadfully bad, the ground so deep in places that Sir William's elephant on one occasion sunk till the mud reached its lower jaw.

*The Prince's elephant charged by a tiger.*

For the first few days the main object of the tiger quest was not successfully accomplished. On Saint Valentine's Day, the camp having moved to Tanda, the Prince shot a bear. Sir William was placed next to His Royal Highness, and observed the brute crouched as if listening. The Prince also saw it and at once fired, the animal dropping to the shot, but it got up again and rushed away, charging an elephant as it did so. Other shots were sent after it, and it rolled over, proving to be a sloth bear of extraordinary size and weight. These animals are exceedingly fierce and mischievous, one of them having been known to kill eight men in two consecutive nights.

On the 15th a tigress was shot, though not by the Prince, who, however, got one next day eight feet, six inches long, together with a sloth bear measuring these figures reversed, six feet, eight inches. On the 17th a tiger was seen swimming a river, and one of the native magnates had a long but unsuccessful shot at it. On the 18th a line of elephants more than six hundred yards long was formed, the Prince being in the centre, and a tiger was roused up, which bounded across in the direction of the Prince, but someone else fired, and the beast turned before His Royal Highness could get a chance at it. It charged the elephant, and soon rolled over, dead, a magnificent beast ten feet long and beautifully marked.

Penetrating farther into the country, the camp moved on to Banbasa. Next day was Sunday, and, after service had been read, a move was made across the river to Nepalese territory, a difficult country of mountainous jungle hardly possible for camels, the elephants being the only means of conveyance. Next day the Prince was not long before he killed his first Nepalese tiger. The hunt must have been remarkably picturesque and exciting.

Great hopes had been formed that the Prince's first day in Nepal should not be a blank, and the expedition set out accordingly. We read of the yells of the *jemadars*, *"Roko!"* [Halt]; *"Chelo!"* [Go on]; *"Baineko!"* [To the left], and *"Dahine-ko!"* [To the right]. Adding to the noise was the blows of the *hircus* [horns], the shouts of the mahouts, the crashing of the branches above and the saplings below that made the forest ring. Suddenly a herd of deer dashed forward and halted like cavalry brought up midway in a furious charge, and directly afterward a tiger appeared, moving at an easy canter, growling as he ran. For a moment, on seeing the elephants, he appeared inclined to charge, but altered his mind and swung round into a small natural shrubbery where he was lost to view.

The Prince and his host, Sir Jung Bahadoor, speedily drew forward. Sir William describes the scene:

> The tiger after two or three growls—the bellow of an angry bull and the snarl of an angry dog commingled—leaped through the brushwood. The Prince fired one! two!—the last shot turned him, he rushed into the covert. His side was exposed to the Prince. The next report of the rifle was followed by a yell of pain; the tiger raised itself, rolled half over, and fell as the second barrel sent a bullet through its body. The apparition of open jaws and glaring eyes sank down into the grass, which waved fitfully to and fro for a second or two; then all was quiet. There was the usual cautious advance of the shikaris, and looking down from their howdahs all saw the creature stretched out dead. He was a full-grown male, nine feet, six inches long. Had he not been stopped just at the right moment, he would certainly have been on to a man or an elephant.
>
> This day one of the wonderful sights was a procession in single file of seven hundred elephants.

Unfortunately Sir William did not see the making of the wonderful bag that the Prince brought into camp on the 21st. No fewer than seven tigers were killed, six of these—including that whose death has been described—having been shot by the Prince. Five were killed in a single beat, which did not last more than an hour. Two of them His Royal Highness got with single shots; the other three took two or more bullets; the seventh fell to another rifle, by whom fired we are not told. The Prince insisted on exercising his own discretion, declining to accept advice that was freely given to "shoot just in front," or wherever it might have been. He would not fire at anything he did not see and chance the result. One of the seven was a tigress whom the experts recognized as a man-eater, clothes and human bones being found near where she met her end.

The hospitable Sir Jung was extremely anxious that his royal guest should enjoy some sport with elephant, and heard with the utmost gratification that a herd was not far distant. On the day after the brilliantly successful tiger hunt, the party accordingly set off at seven o'clock in the morning, the chief taking with him his two fighting elephants. Jung Pershaud, his champion elephant, had his head, neck, and the upper part of his body painted blood-colour in an apparent tribute to his prowess as champion of the Nepalese woods, and Bijli, a great fighter but inferior to the champion. For some hours the party proceeded at the best pace the elephants could muster, a rate of speed that much fatigued the animals, though they sought to freshen themselves up by spouting jets of water from their trunks over their backs; one douche directed by the Prince's mount completely deluged the rider.

At noon they halted, and the news came that the leader of the herd was engaged in a fight with Jung and Bijli, whereupon Sir Jung urged the Prince to mount at once, explaining that the herd might break toward them, in which case no one's life would be safe. They were also twenty-five miles from camp, and it was thought desirable not to go farther away. On the journey back they came upon the captured elephant marching between its conquerors with downcast ears, drooping head, and dejected proboscis.

On the 23$^{rd}$ the Prince killed a tigress, its cub being taken alive, and, incidentally, Sir William Russell did not kill the finest tiger that ever was seen, for just as the fish that escapes is always of phenomenal weight, so the tiger that gets away is of relatively gigantic dimensions. On the 24$^{th}$, the camp, having now reached Mahullea, the Prince shot a leopard, a second barrel that was fired was found to have been unnecessary as the creature was killed by the first, and soon after he had the good fortune to get a fine tigress. She was at first seen only for a moment, and took refuge in some high grass, into which all sorts of things were flung in order to drive her out: oranges, mineral-water bottles, and, amongst other things, the hunting hat of one of the rajas, which Sir Jung seized and hurled into the covert. It is only fair to say that afterward he threw his own pith cap. This appears to have brought her out, and one barrel from the Prince rolled her over.

The 25th February was marked by a wonderful day's sport after elephant, such as, the narrator of the tour remarks, "it comes rarely in any man's life to see." A herd of wild elephants, led by a tusker of enormous strength, size, and courage, was reported to be some seven miles from camp. The Prince and his host set off on horseback, pulling up at eleven o'clock to wait for news of what was going on. It was believed that they could not be far from the herd. The supposition was correct; news of its position was brought by a Gurkha hunter, and Sir Jung gave the word to mount, leading the way through the jungle that was interspersed with riverbeds, boulders, awkward banks, and all sorts of traps that might very easily have brought horsemen to grief.

At length they had to stop; horses could go no farther, and Sir Jung jumped onto the back of one of his Nepalese attendants, with another man on each side to steady him, being thus borne down the rock, across the riverbed, and up the hill on the opposite side, at the rate of a good six miles an hour. Before long he reappeared, still mounted, but exchanged his biped for a quadruped, and after covering some miles, the former halting-place came in sight, where it was suggested that the party should lunch, but Sir Jung knew the risks that might easily be incurred if the elephants came that way. They were all dead men, he declared, if the creatures moved down on them, and requested His Royal Highness and the other members of the party to climb up into trees without loss of time.

The Prince, who at first was inclined to laugh at the idea, presently accepted the advice, and scrambled up to a seat that the Nepalese speedily constructed for him with their kukris [curved knives], some thirty feet from the ground. As it proved, however, no danger was at hand; nothing was seen of the elephants, and if they were to be found it was necessary to go in search of them. Sir Jung, therefore, ordered the tame elephants to advance, but the Prince expressed a wish to ride, and took his seat in the saddle instead of in the howdah.

The host led the way at a gallop, and after some miles had been covered, on the verge of the forest the party saw before them a huge brown back emerging from the surroundings of high grass, "reminiscent of a half-submerged whale cleaving its way in the placid sea." The chronicler surmises the cheer that burst forth, the joyous English hunting "Tally-ho! hark for'ard!" was such as had never been heard before, and will probably never be heard again, in Nepalese jungle, which indeed it is easy to believe.

Startled by the sound, the elephant paused and looked around him, resuming his course for a few moments, and then stopping. The Prince was pressing eagerly forward, and continued to do so in spite of Sir Jung's cry, "*Kubudar!* (Take care!) Look out all of you! You must not go near him in that long grass. You have no chance of getting away!"

But the Prince sped onward just by the outside of the thick grass, and before long headed the tired monster, who came on appearing bigger and bigger as he approached. It is well that Sir William Russell was not absent from this exciting spectacle, or his graphic account of it could not have been written, however well he might have managed from the descriptions of his friends. He writes of the elephant:

> His proboscis extended, his tail straight out, he stood and looked round; suddenly uttering a shrill cry he made a run at the horsemen who were circling before him. There was something so ludicrous in the gait and attitude of the charging elephant that every one, as he bent down on his saddle and rode literally for his life, burst out laughing—all except Sir Jung, who, with one eye over his shoulder, kept calling out, 'Look out, Prince! *Kubudar, Shahzadah!*' (Take care, Prince!)
>
> But though the speed at which his strange, shambling shuffle carried him along was extraordinary, the beast was much too fatigued to continue it for very long. He halted, blew a note of rage, swaying his head to and fro, and flapping his ears. It was of the utmost consequence to keep him in the open, and take as much out of him as possible till the fighting elephants could come up. In a moment the horsemen wheeled and swept round him, Sir Jung shaking his fist and using the most opprobrious terms to the indignant animal. Down went his head, up went proboscis and tail once more.
>
> This time he turned straight on the Prince, who was shaking with laughter as he put his horse, a splendid Arab, to his top speed. Fast as he went the terrible proboscis was not many yards behind for a second or two, but the pace was too great to last. The horses evidently had the pull in this ground, and there was nothing to fear but a fall or stumble, and then—well,

*The Prince, chased by a rogue elephant.*

nothing can save you! Over and over again the bold attack and precipitate flight were repeated; all the party had the honour of a run in turn.

While this was passing, the famous fighting elephants Jung and Bijli were anxiously expected, and after more than half an hour of exasperating anxiety on the part of Sir Jung, their advent was announced, the painted head of the great brute coming into sight above the reeds. The wild elephant heard the clang of the bell that swung round Jung Pershaud's neck, and turning round, swept the reeds with his trunk so as to obtain a better view of his new antagonist. Jung approached; the other, who had only one tusk and the stump of the second, lowered his head. But Jung continued his way, and when close to the wild elephant gave him a blow on the side of the skull with his trunk, followed by a violent ram on the quarter, which wheeled him half over. The thud, we are told, was "like a stroke on the big drum in a silent theatre." Another ram on the quarter followed, and the wild elephant, turning round, bolted with all possible speed, not escaping, however, before he had received yet one more dig in the hindquarters that nearly sent him onto his head.

Sir Jung's apprehension lest the Prince should run into danger was extreme, but His Royal Highness was too greatly interested to take much care, and rode on, expecting to see the fight renewed on some open ground that the wild elephant had to cross before reaching the forest for which he was making. The way was over a deep, ditchlike stream, which the party crossed, Sir Jung's horse getting over after an awkward mistake. There they found the hunted elephant standing against a tree, and at this supreme moment Bijli appeared from the covert a few yards away.

Bijli dashed forward, the other set his forelegs apart, and, lowering his head prepared for battle, the two skulls meeting in a mighty crash. The wild elephant was turning to fly, but Bijli was after him, and having the better speed constantly rammed his enemy's quarters. The wild one presently turned again, and while Bijli gave him resounding blows with his trunk over the head and eyes, some of the attendants passed a turn of rope round the victim's hind leg. It was not enough to detain him, and he broke away once more, but Bijli was after him. Another crashing ram on the quarter nearly knocked him over; "then and then only," Sir William remarks, "poor Miserimus said as plainly as anything could say it, 'I give in.'

"There must be some elephant language as plain as any spoken word. He dropped his proboscis as a vanquished knight lowers his sword point, blew a feeble tootle trumpet full of despondency—a cry for mercy—and stood screening his shame with his huge ears. Bijli accepted the surrender on the instant. He approached in a fondling sort of way, wound his proboscis round the captive's neck, and I daresay complimented him on his very handsome resistance. 'But after all, Miserimus, the odds were against you. There was old Jung Pershaud, and you beat him and did very well, but I am Bijli, you know!' As Miserimus was thinking what answer to make to these compliments, the knaves with the ropes were at work again, and this time they made good their knot."

As one reads, one forcibly appreciates the marvelous intelligence of the trained elephants, who evidently knew precisely what was wanted of them and how to accomplish it. It was presently discovered that the captive was blind of an eye, which he had probably lost in the same fight as that in which he broke his tusk. Sir Jung said that he would let the creature go if the Prince expressed a wish that it should be set at liberty, and it need hardly be said what the answer was. The poor brute felt his defeat, uttering a very bitter cry as he found that the ropes held him fast, and he scornfully declined the succulent sugarcane that was held out to him. The tusk was taken as a trophy and the creature released.

Another week was passed in camp after this thrilling adventure. On 26 February a hunt for tiger was the order of the day. His Royal Highness had no sport though Sir Jung himself accompanied him, but one of the other parties got a tiger after a sufficiently exciting encounter. Mr. Moore, the magistrate of Bareilly, hit the beast, which sprang onto the elephant of the Rev. Mr. Robinson, catching one claw on the rifle so that he could not fire, and tearing the mahout's leg, besides cruelly clawing the elephant. It then leaped onto the mahout of the elephant that was carrying Colonel Ellis, and was tearing him down when the colonel, leaning over the howdah, got in a bullet and ended the fight.

On 2 March the Prince shot a huge tiger upward of ten feet long. On the 3rd he got a couple more, and on the 4th one of the biggest that had been seen, ten feet long and nineteen inches round the forearm. On the 5th a farewell *durbar* [ceremony] was held, and Sir Jung and his brethren rode into camp—the host on a man's back, as was usual when he was not in good health and felt disinclined to ride a horse. The Prince presented him with several very fine rifles, a silver statuette of His Royal Highness in the uniform of the 10th Hussars, of which regiment he was colonel, and many other valuable souvenirs. Next day the Prince, with cordial expressions of the pleasure he had received, bade his host farewell, and set off for Bareilly along a new road that had been made for many miles through the forest.

### Chapter Fifteen

# Charles Gouldsbury
## Tiger Land
### (1913)

Charles Elphinstone Gouldsbury lived a life of adventure. It began at age fifteen when he stowed away on a British ship destined for Canada. After a rough initiation, he spent several years at sea until landing in Calcutta. He almost drowned soon after his arrival, after being pulled into the undertow of the Hooghly River. He then joined the army, right before the Mutiny, and spent several years fighting to suppress it.

The remainder of his career was spent in the Indian police in eastern India, and that is when his hunting adventures began. He shot tiger, rhinoceros, and buffalo, as well as small game in his spare time. Gouldsbury was an intrepid hunter and adventurer who pursued many tigers on foot, as well as by more conventional methods. His hunting tales were personalized because he always interspersed them with philosophical musings and accounts of the various people he encountered on his journeys.

Gouldsbury wrote several books on hunting, as well as an autobiography. This selection is a chapter from *Tiger Land (1913)*. Here he describes his introduction to tiger hunting, a pastime he took up after leaving the military, shortly after the Great Mutiny. It takes place in lower Bengal, where Gouldsbury did most of his hunting during the many decades he spent in India.

#### Bagging My First Tiger

How long I continued in the troop after the fighting was virtually over, I cannot now remember, for when writing from memory of a past so rich in incidents, it is not easy to recall the sequence of events. But to the best of my recollection, the corps I belonged to was disbanded toward the close of the year 1860, to come into existence again almost as a whole—though under a new title—in 1861.

*Organizing the beaters.*

By this time the Mutiny had been finally stamped out, and amongst the changes effected by the government was the creation of a new, semimilitary police or constabulary, as it was called, for the whole of India, manned and officered almost entirely by members of the various yeomanry and other irregular forces that had been raised, temporarily, to aid in quelling the rebellion. I was, amongst some others, fortunate enough to be appointed as a junior officer to this new police force, and found myself posted to the district of R—, in the lower provinces of Bengal, as an assistant superintendent, and lost no time in joining my appointment.

The force, as I have said, was organized on semimilitary lines, and in the district I was appointed to, it consisted of about five hundred in all, including native officers such as inspectors, subinspectors, and head constables, the whole under the command of an officer styled the district superintendent, who, as in most cases, was a military man, and to whom I was in the position of second in command. My life now, though naturally less exciting than what I had been accustomed to lately, was infinitely more interesting, to say nothing of the comfort of living in a house again, being properly attended on by servants, and having proper food, instead of living nowhere in particular, waiting on myself, and foraging, often unsuccessfully, for a meal. My CO, or superintendent, a recently promoted major, was one of the nicest men I have met, and, being an Irishman like myself, we got on excellently together.

Our duties were fairly heavy as was only natural considering the condition of the country and the fact that both native officers and men, being quite new to their work, had to be continually instructed in the rules and regulations that we had first to learn ourselves. In my case, I also had to pass certain tests, for before being confirmed in their appointments, all assistant superintendents were required to pass an examination in law and the language of their district, within two years of being appointed. Indeed, so overburdened was I with work that after the first month or two I often found myself regretting having given up my past life, despite all its discomforts. It seemed a preferable occupation to be shooting sepoys in the open—even when being shot at in return—to confinement in a stuffy office all the day, or in my room at nights with an oleaginous Munshi [honorific for a teacher] endeavouring to instill into my mind some knowledge of his abominable vernacular.

But, later on, when his efforts had to some extent succeeded, and I had gained more experience in my duties, my good-natured superior, seeing my dislike to a sedentary life, sent me often out into the district. Ostensibly these forays were for investigation or inspection duty, which I performed to the best of my ability, though not, I fear, with any extraordinary results. These inquisitorial excursions were made once or twice a quarter, each occupying about a week, during which period I was continually on the move, sleeping in village huts or at a police station, and at times even under a tree with my saddle for a pillow—two such occasions being, I remember, a Christmas and New Year's Eve of the same year.

It was in these wanderings round the country that I acquired a taste for big-game shooting that eventually developed into a passion. Tigers and leopards were plentiful in those days and were destructive in proportion. *Khubber,* or information, of cattle and sometimes human beings killed by them was constantly brought to me by the villagers and police, the reporting of such matters being a portion of their duties. Often, too, while seated of a morning under a tree examining witnesses in some case or poring over musty registers at a station, the distracted owner of a cow or buffalo would present himself. The owner of the animal killed during the night and dragged into an adjoining jungle would come running in himself and, groveling at my feet, insist on "the preserver of the poor transferring his august presence" to the scene of the disaster and slaying the *bagh* [tiger] at once!

I seldom declined these invitations, for the destruction of dangerous game was, I had been told, a part of my business. It was also one I felt better qualified to tackle than witness and registers since the first I could barely understand and of the purport of the latter I had but the vaguest notion. But, diligently as I followed up each piece of information received, I was invariably unsuccessful, sometimes because the so-called kill would, on inquiry, be found to have died a natural death, though more often, as I know now, the failure was due to my ignorance of the habits of the beasts I was attempting to locate. It was not till many months later when I was acting for my CO, who had gone on three months' leave, that my perseverance was rewarded. The incident happened in this wise.

One morning, shortly after I had taken charge, I was hearing the usual daily reports from all the police stations. Amongst them was one from the officer in charge of a frontier post urgently requesting to be supplied with some more rounds of ball cartridge. That being a somewhat unusual demand and one I considered dangerous to comply with without further inquiry, I dispatched a mounted constable at once to the post, some seventy miles distant, to demand further details. In the course of four or five days I received a reply stating that a tiger had for some weeks past taken up his position in a jungle close to the outpost and had not only carried off several head of cattle belonging to the villagers but also had become so bold and reckless that it was feared he might take to attacking human beings. Hence the request for more ball cartridges.

On receiving this news, I sent orders immediately to the sporting official to collect as many elephants as he could lay his hands on and have them assembled at his outpost within four days, adding that as I would be there myself as soon as possible, he was on no account to take any action calculated to frighten the tiger away before my arrival. My gun and cartridges, together with the food and clothing necessary for a couple of days, I dispatched in charge of my factotum on an *ekka*—a light, two-wheeled conveyance of the country. I also sent three ponies for myself to different stages.

Giving time for my impedimenta to arrive, I started myself, overjoyed at the prospect of seeing a tiger at last, and perhaps shooting it! On my arrival at the outpost I found a large and excited crowd assembled and learned that a

*The author on his pad-elephant.*

night or two since the tiger had actually come into the centre of the village, and, jumping a bamboo fence, had carried off a fair-size cow from the enclosure.

This news was highly satisfactory from my point of view, showing as it did, firstly, that what I had come in quest of was a tiger and not a leopard, as I had feared, and secondly, that there was every probability of his being found lying up with his kill. I saw that my instructions as to elephants had been carried out, as six were drawn up awaiting my inspection—and a motley crew they were! In shape, size, or build, no one animal resembled another, though all had the half-starved and draggled appearance suggestive of improper food and utter neglect. The tallest, which carried an apology for a howdah, was perhaps eight feet, the rest anything from seven to four, their drivers being as strange and weird of appearance as the animals they bestrode.

The howdah, too, was well in keeping with the rest of the entourage, for never was such a marvelous structure seen before, except, perhaps, in some museum of antiquities. Two hundred years since it had possibly graced the triumphal procession of some royal potentate, but its splendour had now departed from it, and the relics merely served to accentuate the contrast with its past. There was little of the original left, what there was being held together with recent bindings of red tape—a fit emblem of its prospective occupant! However, a howdah, even though an antiquated one, is not to be despised

*The end of a successful hunt.*

when one is in pursuit of such dangerous game as tigers, especially so active an animal as this one had proved itself to be. So, thankful for small mercies, I clambered into it as gingerly as I could.

The cover was about half a mile distant, and we were just about starting for it when, much to my surprise, the inspector of the division, an enormously fat and most unsportsmanlike individual, came puffing and panting up, mounted on a diminutive pony, and, having made his obeisance, requested permission to accompany me on the plea that he had never seen a tiger and was most eager to do so. Permission was readily accorded, though I confess I was at a loss to imagine how my valiant but extremely obese subordinate proposed elevating his huge, unwieldy person onto the back of an elephant. However, he had evidently grasped the situation, for, selecting one of the small animals, he first sent up a stalwart constable. Then, ordering two others to push from below, he was gradually, but painfully, hauled onto his perch, maintaining his position by sitting astride the narrow pad instead of sideways as usual.

We now started, and soon reached the jungle—a comparatively small one, though connected by a narrow strip of grass with a much larger patch about two hundred yards off. Taking up my position in the centre of this grass,

I directed the inspector, who, in virtue of his rank, I appointed second in command, to take himself and his forces to the far side of the cover, and to beat it up toward me. He marched off, full of importance, and, having marshaled his five elephants into something approaching a line, proceeded to carry out my instructions. From where I was posted I could see the taller elephants of the line, and I was expecting every moment to hear the tiger break.

Suddenly there was a loud squeal from one of the elephants, followed by a general commotion all along the line, caused, I guessed, by the tiger having been either viewed or scented, so I made signs as well as I could for the line to be pushed on. The drivers did their best to obey, but, in spite of all their efforts, not an animal would advance—and small wonder, for there, barely ten yards in front of them, was the tiger, growling savagely! At last one elephant, less timid than the rest, was induced to move a step or two forward. The next instant there was a savage roar, and every elephant, big and small, rushed helter-skelter back through the jungle, and soon the whole line could be seen careering madly across the open on its way back to the village, the inspector's charge, more nimble than the rest, leading the van!

I have seen some comical sights in my life, but never in all my experience one more utterly ludicrous than what now was before me—that is, the huge jelly-bag figure of the unfortunate official, encased in a tight uniform, poised on the highest point of the little animal he bestrode, clutching frantically at anything he could find in his efforts to maintain his seat, and shouting at the driver to stop, yet betraying his anxiety to get on as quickly as possible by digging his heels into what he probably imagined to be the ribs of his pony, forgetful for the moment that he was now mounted on an elephant! The latter, with his tail in the air and his trunk upraised, bustled along as fast as his sturdy little legs could carry him, squealing with terror. Indeed, elephants and men lent themselves to making up as droll a scene as it is possible to conceive.

However, I had little time to enjoy this impromptu burlesque, and soon had graver matters to attend to. For, while still laughing, I heard a loud coughing snort in front, and before I could raise my gun to my shoulder, with a quick rush through the grass the tiger had passed behind me. I turned and fired both barrels into the moving grass, but apparently without result, and ere I could reload he was out of range.

I now looked again for the elephants, only to find that I could hope for no assistance from them. They were still going, and likely to continue doing so. In despair I consulted my driver, and, acting on his advice, having no experience of my own to draw on, decided to go in pursuit of the tiger, in the faint hope that one of my shots might have taken sufficient effect to prevent him journeying far.

But to pursue an angry tiger on a timid and untrained elephant was not so easy a matter, for to do so it was obviously necessary, in the first place, to make a start, and this the terrified animal absolutely refused to do. In fact, it was only with the greatest difficulty that we succeeded in making him even face in the proper direction. At length thoroughly exasperated, I allowed the driver to use his *gujbar*, or goad, a terrible weapon resembling a monster fishhook, the shank projecting beyond the curve and terminating in a sharp spike. But this only made matters worse, for, instead of moving forward, the animal now commenced to back, and then to "shake," a term applied to elephants and denoting one of their most dangerous vices. In effect, it is much the same as buck-jumping on a horse, but the motion, instead of being longitudinal, is from side to side, and so violent that a really proficient "shaker" will often rid himself of his riders, literally "in a brace of shakes." This is what would have probably happened in our case. Providentially, a peacock, rustling through the grass behind us created a diversion, for the elephant, thinking the tiger was now behind him, started forward, and away we went, a great deal faster than we wanted, but in the right direction.

We had flashed through the grass and reached the larger covert before we could pull up our runaway mount, and, having soothed him into a more suitable frame of mind to negotiate the dangerous tree jungle now before us, entered it, proceeding cautiously, for we might come upon the tiger at any moment. We had proceeded in this manner about two hundred yards when we came to a small clearing some thirty yards wide.

Traversing this we were about to re-enter the jungle when, without the smallest warning, the tiger, with a roar appalling in its volume and ferocity, sprang at the elephant's head. Rendered wary by the extreme suddenness of his previous appearance, I was fortunately prepared. As he sprang, I fired both barrels almost simultaneously, but the next moment I tumbled backward into the howdah as the elephant, turning sharply round, made off for all he was worth in the direction from which we had come.

Now came the most unpleasant half-hour I have ever gone through. The jungle, as already stated, was what is known as tree jungle, and therefore one to be traversed with extreme care and caution, and of necessity very slowly, when in a howdah. The reader may, therefore, imagine my feelings when, on recrossing the small clearing, we dashed into the cover at railway speed, regardless alike of branches, thorns, and creepers, and tore through them at a rate which, though necessarily reduced, was yet sufficient to sweep off howdah, guns, and riders, landing the latter, perhaps, into the very mouth of the tiger, who, for all we knew, might be pursuing us!

How we escaped being brained, or at least swept off, I have no conception, for, as in most situations of the kind, it all seemed to happen so quickly that we never quite knew what actually did happen. One very vivid recollection, however—which a bump the size of an egg on my forehead helped me to recall for some days after—was a violent collision with a large branch. The bump aforesaid was not the only evidence of this rencontre, for on looking for my pith hat afterward, all I could find of it was the rim, the crown being found later in the branches of a tree! We had also apparently collided with one or two other hard substances, for my coat was badly torn about the shoulders, both of which felt extremely sore. The mahout, being seated much lower, had come off comparatively scatheless, except for some scratches on the face and hands, and a deep one on the side of the foot, evidently, as he said, from the tiger's claw.

Our elephant, even after reaching the open, had continued its headlong flight. In fact, he did not pull up till he met the others, now returning from their little excursion to the village. Giving the elephants, including my own, time to recover from the fright and to pull themselves together, I returned with them to the scene of my late encounter with a view to renewing hostilities.

Reaching the place, the first object that met our gaze was the tiger, or, rather, tigress (for so she proved to be), stretched out, stone dead, on the very spot where my elephant had been when she charged. Quickly dismounting, I examined the body and found one bullet hole just below the throat, and another in the fleshy part of the thigh, the first obviously the shot that had killed her, and the second one of the two fired as she dashed past me on her first appearance.

Both of these shots could only be regarded as unusually lucky flukes, especially the first, which had probably saved us an extremely unpleasant, not to say perilous, quarter of an hour. As it was, the tigress must have completed her spring, judging from the mahout's statement, corroborated by the claw wound.

We now measured our prize and found her to be nine feet, four inches from tip of nose to tip of tail—a rare length for a tigress. Being in the prime of life and condition, her skin was an exceptionally fine one, and, when cured and hung up in my bungalow, served to recall for many a year after the pleasant and exciting incidents connected with the slaying of "My First Tiger."

## Chapter Sixteen

# Robert Baden-Powell
### Memories of India
### (1915)

*Lt. Gen. Robert Stephenson Smyth Baden-Powell, also First Baron Baden-Powell, was one of the most illustrious Englishmen of his day. He was a soldier who was posted to India and saw action in Africa, and he was a writer of several books on soldiering and sport. But he is best known as the founder of the Boy Scouts.*

*Baden-Powell began his military career in India after joining the famous 13th Hussars regiment. He later went to Africa and saw action in the Zulu and Boer Wars. Baden-Powell was the youngest man ever to become a colonel, but he was best remembered for his spying escapades. He often disguised himself as a butterfly collector who coded specimens' wings with military secrets. When in India he was known for his love of pig sticking and wrote a book on the subject. And, like most British soldiers, he hunted tigers—but not until he had been in India for five years.*

*Here he describes his very first tiger hunt in the Nepalese Terai, in an excerpt taken from a chapter of his book* Memories of India *(1915). He is obviously a tyro, something he reveals with typical humor and humility. Baden-Powell was also a skilled artist who drew all the pictures in this and many of his other books.*

### Tiger, Tiger Burning Bright

When I had been in India for some five years, I began to think of the future. Someday I might die, and I should look exceedingly foolish in the other world if, on being asked how I had enjoyed tiger shooting when I was in India, I had to confess that in all the years I had been there I had never tasted this form of sport.

April is the month for tiger shooting. It is also the month for pig sticking, and hitherto I had always indulged in this last form of sport. So I determined

*The genius of a pad-elephant overcoming difficult terrain.*

to break away from my usual pig sticking and to take a turn in the jungle. I had an excellent opportunity offered me because there was going to Nepal a party that, in the previous year, had had exceptionally fine sport, bagging over thirty tigers in a fortnight. Sir Baker Russell, one of the party, was not able to go on this occasion, and I was therefore to take his vacant place.

On 12 April 1898, I left Meerut and reached Bareilly the next morning. With the usual perverseness of Indian railways, the train that was to take me on from that place to Pilibhit on the Nepalese border started half an hour before my train got in, which condemned me to wait more than ten hours before there was another train. However, I did not much mind the delay, as it gave me a chance of seeing my friends in this station, including Smith-Dorrien of the Derbyshire Regiment, who had just returned from the front in Chitral and was shortly to go off to Egypt on service there. I will not say he was a lucky beggar because I felt that of all men he deserved to get on.

During the few days that he was spending with his regiment between the two campaigns, he was hard at work for the welfare of his men, working up their coffee-shop and canteen comforts and his cycling club, through which they could develop health and amusement. I was glad of the chance of seeing how he worked these things, and I afterward cribbed many of his ideas for doing the same in my own regiment. In fact I arranged, then and there, for the purchase of a dozen bicycles toward starting our regimental biking club. It proved an enormous success because we developed it into a dispatch-riding unit, which effected a great saving of horseflesh and became a most efficient means of carrying out communications.

At Bareilly I picked up two more of our party, Major Ellis and Major Olivier, Royal Engineers, who were both of them old tiger shooters. A few miles down the line we were joined by McLaren, of my old regiment, and St. John Gore of the 5th Dragoon Guards, and these completed our party.

During the rest of the journey we three beginners sat agog while Ellis and Olivier told yarns of tiger shooting and of its dangers, each capping the other with something more wonderful in the way of adventures and close shaves. When they had worked us up into a complete state of trepidation, some of us volunteered to shoot quail for the pot while the rest were out tiger shooting, and being of a modest disposition myself, I agreed to look after camp for the whole lot of them, as it seemed to me that in a jungle so full of tigers as this one appeared to be, you had every chance of coming upon a tiger even when you were merely harmlessly quail shooting. For my part I felt inclined to let sleeping dogs lie.

We arrived at the end of our railway journey late in the afternoon and found that our faithful servants, who had been sent on before with our camp equipment, had gotten dinner all ready for us at the side of the line, and after a few more yarns on the subject of tiger shooting we turned in. It was warm weather, and we slept in the open—that is, we slept as well as the yowling pariahs would let us. Next morning we went on to our camp, which we found pitched in a temporary native cattle village, just inside Nepal. Native servants may always be trusted to find the dirtiest bit of ground in the country to pitch your camp—only if they cannot find a cattle-standing they will choose a native village, and in time you become an epicure in odours.

Bala Khan, a local native gentleman and sportsman, joined us here. He reported twelve tigers to be about in the district, but probably none in tomorrow's beat. At dinner somebody remarked that I was wearing **MCC** (Marylebone Cricket Club) colours without being entitled to them, but "the Boy" (personal servant) explained that I probably did belong to the **MCC**—namely, the Margate Cycling Club! It was a great delight to be in shirt-sleeves and cowboy hat—in camp once more. Our kits were generally much alike, especially as regards thick pads on the back to prevent sunstroke, a very necessary precaution.

Half our elephants had not yet arrived, so we went out with the fifteen we had, each of us in a howdah on top of an elephant. A howdah is a cane-sided, boatlike car with a seat for yourself and one behind for a native. It is fitted with gun racks, cartridge pockets, and the like. My general armament consisted of a .500 Express and a Paradox, or 12-bore, firing ball. The other equipment carried in the howdah was a *chagal,* or water bottle full of tea and lime juice, a blanket to roll up in if attacked by bees, an umbrella, gloves, and blue spectacles for protection against the sun, a dry shirt, a towel, a camera and sketchbook, a yard measure, and a skinning knife.

Off we went, across country very like English parkland, but without the "antlered herds," and then there was the scent of flowering grass—a scent just like that of the powder some women use. It reminded me at once of—well, to continue. All the country here had been under water during the rains for a width of ten miles and to a depth of twelve feet. All green, wild, and gamey looking, very like Mashonaland.

At a small straw-hut camp of cattle grazers the natives, women as well as men, came out quite cheerily to talk and told us they had that morning seen a tiger nearby. We went into the sal forest, with its long stems, small branches, and big, fresh, light-green leaves, and on reaching a boggy stream with a tropical jungle of canes, ferns, and reeds, we took up positions for finding a tiger. Gore, Olivier, and I were posted: I in the stream, they on each bank. The line of elephants beat up the stream from about a mile lower down—the Boy in advance on one flank, the Khan on the other, and Ellis working the line.

There we sat for an hour—watching. The twitch of a leaf or the rustle of the beautiful dark peacock-green doves pricked our excitement. But no tiger. At last we could hear the line of elephants crackling along, but very cautiously. Then, silence again. Suddenly there was a bellowing roar—the screaming trumpeting of elephants, yelling of mahouts, banging of rifles jabbering, shouting of orders, and the coming on of elephants. It was crash, splash-bang, bang. Something tears through the bush across my front, and then fifty yards to my left a grand, great tiger springs gaily across the pathway. I banged at him as he disappeared into the jungle, and then turned my elephant and followed up with all speed. I saw him canter, tail up—and enormous he looked, too—into a fresh patch of high grass and weeds. Again we formed to beat him out, three of us going on about half a mile. Presently we in advance heard a rifle report and then a second. The mahouts shouted to each other, and we learned that the old brute had turned and charged the line of elephants and had fallen to Ellis's gun.

It was now three o'clock, and, while the mahouts got a great net round him (the only way to get sufficient hold of him given how enormously massive a brute he was) and hoisted him onto a pad-elephant, we squatted down to lunch on cold chicken and lime juice and soda. We found our new camp situated on a knoll in the sal forest with a glimpse of the hills between the trees. It was known as Sinkpal Guree; Stinkpal would have been more appropriate. Voltaire said, *"Le corps d'un ennemi mort sent toujours bon."* (The body of a dead enemy always smells good.) He cannot have smelled a tiger the day after it was shot! The next morning we were quite reconciled to leaving our beautiful camp on this account.

When necessary to move camp, we would select a spot and leave the rest to our native servants. When the beat was over, we would rush for the new

*A Hindu temple.*

spot and find everything in readiness. The tents and other paraphernalia were carried on our camels and bullock carts, and our drinking water (we brought our own in iron tanks) on a bullock dray.

During the night of the second day our missing elephants arrived in camp, which was very satisfactory, as it meant a far better chance of sport. To counterbalance this good fortune, we found Ellis looking very gray and tired; he had got a touch of fever and had to lie up for the day in camp. We others started with twenty-seven elephants in a blazing hot sun. Our pad-elephants carried us at first, this being far more comfortable both for elephant and man than a howdah, for a longish ride. These are elephants with big mattresses or pads fastened on their backs that are used for beating the jungle and for carrying home the game when shot.

Although the days should have seemed long with so little shooting, as a matter of fact they did not. The sun was blazing hot and the elephants moved slowly, but they are such interesting beasts to watch that the time slips by very comfortably. Also, one lives in constant hope of a tiger, and there is always a world of pretty scenery about.

The few small patches of cultivation had machans, lookout platforms from which the natives watch their crops and flocks to protect them against wild animals. The natives were wilder looking than those of the plains, the men with shock-heads of hair, yet their huts were much neater and more comfortable, having a small veranda in front, clean wattle and daub walls, and a small "hall" inside the door with a room opening off to each side.

On reaching the forest, we got off our pad-elephant cover-hacks and onto our howdahs. Again the same plan of beating, two of us as stops posted at the mouth of a swampy stream, the remainder of the elephants beating it in line toward us. This waiting for a tiger *"donne une emotion"* [stirs the feelings] as the Frenchman would say, especially when the line approaches and you hear the elephants breaking down small trees and dead branches, with a noise just like guns firing in order to frighten the tiger, and then they come in sight in a close and formidable line that must push the brute on to you if he is there.

This time he was not, but at the last moment, when the line was only about thirty yards from me, a panther jumped up close to Gore. He got in two shots at him in the long grass, but though we beat carefully for him we did not see him again. Then we moved off two miles and halted for lunch on the bank of a river, where our elephants bathed while we enjoyed the scenery and a cool breeze.

About sunset we turned homeward, doing "general shooting." Beating out one bit of cover we got shots at a lot of jungle fowl. Just like small English fowls, they cluck and crow the same, except that they say *cock-a-doo* instead of *cock-a-doodle-doo,* but they fly like pheasants. We got seven of them. On the way home my elephant trod on a thorn. He stopped and held up his foot and would not budge till the mahout had got down and examined it. The mahout saw the thing, but it was broken short off in the foot, so he could not get it out. He told the elephant it was all right, and the old brute went on quite happily again; we got back to camp after dark through a crowd of dancing fireflies.

As Sir Baker Russell had not come on this shoot, the other fellows took to calling me "the General-Sahib." But one night Olivier appeared at dinner in a black velveteen coat! We could not live up to such form. As a matter of fact, I had not any coat to wear in camp, so I felt I could not pretend to the exalted position in the face of such rivalry, and I determined to resign.

Although the sun was very hot in the day, yet the air was cool whenever there was a breeze, whilst at night it was quite cold. I put on a blanket about midnight and a *resai* [quilt] about 3:00 A.M.

One morning before breakfast the Boy and I drove off on a pad-elephant to the neighbouring village of Dais to see how the people lived and whether they had any curios worth buying. The houses are very neat and clean inside as well as out. They were divided by partitions into several rooms, one of which is the kitchen, well kept and tidy, which, however, they did not like us to enter. They had a few muzzleloading guns and some inferior *tulwars* [swords]. Their ordinary working tools, axes and *koorpies* [grass-cutting chisels], they would not sell, but the Boy bought a cow bell, and I got a carved club and a quaint iron lamp. We gave them two rupees for the lot, at which they grinned and examined the rupees as if they had never seen such things before. The women and children were quite friendly, and, after getting over their first shyness, they crowded round and grinned to see us so interested in their household odds and ends. These people have the Chinese eyes of the Gurkhas and Tibetans, but the taller physique of the Hindus. The women wear two braids of hair looped across their foreheads.

That day we beat a large swamp south of the camp where the grass and reeds were so vast in extent and thick and high that the elephants were often completely out of sight in it. It was on our return to camp that the incident occurred that nearly brought my life and my diary to an abrupt termination. Another sportsman riding up alongside me on his elephant with his rifle lying across his howdah accidentally let it off. Fortunately I was thin, and the bullet passed across my front without perforating my corporation. I do not think I am fated to be shot accidentally, for this is not the only time that I have escaped that sort of an end.

Apart from the ordinary shaves incidental to cover shooting at home, I have had others. I was missed by a mule once. I am probably the only man who has been shot at by a mule, although many have experienced narrow escapes from asses. We had just buried a man during a fight in the Matopos, and no one had noticed that his rifle, loaded and at full cock, had been strapped onto the pack saddle of a mule. We noticed it a few moments later when the mule walked on and in brushing past a bush caught the trigger of the rifle on a twig. The bullet passed "between my ear and my skull," as the Zulus say when they wish to indicate a narrow shave.

When forming a force for the defense of Mafeking, I once went to inspect them in the manual and firing exercise. They were put through the actions of "Ready," "Present," and "Fire." Two or three of them did more than merely go through the action; they actually did fire, having forgotten to unload their rifles after a previous lesson in how to load. As I did not happen to be standing in front of a firer, I got nothing out of it, but the firers got a good deal of advice.

*******

It was evident that the floods or something had vastly changed this country since the previous year. Smith-Dorrien's diary of his party's trip shows that in addition to a total of twenty-three tigers, they also used to shoot several buck every day, besides seeing unlimited numbers of them. We would see only about five or six in a whole day. One beast that I saw every day, and would have liked to get, was a very handsome little dove. I had never seen him anywhere before. He lived only in the thickest swamp jungles and was very shy. He generally dashed away the moment the elephants began beating, and there was seldom more than one of him in a beat. I was often tempted to have a whang at him as he came whizzing past, but no general shooting was allowed during a tiger beat, and I never saw him at other times.

After dinner our skin curer was showing us the small bones, said to be rudimentary wing bones, that he had cut out of the previous day's tiger, when one of them was dropped on the ground. For a long time we searched in the grass with a lantern, but in vain, till, going down on all fours, I played at being a dog. After a little "sniffing" about, I soon winded the missing link. These rudimentary wing bones are said to connect tigers with the griffin.

Our want of luck now resulted in a council of war, and it was resolved to move on to Calcutta (not *the* Calcutta), where the jungle had been burned and two tigers at any rate were known to be. This was two marches from Camp Akadbully, where we then were. Although we were getting no sport, yet the time was very enjoyable and slipped by very quickly. Every day was exactly like the last, and this was our routine as noted in my diary.

At dawn we awoke and had tea, during which we would lazily chaff each other and enjoy the cool air. The country round was full of the noise of birds, the jungle fowl, especially, making it quite civilized with their cock-crowing. The blue, misty view was very good, too. About 8:00 we would think of dressing, after which we breakfasted in the open. By 9:00 a dead stillness would come over the forest, and the sun would already be high and strong. Half an hour later the howdah elephants came round to our tents to be loaded up with guns, water-bottles, and so forth. Then came the pad-elephants and we mounted and rode off, umbrellas up and goggles on, Ellis and the Khan on one elephant, Gore and Olivier, and the Boy and self.

This was the worst part of the day. From ten to twelve it was dead, sweltering heat and no breeze. About an hour's ride would bring us to the cover. Here we would mount our howdahs and carry on the beat. This was rather like a game. As in all games, including the game of soldiering, you ought to play for your side and not for yourself, the aim being to get the tiger killed by the party, not merely to get a shot at him yourself.

A line of a dozen pad-elephants beat out the cover. The two forward guns or stops are sent ahead to head him and stop him going away forward. Two side guns act principally as stops at all likely points of escape on either flank. Guns with the line prevent him from going back. The thing is to hold him until the guns are in a circle round him and he cannot escape. We did it awfully well, but then we never had the tiger to put in the centre. The elephants move very

*Beaters at rest.*

slowly in the jungle, about one and a half to two or three miles an hour, thus much time is wasted in getting from one beat to another.

About two o'clock we would halt for lunch under a tree. One elephant carried a box of eatables and drinks, claret and two bottles of soda-water per man, and ice, which we got every two or three days from the railway thirty miles distant. Lunch never took more than half an hour, and then on we would go, beating till sunset. Then back to camp to tea. The Khan would sit and talk and drink soda-water and ice, while we had Angostura Bitters and soda. After tea there was the tub, then dinner at 7:30 and bed at 9:00.

During the heat of the day I wore a handkerchief dripping wet under my topee [pith helmet], and it kept the back of my neck very cool, which is important when the sun is so powerful that your guns are too hot to hold without gloves. You cannot carry your white umbrella while shooting; it is too conspicuous.

Olivier left us early on the 24th, his leave being up, and to signalize his departure Ellis, who had been getting gradually better, in spite of my medicines, now complained of feeling very weak and knocked up. So we left him in camp with mosquito curtains and a book, and with orders to move to the new camp after the heat of the day was over. Of course, he started bang in the middle of it after all.

The men of this country are lithe, well-made chaps, not so squat as the Gurkhas we enlist into our regiments but with the same Chinese face. Their dress shows off the symmetry of their limbs, at any rate. On nearing our camp in the afternoon, Bala Khan called at a village where a good, local shikari lived. This man, a cheery, well-fed Gurkha, was delighted to see us, as a tiger had killed one of his cows the previous day and another the day before. It lived about a mile away in a little gully, and drank at a certain stream. He knew all about it and climbed onto an elephant to show us the way. What a change he brought on us. The day was no longer hot, or the way long. We were all very wide awake. When we got to the forest he showed us the stream where the tiger drank, as a kind of proof of words.

"Where is his lair?" we asked.

"Oh! there," he replied, pointing generally all over the forest.

"And where shall we post ourselves?"

"Oh! anywhere. He'll walk past, all right." A most confiding tiger, this! "And the biggest you ever saw," etc., etc.

Needless to say, we beat and beat and never saw a sign of him.

Next we moved from Daka-ki-garhi to Calcutta, Ellis going with the baggage. Calcutta was a big, open plain south of the forest in which we had been. The people were more like the ordinary Hindus; they lived in wretched straw huts, had less cattle and more cultivation than our late neighbours. The plain was dotted with solitary peepal trees, and big antheaps five to eight feet high, similar to those in South Africa. I was sorry to see the mountains dropping away into the distance again.

It is wonderful how the mahout drives his elephant. He sends him on by digging his toes in behind his ear, stops him by digging his *ankus,* or hook, into the front of his forehead and pulling backward, hits him hard with the flat of the hook on the side of the head when correcting him, and does much by word of command.

On the 6th Ellis left for Bareilly, unable to get better in camp and evidently wanting better medicines than I was able to give him, though better doctoring he could not get.

One day we mounted our elephants and, for a change, beat outside the forest, a swamp that runs for three or four miles along the edge of the forest. It was about two or three hundred yards wide with reeds ten to twelve feet high, in most places dangerous bog. Having beat a lot of it without result, we were wearily on our way to beat the same bit again. At last I felt hopeless and was dozing in my howdah as my elephant, Dandelion, plodded slowly back to our post when I was suddenly awakened by a rifle crack, quickly followed by others from the people away behind us.

This is what had happened. A tiger, tired of being hunted by us, changed places and quietly followed us in our procession across the open plain. The Khan happened to see him, and he and Gore saluted the beast with a volley at two hundred yards, which the tiger acknowledged with a whisk of his tail and a smile as he lightly slipped away into the jungle.

Boiling with impotent rage, we set to work and fired his jungle-home and watched for his coming out, but it was a hopeless job in the huge bog. As a bonfire, it was a great success. The forest took fire, and the view from camp that night was very fine. Gore remarked: "By Jove! We shall be put down for six new Nepals, as sure as fate." (Nota Bene: It is customary, when through your own carelessness you damage any article in the mess, that you pay for six new ones to replace it.)

After our return to camp, between tea and sundown, we three, accompanied by Bala Khan, walked out and shot a few quail. Quail shooting is a nice sporting pastime, but these asses with me must needs make foolery of it all by pretending that we were tiger shooting. When a quail fell wounded, you would hear: "For goodness' sake, don't go in on foot to him. Wait till the elephants come up," and so on. Even the Khan himself entered into the spirit of the thing. I did expect better sense from the Boy, for he could play golf without even wanting to put on black crepe weepers, and that's more than I could do.

We greatly missed Ellis, with his rich Hibernian intonation and his: "Now, what I'm going to tell ye is thrue, Johnnie. There's only three sardines left for the five of ye, so it's no use for any Johnnie to take more than his fair share, or there won't be enough! Oi'll take wan, and that will make the division easier for the four of ye."

We were not to get any more of his surprise delicacies, which were brought specially for Sir Baker Russell's benefit. One night we had mince pies made with apricot jam and pie crust; they had got pounded on the journey into a solid mass and were served up scalding hot. Luckily we dined in the open and so had no carpet, and were able to say with Dr. Johnson, to his hostess, when he had done with a cup of overhot tea: "A fool, madam, would have swallowed it." A fool might also have swallowed the oysters that figured on our bill of fare another night, but he would have been a number-one-size fool.

While sitting in the howdah during a beat, one is visited by many strange characters: spiders with gold spots, spiders with long bodies with a splash of whitewash on them, opal-coloured spiders, praying mantises looking like dead straws, and a, to me, new kind of mantis, which I called the "Interested Mantis" because he looks about him. All these and many others come to one, not to mention flies, fleas, bugs, and bushticks.

On 30 April we were back again in civilization, and our shoot was ended. We reached Bala Khan's villa at Sherpur before noon, where he made us at home during the day. The villa appeared like a small square room, full of chandeliers and lamps and coloured glass balls, with little rooms round it. We lunched, dozed, and talked to the Khan and his sons. One of them could speak English and would suddenly spring upon us, *a propos des bottes* [without rhyme or reason], such a statement as: "The wind is now blowing very furiously."

At Puranpur we were seen into the train by the Khan and his sons, after being decorated by him with tinsel necklaces and having our handkerchiefs perfumed with pungent sandalwood scent. We noticed while at the Khan's house that the hot weather had really begun, but by living out in it we had gotten acclimatized. Now that we were in a house and looked out at the glare or went out into it, we realized that summer had set in.

## Chapter Seventeen

# Nigel Woodyatt

### My Sporting Memories
### (1923)

Maj. Gen. Nigel Woodyatt spent more than four decades in India as an officer in the fabled 3rd Gurkha Rifles, whose Nepalese recruits helped the British crush the 1857 Mutiny. The Gurkhas saw action in many places around the subcontinent in Woodyatt's day, which gave him many hunting opportunities.

Woodyatt was a sportsman in the truest sense of the word. For him it was the entire hunting experience, not just the thrill of the chase and kill, that mattered most. He loved India's diverse forests, organizing the hunt, and, perhaps, most important, the comradeship. Naturally, he was critical of hunters whose sole purpose was bagging the biggest trophy or racking up the greatest number of kills. To him that was not sportsmanship but selfishness. And he met hunters of both types during his many years in India, and he made known his preference.

Most of Woodyatt's hunting adventures took place in the Terai of the Himalayan foothills, which is where the 3rd Gurkhas were based. This selection is from a chapter in My Sporting Memories (1923) devoted to hunting from elephant back. The Terai was known for its many big, boldly striped cats, so it always attracted international trophy hunters and dignitaries. The Terai was always on the itinerary of an official British royal visit. England's King George V came for his 1911 India tour and allowed Woodyatt to publish the pictures.

#### Beating for Tiger with Elephants

Beating for tiger with elephants and when shooting from a howdah, you must take your chance of the elephant being unsteady at the shot. When standing as a "stop," it is wonderful how motionless a good elephant can be, provided it has a good mahout. When Herky Ross (a friend) missed that sitting shot, he put it down to his elephant moving. I have told the tale of L.

*Chandra Sher, ruler of Nepal, and King George V with a trophy tiger in 1911.*

and the tigress. He had his rifle at the "present" for an interminable time. I am not sure his elephant was so very unsteady. If it was, the slow, measured tread of the tigress in the open, that may have disconcerted it.

Then there was the case of the colonel, on the day I shot my ten-foot, two-inch tiger. This was not a case of being unsteady at the shot, but of an elephant being generally unsteady while on "stop." Lowis was not in the habit of giving his guests unreliable elephants. I knew this particular one quite well, for I had often ridden it.

Elephants are very peculiar animals. It almost appears as if, on the above occasion, the beast knew it had been posted in the riverbed and resented any change. It may have felt also that it was a darned silly thing to go and stand in high grass.

When shooting from the line, or otherwise on the move, a mahout stops his beast dead for the shot by uttering the word *datt,* and he starts it off again by saying *myal*—both commands accompanied, of course, by the necessary legwork. Shots from the howdah in a moving line are just "snap shots." For birds you never stop your mount, but for all animals the mahout usually halts the elephant on his own initiative. For a second or two the majority of trained elephants are quite rigid. With a lot of commotion in the line, or in the case of a melee, you can hardly expect absolute steadiness.

I remember a Bettiah hunt where there was at the end of the beat a sunken road fenced on both sides by thorns. I was placed as centre stop on the far side of the road. Lowis had himself seen a tiger enter the patch of grass to be beaten, which was not more than four hundred yards long.

The tiger was got on the move very shortly after the beat commenced, but no one saw anything except moving grass. It was a very queer tiger, going ahead of the line for a few yards without exposing itself at all, and then stopping. This was repeated time after time, and seemed for some reason to upset the elephants.

It was peculiarly irritating for the stops. We heard the shouts of the mahouts, and the trumpeting and trunk thumping of the elephants. Every second we expected to see the tiger break covert, but nothing happened, beyond, after a few minutes, a further repetition of the same hide and seek game. The tiger was evidently looking hard for an opening through which to break back. At the same time, it took no steps to make one by a charge.

Lowis was afraid the tiger would slip out somehow, as the elephants were not playing up. He determined to "ring" it, and called me, with the other stops, to complete the circle. I had some difficulty in breaking down the thorn fences but got through both eventually, with my right and left stop almost on top of me.

I had a steep rise to manipulate. Just as my elephant's head reached the top, and while I was hanging to the handrail of the howdah to keep my balance, the tiger moved forward again. I could see it, but was quite unable to fire from the position I was in, and the elephant was on its knees. As the elephant rose, the tiger charged, striking out with its paws. Half-a-dozen of the nearest sportsmen fired, one, immediately behind me, with a heavy rifle with which I thought he had blown off my head. The explosion was deafening!

All the elephants were now very excited and making a tremendous noise. The tiger stuck to mine, but although unhit, the hail of bullets had disconcerted it, and it had no real hold. My elephant was trying to get the tiger under its feet, and actually kicked it over onto its back. In this position the tiger tried to claw the old lady's belly, by striking upward with its hind feet, but was unsuccessful.

All this time I was endeavouring to get a shot, but my wife and I were being shaken to bits. At last, leaning right over the side of the howdah, I got one, but the muzzle of my rifle was wobbling up and down with the elephant's movements, like a cutter in a choppy sea. After that shot the tiger disappeared, sneaking somehow through the confused circle of elephants. We never saw it again.

Such incidents are very disconcerting. One never knows what the end may be. This I can best illustrate by the account of an adventure that befell Sir John Campbell in the Kumaon Terai in 1912, when he was forward as a "stop" to a line of elephants beating a tiger up to him.

Sir John wounded the tiger as it passed him. The animal went on for a short distance, then turned and broke back through the line. The beat was re-formed the reverse way, Campbell joining the line. He had seen, more or less, where the tiger had gone into the long grass, and made for the spot, the line conforming to his elephant's movements.

As they neared the place, Campbell heard spitting and cursing, like the noise of an angry cat, but he was then too close to draw a charge from the tiger by using his shotgun (a sure way of making a wounded tiger charge, so as to get a fair chance at the animal). Therefore, he told the man behind him to throw a bottle of barley water into the place where the noise came from. Out charged the tiger, but it turned to Campbell's shot and galloped down the line, where it clawed a small female elephant. After this it went off and lay down near one of the "stops." This sportsman could not see the tiger, but directed Campbell to where it was. The latter, spotting it under some bushes, inflicted a mortal wound, just missing its spine.

Then the little elephant that had been scratched by the tiger (she was carrying a load of soda-water and a man who had been told to keep water cool by wetting it) lost her head completely. Charging out of the line, she went straight for the tiger, trying to kneel on it and butt it with her head. The result was that she got badly bitten in the trunk and mouth, while the soda-water man and most of the bottles were hurled into space.

Next she tried to roll on the tiger, with all her four feet in the air—a very thrilling spectacle for the line, which stood looking on, agitated but helpless. At the first attempt to roll she got the mahout's leg between her weight and the tiger. This snapped the limb in two. The mahout, poor devil, did not tumble off, as the other leg being hung up in the stirrup saved him from falling.

At the second attempt the elephant planted the broken leg into the tiger's mouth! As she got up, the tiger came with her, hanging onto the mahout's broken leg with its teeth and claws. Then the tiger let go, and the elephant ran back to the line. But on the way she had another roll that left the poor devil of a mahout standing on one leg in the grass. By this time the young female elephant was just mad with fear and excitement. As she saw her mahout standing there, she began to squeal and throw out her trunk toward him, evidently meditating an attack.

Campbell got forward as quickly as he could. Realizing, however, that it was impossible to reach the spot in time to stop her, he slipped a solid bullet into his rifle and shot the elephant stone dead through the temple. Yet Campbell will tell you he is not really a good shot! Perhaps he will say next that his brain is not apt to work quickly, or on sound lines!

This was a truly marvelous shot. Think out the whole situation, and the stirring incidents that occurred, one after the other. The suspense, the intense excitement, the spilt soda-water bottles exploding in every direction from the heat, the roaring tiger, the trumpeting mad elephant, the maimed mahout, and the line waiting for someone to act. Then there was an instantaneous calculation to be made of where the elephant's tiny brain was, for a shot from above out of a howdah, instead of one almost on a level from the ground.

Sir John Hewett first told me of this extraordinary incident, and then I managed to drag the details out of Campbell. I am glad to be able to add that, although the poor mahout lost his leg, he was well and flourishing when Campbell last saw him, in the year 1918.

One tigress with three big cubs at Bettiah gave us a great day's sport. She was in a very big strip of high grass with fire lines (a wide track cut through the grass to prevent a forest fire from spreading) running through it at the western and northern sides. Beyond the northern track was a large area of scrub jungle covered with shortish grass and stunted forest growth. Five of us were posted on the fire lines, while the beat went a mile off to drive the tigress toward us. The tract of grass was so wide that Lowis decided to make three beats of it in strips, taking the western side first, and driving from south to north.

I was posted at the corner where the northern and western fire lines joined and had a clear view along each. The beat was a long time coming, for the grass was very thick and high. When the line was about two hundred yards from me, Lowis *"cooeed"* and made signs that the tigress was on the move in front of him.

*The bag of King George V's Nepal hunt, 1911.*

Then she charged the line with much roaring, but two or three shots turned her. Every second I expected to see the cubs break across one of the fire lines. But nothing happened, and when the beat emerged onto the northern fire line we agreed she must have managed to keep the cubs with her and had taken ground to the east. Back went Lowis with his line for the second strip.

After another tremendous wait, we saw them coming through the sea of grass like little figures sitting on a hay cart. Even the heads of the mahouts driving some of the smaller elephants could not be seen at all. The beat was a barren one.

The elephants were quite done, and we felt it would be impossible to do the third (eastern) strip without watering them. There was also the matter of our own luncheon, and Lowis and his wife were both looking fagged. The danger was that if we made much delay the tigress might either cross the northern fire line in our absence, or move back into a portion of the grass already beaten.

After some discussion we agreed that, as it was after 2:00 P.M. and very hot, the tigress was most unlikely to move to a flank in the stifling grass, but she might move forward. Lowis decided not to put about six of the youngest elephants into the beat again, as they were quite cooked. We used them to watch at intervals the eastern side of the northern fire line while we watered and fed.

For the last beat I was No. 1 stop—that is, on the right facing the drive. Four more were along the northern fire line. Lowis brought the line along "left shoulder well up," to keep the tigress from moving to the strips on his left, already beaten. I realized that I was not likely to see much, but that did not prevent me being intensely interested. On the eastern side of the third strip (that is, to Lowis's right) was the high bank of a dry riverbed.

When the left of the line was about a hundred paces from me, with the right of it well thrown back, the tigress began charging at the centre so as to distract attention and allow her cubs to get away. Lowis had a shot at the moving grass, but with no result. Then she charged the left of the line near me with tremendous roars. She could easily have got round this left flank and escaped, but she was not thinking of herself, poor thing, only trying to save her cubs.

Soon after she retired from the second charge, the gun on the left of the line shouted to me to look out. Within a few seconds she bolted across the fire line twenty yards in front of my elephant with a tremendous rush. I swung round like a flash and fired.

Almost as I pulled the trigger, I realized that it was not the tigress at all, but one of her cubs. It looked so big in its rush that I was quite deceived for the moment. Luckily I missed it. I hate shooting a cub. Then came a bang in the fire line to my left. The next stop had done exactly the same thing with another cub! Fortunately he missed, too. The third cub broke higher up, and was not fired at.

By this time the left of the beat had reached me and halted on the fire line. The poor old tigress was now hemmed in. A close line of elephants was behind her in the form of a half-moon, for the right flank had been pushed on by Lowis. In front of her a fire line to be crossed bristling with rifles awaited her destruction. At the northeastern corner was a loophole, but leading only to bare, open ground. Moreover, and she probably knew it, there was the left stop keenly watching his left, and guns on the right of the beat ready to fire that side if she broke in the open.

Strange to relate, she seemed to know her cubs were safe, for she made no attempt to charge again. Once she came to the edge of the grass and looked out near No. 2 stop, who fired and nicked her cheek. Even then she did not speak. As the inexorable line closed in she moved toward the centre, eventually bolting across the fire line with mighty bounds, between Nos. 2 and 3 stops. Both fired, but she was too fast for them and reached the scrub. As she entered it, she became visible to Jack Lowis. With a magnificent shot he hit her between the shoulders, and she dropped dead in her tracks.

Someone said that another tiger had crossed into the scrub, and that it was not a cub. Though ladies, men, and elephants were all dead tired, we made one line through it. The three cubs kept bolting like rabbits. They were quite big, and well able to look after themselves, which made one more contented. There was no other tiger.

This tigress had frightened the shikaris a good deal the day before. When going to look at the bait, which she had not then killed, they stumbled on to one of her cubs. The tigress roared, and the men shinnied up trees very quickly. Then she came out at one couple climbing the same tree, and nearly got the lower man. This tale being exaggerated, as usual, led to the rumour in camp that she had climbed the tree! Tigers do not climb trees. They are much too heavy and quite well know it. A few words about tree climbing in general may be of interest.

We all know that the lynx almost lives in a tree because its favourite method of attack is to drop on its prey from the branches. We also know that the small clouded leopard (usually less than six feet long, including a tail of about half that length) is entirely arboreal in its habits. Also that bear and panther climb trees with the greatest ease. I have only heard once of a tiger climbing a tree, although I have known it to make frantic efforts to get at a man in a tree. Instances have been recorded of a tiger "treeing" a man, and then waiting below to get him when he came down. This does not look as if the tiger thought much of its own climbing powers. At the same time, I am quite certain that a tiger could climb a tree quick enough if it had to.

The exception was told me by Sir John Hewett. It was the case of a man-eating tigress very old, emaciated, and shriveled, and therefore light. The tigress had killed a woman, and was then driven off by villagers who placed the body in a rhododendron tree. When the villagers went away the tigress climbed the tree and carried off the corpse. Colonel Patterson gives us his experience of a lion climbing a tree (in *Man-eaters of Tsavo*, I rather think). Elsewhere in this volume I tell the story of how Sir John Goodwin actually saw a wild goat (markhor) not only climb a tree but also walk along a horizontal branch.

I cannot think of any more tree climbing incidents of interest, except one that relates to a horse climbing a tree! The late General Sir R. Low was inspecting an Indian cavalry regiment and with his usual thoroughness was asking the history of each animal as he walked through the horse lines. The squadron commander being away, an Indian officer was giving the required detail. They came to a nice bay mare, which Sir Robert admired.

"Yes," said the *ressaldar* [military commander], "she is a well-bred mare and of a good stamp, but unfortunately she is mad."

"Mad!" retorted the general. "What do you mean? Is she not normal? Is she an awful handful in the ranks, or what?"

"Oh, no, sahib," answered the native officer. "It is not that, but last night she broke loose, and we found her trying to climb a tree!"

What had happened was this. Near the water troughs was a great tree with a flattish trunk running out almost horizontally for a bit, and then sloping gradually upward. About seven feet from the ground the tree had thrown out branches on which, at that time, were some new shoots. The mare had climbed on to the lower portion of the tree to try to nibble the young shoots.

*Hunters on elephants proceed through the thick grasses of the Nepalese Terai.*

On more than one occasion have I been "let down" by mahouts who have been unable to strengthen the line properly with their howdah elephants. I have already written fully on this matter and explained that no one but a sahib—and a pretty masterful one at that—can keep mahouts in order and see that they ride their elephants the whole time for all they are worth. Not even Samander, prince of shikaris and greatly looked up to and respected by all his own sect, could prevent one or two lagging behind and thus causing a gap for the tiger to slip through.

I remember one occasion of a line wonderfully controlled by a forest officer alone in the centre, and I remember it well because of two or three extraordinary incidents that mark the day forever in my memory. We were beating the Maler swamp near Dehradun in the Uttar Pradesh, and four of us went forward on a pad-elephant to take up our places as "stops." On the pad we drew lots for the machans, and I drew number one, which was looked on as a certainty being on the direct line the tiger was expected to take. Moreover, being on the extreme right, I got a double chance of the tiger breaking out to that flank, or coming between number two "stop" and myself. That was the line the animal would naturally take.

*A wounded tiger mauls an elephant.*

The drawer of number four (extreme left) was a huge man, and perhaps not too pleased at the post he had drawn. Presently we reached his tree, and all three of us became convulsed with silent laughter. It was extremely small with a forked branch about eight feet from the ground on which two slender poles had been loosely lashed. It was no proper machan at all, and the tree impossible except for the lightest weight. I was regularly holding myself to keep from laughing out loud when my mirth vanished like a shot on hearing a voice say, humbly and pleadingly:

"I say, Nigel, old man, do you mind swapping places with me, for I cannot possibly, with my weight, get into that tree?"

As no one else offered, there was nothing for it but to acquiesce with the best grace possible. I may add, that in addition to my bitter disappointment at losing my good post, I was never more uncomfortable in my life! The only way to sit facing the beaters was at the foot of the branch with my back against the trunk, the rest of the branch between my legs, and the poles utilized as stirrups. This gave me a half-left frontage that seemed all the better (on the left flank as I now was) in case the tiger broke that way, but I had little or no hope of seeing any tiger at all.

The line came up quite close and I thought the beat was over when a tiger suddenly lolloped out of the swamp on my right front and only thirty feet away. How the "stop" on my right missed seeing it I never could make out. It being impossible to "put up" at the animal from my position, there was nothing for it but to slew round, changing my left foot over the branch between my legs. This sudden movement attracted the beast's attention, and it stopped short, growling horribly, to stare at the strange apparition in a tree. Being broadside on I planted a shot with my .450 Express behind its shoulder, and distinctly saw a red circle the size of a five-shilling piece form over its heart.

The tiger made one half-bound toward me and then, changing its mind, continued up the slope in the direction it had been going. The slope was at least 150 yards to the top, and the going was fairly steep.

I have said that the day was marked by two or three extraordinary incidents, but there were more than that. Firstly, there was the bit of luck in getting the tiger from the most unlikely machan of the four, after being "outed" from the best one. Secondly, there was the still greater piece of luck in not being charged, for the beast had me at his mercy. I should of course have fired my left barrel immediately. I had heaps of time to do so at a standing tiger, ten paces away, broadside on.

Ordinarily I should have done so, even at that period when I was much less experienced. Now, I would never dream of hesitating. But that red circle so fascinated me that I could do nothing but stare at it, expecting every half-second to see the tiger drop down dead, for it was directly over its heart. That was the third incident—namely, that the beast did not seem even to flinch. The fourth was the vivid scarlet spot so plainly visible, and which I have never seen on any other occasion. Of course, I was at very close quarters.

Finally, there was the tiger's marvelous vitality after being shot through the heart: It had gone up a hill and disappeared out of sight. As we got into our howdahs, I was subjected to a great deal of chaff about what the others were good enough to call my "scarlet bull's-eye, very similar to the red miss-flag on the range!" I was not too comfortable about it all, until in a close line we topped the slope and fifty yards down the other side found the animal lying with its great head between its immense paws, but otherwise fully stretched out and looking very magnificent even in death.

I have not much to add to what I have already written about driving tiger toward the guns by means of beaters. For this method I cannot do a sportsman a better turn than to recommend him to read and digest all Mr. Best has to say in his book *(Shikar Notes)*, to which I shall refer more than once.

There is one hint I can give though, and that is to be thoroughly prepared, before you indulge in this form of sport, to finish off the tiger yourself on foot if you have not killed it. I refer to occasions when not a single elephant is available, which is sometimes the case. It is following up a wounded tiger on foot where the extreme danger comes in. You have by your shot changed a very much surprised and frightened animal into a perfect devil of a beast that sees red. Yet you are bound to finish it off, for, even apart from feelings of compassion, you cannot possibly leave the poor, unarmed villager and his family to the tender mercy of a dangerous animal like that.

Always wait at least half an hour, even if you feel sure you have mortally wounded a tiger or panther, and twice that period if you are uncertain. I think an abdominal wound is the worst one to compete with in either of these beasts, for the animal not only appears to lose no vitality, even if its stomach is half out, but it enrages it more than any other. Such a wound also seems to dull all feeling to the shock of further shots, unless you hit an absolutely vital spot. When speaking of panthers later on, I give a typical instance of a female of that species when practically disemboweled.

When you are following up, take plenty of stones in your pocket to throw into every atom of cover, and under the aegis of your rifle or gun send picked men up each tree ahead of you, and to each flank. This should prevent surprise by a sudden charge from covert. For this kind of stalking, I think lethal bullets in a 12-bore gun are best.

If you have hit the animal mortally—that is, say, in heart or lungs—you ought to locate it under a quarter of a mile. If not, it is a most unpleasant business. A very good precaution is to get hold of a herd of buffalo. They will follow the blood trail. I have never heard, authentically, of them actually attacking a wounded tiger, but they will certainly locate it for you.

### Chapter Eighteen

# Bernard Ellison
## HRH The Prince of Wales's Sport in India
## (1925)

*E*dward, like his father and grandfather (King George V and Edward VII), made a lengthy tour of India in 1921–22 while heir to the British throne. He traveled in typical royal style on his four-month venture, which took him through central, eastern, and southern India before embarking from Bombay.

The Prince covered more territory than previous tours, allowing him many hunting and fishing opportunities. He shot tigers in the Nepal Terai, the hill country of Gwalior in central India, and the dense forest of Mysore in the south. He was only twenty-seven when he went to India, fifteen years before his fateful marriage to Wallis Simpson, the American divorcee for whom he abdicated the throne. The couple spent most of their life overseas, where Edward lived the cafe society lifestyle, more than that of a gentleman hunter.

This piece is on the Nepal hunt in the winter of 1921. Edward and his party killed seventeen tigers, ten rhinos, leopards, bears, and a ten-foot king cobra, shot by the Prince himself. The selection is part of a chapter from Bernard Ellison's HRH The Prince of Wales's Sport in India *(1925)*. It is one of the most comprehensive books on Indian sport ever written, with numerous maps and more than a hundred photos. Ellison was curator of the Bombay Natural History Society and the tour's official naturalist.

### Big Game in Nepal
### First Day—14 December

At Bikna Thori the camp was aglow with excitement from the early morning. I was awakened by the trumpeting of elephants and the shouts of an army of Nepalese attendants. I watched the little Gurkhas passing to and fro near my tent. What a noise the stout little fellows with the kukris made!

Talk was of nothing else but the arrival of the Prince and the prospects of the shooting. A very large tiger had been seen, and it was hoped that it would fall to the Prince's rifle.

Shortly after 9:00 A.M. a fanfare of bugles announced the arrival of the Prince. The Nepalese guard presented arms, and the royal car swept into the camp, followed by the cars of his suite. The Prince stepped out, looking remarkably well and boyish in light khaki jodhpur breeches, shooting coat, and sambar leather shoes. A few minutes were spent in introductions. Then off we all went in the cars to the shooting beat, which was quite near the camp, at a place called Sarasoti Khola.

We got out of the cars and mounted the pad-elephants, which took us to the line of howdah elephants, in position by the riverbed. His Royal Highness mounted into his howdah, which, by the way, was the same as was used by his father when he last shot in Nepal. The rest of the party were the Earl of Cromer, Admiral Sir Lionel Halsey, Colonel Worgan, Lord Louis Mountbatten, Captain the Hon. Piers Legh, the Hon. Bruce Ogilvy, and myself.

Everybody was expectant, though nothing happened for some time. On the other side of the huge riverbed, now reduced to a narrow stream, stretches the jungle for mile on mile. It is very hot, the elephants are impatient, and every now and then one of them gives utterance to restless trumpeting. Suddenly there is a movement on the left-hand side of the line. General Sir Kaiser, the master of ceremonies, who had organized all the shikar arrangements in connection with the shoots, rides in on a fast-trotting pad-elephant with news of a tiger, and off we start.

The elephants move forward with their weird, lumbering gait. HRH leads the procession, followed immediately by the party, and then an army of pad-elephants, and still more pad-elephants to be used in case of accidents. Ponderously the line proceeds through the dense jungle, crossing many a placid stream, and emerging at times from the cool shade of the giant trees into some glade where the sun beats hot and fierce, only to plunge again into the cool depths of the evergreen jungle. One cannot but be impressed with the calm and twilight grandeur of these gigantic forests. Within their depths all is stillness, and no movement is discernible. There is nothing to break the monotonous tread of the elephants, save an occasional burst of drumming from cicadas whose shrill music subsides as quickly as it rises.

*The Prince of Wales's mess tent.*

Suddenly there is a stir in the line. All the elephants begin to close up, shoulder to shoulder, and the great beasts stand to form the ring. All is expectancy: There is an outburst of shouting from the beaters, and out rushes a deer that escapes terrified into the jungle, to be shortly followed by another and another. Then the real thing happens, and there is a cry *"Bagh! Bagh!"* from the beaters. The tiger at last!

A glimpse of a yellowish form is seen in the long grass for the space of a few seconds and is at once lost to view. Once again it is seen behind a tree trunk. Closer advance the beaters, the tiger charges out, but he is a wary beast and seems to know intuitively where the guns are posted and gives them a wide berth. Again and again he is driven out, only to seek cover in the long grass away from the guns. A shikari climbs a tree and pelts him with stones. The maneuvre succeeds, and once again we get a half-length view of the tiger as he makes a spring at his tormentor in the treetop. The ring closes in upon him, but with a roar he dives into the long grass; another roar, and he shows himself quite near the royal howdah. A moment's suspense, and HRH fires, and a second afterward two more shots ring out. The Prince has a hit. The

*"Ringing in" the kill after a tiger shoot.*

tiger, though mortally wounded, has plenty of go in him, and charges to the opposite side and is buried once more in the heavy cover. The ring closes in. A shot rings out, and the tiger rolls over dead.

As I descended from my howdah to measure him, it was a striking scene: this great circle of sportsmen, beaters, mahouts, and elephants, waiting in silence while the measuring was done. The tiger taped nine feet, but he was a royal beast, and looked splendid when I saw him later stretched out for the Prince's inspection near the great log fire in the royal camp.

In the evening we had news of three more tigers having been shot by another party who had gone farther afield. There appears to have been much excitement, and no little risk, experienced on the occasion, as several of the party were filled with more zeal than experience of tiger shooting. Guns were pointed in all directions, and the poor tigers eventually succumbed to a perfect fusillade of bullets. One of the members of the party contributes the following description of one exciting episode:

> The tigress came out straight toward my elephant but turned very quickly to its own right, and I fired just as it turned back into the jungle. I hit it on the near quarter, and broke its hind leg with the first

barrel. The second barrel I fired as it was disappearing into the jungle, and from what we found afterward apparently hit it on the tip of the tail! There was great difficulty in stirring the tigress out again from the jungle, so we went in on our elephants. She suddenly came out and charged the elephant P. was on, which turned round so quickly that P. sat down on his topee and squashed it flat. The tigress was finished off, I think, by H., but I am not quite certain.

The menu card below shows the lavishness and wonderful care taken in everything by the Maharaja of Nepal to entertain the Prince of Wales. This dinner was served in the impenetrable jungles of the Nepal Terai, miles away from any civilization.

### DINNER

| | |
|---|---|
| Consommé Printanière | Haricots verts à l'Anglaise |
| Saumon a la Grand Due | Crème Viennoise |
| Suprême de Poulet Mascotte | Petites Rissoles Nantua |
| Selle d'Agneau | Dessert |
| Perdreaux sur Canapés | Café |

After dinner I went down to the skinning camp to see what had been done in the matter of the disposal of the trophies. It was an eerie experience tramping through the heavy jungle after nightfall. Of course, in the present instance, with so many people about, there was not much danger, though everywhere one saw the pug marks of tiger and the tracks of elephants. Thanks to the efforts of my men, the work of skinning the various trophies had been satisfactorily concluded, and so, with an easy conscience, I went to bed.

### Fourth Day—17 December

HRH spent the morning after small game, and with his party accounted for some twenty-five head. Admiral Sir Lionel Halsey, Colonel Harvey, and Lord Louis Mountbatten motored to Kasra (thirty miles) after rhino. They saw none, and had a tiger beat that was also blank.

The same morning Captain Poynder and Captain Dudley North both had a shot at a rhino that fell to the former's rifle. She was found to be a gravid female. When she was being skinned, a calf was found in utero. The animal gave no trouble, and did not charge, but, as Captain Dudley North afterward said, "She took a terrible lot of killing."

The rhino shoots in Nepal showed very clearly the extreme difficulty of bringing these animals to bag without a vital shot. In the dense swamps of the Terai a wounded rhino is practically impossible to track and recover. In the present instance, the rhino was spotted in a strip of grass jungle, flanked on three sides by forest and on the fourth by a watercourse. "Stops" were posted in trees on two sides, and Captain Poynder and Captain Dudley North walked their elephants through the thick grass to a point from which the animal could be seen. The rhino moved off on their approach but was turned back by the tumult raised by the stops, and it blundered back to within ten yards of the guns. It was extremely difficult to see in the heavy cover, but both Captain North and Captain Poynder fired, putting four high-velocity .470 bullets into it. The rhino lurched forward but got away, and was again turned by the stops, some two or three hundred yards off, when the brute was finally dropped with a shot through the neck from Captain Poynder's rifle.

All five shots had taken effect, four of them in the region of the shoulder. The shot in the neck had finished it. But for this and the "stops" posted in the trees, the animal would in all probability have gotten away to perish miserably in the trackless swamps. A shot in the vertebrae in the forepart of the neck will drop a rhino in his tracks. This and the brain shot would seem to be the most effective.

Another party, consisting of Colonel Worgan, Mr. Pettie, Sir Godfrey Thomas, Commander Newport, and Captain the Hon. Piers Legh, left camp on elephants late in the morning. They went down to the riverbed from Bikna Thod Station about four miles, and changed from the pads onto howdah elephants. The ring was formed, and very soon a fine tigress gave Sir Godfrey Thomas a shot. Later Sir Godfrey wrote:

> It was not a difficult one, and Rushbrook Williams, who was in my howdah, is certain that I hit it. Personally I am not at all sure, as my elephant had no guts and turned round and more or less bolted as soon as the tiger appeared. I was on the floor of the howdah, and Rushbrook Williams nearly fell out while the elephant began to make for the woods. Luckily the mahout stopped the brute, and we got back

The Prince (center) with his first tiger back at camp.

near the line to see the tiger down, with everyone shooting at it. It took an awful lot of lead to kill it stone dead.

An uproar then began down the line, and we discovered that there were two cubs outside the ring. The line closed in upon them, as we had an idea of taking the beasts alive, but they were too big to catch without nets and a good deal of preparation, and too young to leave, as in all probability they would not have lived without their mother. Colonel Worgan got one, and Commander New port the other. All the way home the jungle was beaten, but nothing was seen.

A tiger measuring nine feet, two inches was also shot by Captain Bruce Ogilvy on this day.

## A Day of Rest—18 December

It being Sunday, there was no shooting today, and this was rather a relief to my skinning department, which had been working at high pressure for the last

*The skinning camp.*

few days, getting rid of the great mass of material that had been sent in. I was up all night with my men, as, with so much already having come in, and with great disarticulated limbs of rhino arriving continually, I had to work against time to prevent anything being spoilt. Day and night operations thus became the order. We had a generous supply of disinfectants that were scattered with a lavish hand, but even so it was an obscene business, and not to be dwelt on more than is necessary. An entry I saw in the diary of a member of the staff succinctly describes the case: "I visited the skinning camp where Ellison is dealing with the stuff; there was an appalling stink there!"

The skinning camp was guarded day and night by Gurkhas. Tigers' claws, whiskers, fat, and kindred articles are of much value to the native, who has uses for them not dreamt of in our philosophy, and with such a profusion of riches lying about, one had to guard against the intrusion of the snapper-up of unconsidered trifles. One such gentleman we caught red-handed, and his subsequent fate at the hands of the Nepalese officials was a sufficient deterrent against further attempts of this nature.

Anent the tiger fat: Divers petitioners came to me pleading for a modicum of the precious adipose, reputed to be a panacea for many ills, but like Pharaoh of old to his starving Egyptians, I commended them to Joseph, in this instance Baptista, my head skinner. To him in the course of his labours had fallen a bountiful harvest of the desirable unguent, and to the waiting multitude he bestowed his favours, with, I am afraid, a somewhat niggardly hand.

Sunday afternoon was spent in the distribution of gifts and mementos from the Maharaja to his guests. Among these were a number of beautiful silver-mounted kukris, which were presented to various members of the party, a fitting memento of their days in Nepal. According to time-honoured custom, HRH was the recipient of a number of live animals and birds, a list of which is printed elsewhere in this volume. Among the animals was the famous "unicorn" sheep of Nepal. These are normally two-horned. When quite young the horns are bound closely together, so that they grow up in contact with one another, giving them the desired "unicorn" effect. The birds included a very fine series of pheasants. Particularly striking were the gorgeous monauls, the tragopans with their crimson, white-spotted breasts, and the little blood pheasants with their green splashed over with blood-red markings.

After being inspected by the Prince, the collections were handed over to the writer, and at the close of the shoot in Nepal, were brought down to Bombay, where the animals and birds were temporarily housed in the Victoria Gardens previous to their being shipped to the London Zoological Gardens, their final destination.

## Eighth Day—21 December

This was the last day of the Nepal shoot. HRH rode out after lunch with Colonel O'Connor, the British envoy, Sir Godfrey Thomas, and others. In the course of the evening, near the village of Persanni, in British Territory, the Prince encountered a hamadryad, or king cobra, which he luckily killed. The party were walking up jungle fowl at the time. HRH's first shot at the snake was as it was moving away, and apparently hit it, for the brute turned and appeared to be about to attack him when he killed it with his second barrel. The snake was brought into camp with the rest of the day's bag. It was first assumed that it was an ordinary rat snake, or *dhaman*, when examined in the fading light. Subsequently, when the skin was examined at the Bombay

Natural History Society's Museum in Bombay, the identity of the reptile was revealed. The Prince's king cobra taped ten feet, three inches.

The hamadryad, the largest known poisonous snake in the world, grows to over fifteen feet in length. In the Sarawak Pavilion, at the British Empire Exhibition at Wembley in 1924, a hamadryad was shown measuring fourteen feet, four inches, and said to be the "largest specimen known," but the record specimen measures fifteen feet, five inches, which is now in the museum of Bombay Natural History Society.

Much has been written about the ferocity of the king cobra, and its propensity for making an unprovoked attack. When cornered, a king cobra may show fight, or a female will very probably attack, should her nest or eggs be endangered, but experience has shown that these serpents, like others, under ordinary circumstances usually seek safety in flight. One writer says:

> The "scourge of the jungle" it has been called. It lives largely in the trees, but takes to water readily. There used to be a living hamadryad in the possession of the Bombay Natural History Society, which was said to be twelve feet long. It did not look it. But the incredulous were invited to run a tape over the creature to satisfy themselves—always provided that they first deposited with the Society a sum to cover their funeral expenses.
>
> Happily the hamadryad is comparatively rare. Happily, too, though so equipped as to be able, if it chose, to prey on any living thing, it has the commendable good taste to confine its diet almost entirely to other snakes.

On the morning of the 21$^{st}$, a party consisting of Lord Louis Mountbatten, Sir Godfrey Thomas, Admiral Halsey, Colonel Worgan, Commander Newport, Colonel Harvey, and Mr. Metcalfe, went down to Dhoba near the twentieth milestone, where a tiger had been ringed. The following is another extract from Sir Godfrey Thomas's diary:

> The ring was in very thick jungle, and we spent some time in getting the elephants to trample down a patch in front of each gun. Nothing happened for some time till we got a fright when a big pig suddenly dashed out. Shortly afterward we heard a tiger woofing in the middle, but he could not be seen.

Suddenly he appeared in the same place as the pig, and was just coming out when Metcalfe got him with a very good shot in the head. We could not see where he fell, but he subsequently proved to be stone dead. Metcalfe was all for getting down to have a look at him, but as they shouted out that there was another tiger in the ring we quickly resumed our places.

Sure enough a tigress came dashing out again by an extraordinary coincidence right in front of us. Metcalfe missed with his first shot, whereupon the beast charged the elephants on our left. There was a regular mix-up, elephants trumpeting, squealing, and going in every direction. I did not dare fire, but Metcalfe took what looked like a pretty dangerous second shot, apparently without result. By then all the elephants had cleared off, and seeing a gap, the tigress went straight through. I turned round in my howdah and got a broadside shot just as she was disappearing, and thought I hit but couldn't be absolutely certain.

However, they swung the elephant round and made a big ring round the place she was going to. They beat about in the middle for some time without anything happening. I thought she had probably slipped right through, as, had she been wounded, they would have known it. However, they suddenly discovered her quite dead, having burrowed right under some grass so as to be practically invisible.

Metcalfe and I were lucky in getting both beasts from the same elephant. My shot had gone right through about six inches behind the shoulder.

All the shooting was finished by 6:00 P.M., and the remaining time was spent in saying good-bye. HH the Maharaja and his sons went down to Bikna Thori Station to see the royal party off, and the royal train steamed out of Bikna Thori Station at 6:30 P.M.

Thus ended HRH the Prince of Wales's shoot in the Nepal Terai, which for the colossal scale on which it was carried out, is to be ranked among the greatest in the annals of big-game shooting in India.

# Chapter Nineteen

# Arthur Stewart
## Tiger and Other Game
## (1928)

"*Every officer in the regiment should be able to say he has shot a tiger, panther, and a bear.*" *So proclaimed Col. A. E. Stewart in his book* Tiger and Other Game *(1928). His was an unusual work in that it was oriented to the amateur, especially the novice officer in India, rather than the experienced shikari.*

*Stewart spent much of his career in central India, which is the book's focus. Because it is a guide for new hunters,* Tiger and Other Game *describes every detail of the hunt, from requesting a governmental shooting block and finding a campsite to skinning and cleaning the dead cat. He prides himself on always making his own bundobust, or preparations, preferring to walk or take a bullock cart rather than an elephant or car. He encourages young hunters to do the same. He tells his readers to "study the jungles, learn from experienced hunters, read their works, and you will master the art of tiger hunting."*

*This is an edited part of a longer chapter on beating, the age-old method of hunting tigers in India. In a beat, the tiger is driven out of the forest by a line of "beaters" between two lines of "stops" toward the waiting hunters, who are perched on the backs of elephants or in treetop machans. Stewart describes the planning and execution necessary for a successful beat, which requires more skill and perseverance than many believe.*

### The Beat

Beating for tiger is an art; read all you can about it, and make careful observations of every beat you have, whether successful or not. The object of the beat is to rouse the tiger and maneuvre him slowly up to your machan from the place where he is sleeping near his kill. It is obvious that if you frighten him, he will charge away in any direction and will refuse to be driven in the

*Author with an 8-foot, 4-inch tigress.*

manner you desire. No stops will turn an angry and frightened tiger; you must gently humour him forward in the required direction. This is the secret of a good beat. In a beat there are two distinct kinds of tiger: the suspicious tiger and the frightened tiger. Do all you can to keep him in the suspicious temperament and avoid anything likely to arouse fear.

As I have said before, he must or should have a "lead," and this should take him to good jungle. In fact, the direction of the "lead" should be to his liking. To try to drive him into open or thin jungle would be hopeless; he would refuse to go and would charge through the stops. The distance covered by a beat from start to finish depends on the ground, the jungle, water, the information you have obtained, and so forth, but an average would be about 750 yards. More than 1,000 yards involves more stops and beaters. If less than 500 yards, you risk going too close to the kill, disturbing the tiger before the beat, and, in addition, not giving the tiger room for his preliminary maneuvre, which I consider to be essential.

I am strongly of the opinion that the tiger must have "breathing room," however small, at the start, and before he gets into the neck of the bottle—that is, free movement after the first sounds of the beat to allow him time to appreciate the position from his point of view and select his line of retreat in peace. If you have worked out the problem correctly, that line of retreat will be to your machan. However, the distance you decide on must greatly depend on how far the tiger is likely to have dragged, where the water is, and the type of jungle.

As I have mentioned before, the near stops are important; they are the neck of the bottle, and no matter what the other stops do, the near stops must remain dead silent until the tiger comes toward them. When the tiger approaches one of them, the stop must try to turn it with a gentle low cough, to create suspicion and not fear. Should this not be effective, he can increase the sound accordingly or drop a cloth or puggaree.

All other stops should cough, clap, or tap a tree with a stick, and turn the tiger at all costs. No stop should utter a sound until the beat starts. Never have anyone in the machan with you; for certain they will hinder or cramp your free movement if you have to turn quickly. If a nonshooting friend is with you and he or she is out at the beat, make them No. 1 stop on the right or left. From there they can take an active part in the "stopping" and see everything. See you leave nothing on the ground, such as a Thermos, a camera, or clothing; these might act as a silent stop.

After the shikaris line up the beaters, all is ready for the beat to start. Up to this time, say 1:00 P.M., the tiger is asleep in heavy shade, and the first thing to do is to waken him. The beaters should remain where they are for three minutes, and shout as loudly as they can. This will rouse him from his slumbers, and he will sit up and prick his ears. This sudden disturbance of the peaceful jungle will start him thinking; he will get suspicious, and commence to move gradually away from the noise.

The beaters then advance, shouting and beating trees with sticks, all stops coming to ground and joining in as the beat passes them. The noise the beaters make should gradually decrease in volume as they advance, and when they reach No. 6 stop (counted from the machan), shouting should give way to talking and tapping of sticks on trees. By this time the tiger is in a much more confined space, so you do not want to frighten him or make him realize that he is being cornered.

On the first shouts of the beaters you come to the "ready," and you should be all eyes and ears. Make no movement; just listen and watch for the first sign or information from the stops. The tiger may come straight without bumping a stop, and you will get no information from the right or left. He may come up early and lie down unobserved fairly close to your machan, remaining there until the beat is almost on him. So, until you get some information you must remain dead still and not give yourself away by movement. Although you do not know it, he may be lying up within twenty or thirty yards of your machan.

No cover should be missed by beaters; they should throw stones or sticks into what they cannot go through. With the commencement of the beat comes the excitement. Human nature is the same all the world over, and I admit that I am always excited when I hear the first sounds of the beat commencing.

However, you must "pull yourself together," as fluster and excitement are dead enemies to a true aim. Remember that the jungles contain more than tiger. You will likely have monkeys, peafowl, sambar, chital, nilgai, and pig rushing about, all disturbed by the beat; you may hear them crashing through the jungle unseen, or see them dash past you. Let them all go as if unnoticed. Keep your eyes and ears open for the warning cough or tap of the stop, or the gentle rustle of the dead grass and leaves. If you hear a stop give warning, you must get into position at once. If the right stop warns, get your legs over and face the right. This puts your right shoulder in position for the right or front. If the left stop warns, face your front and your shoulder in position for the front and left. A tiger turned by a stop, and especially after having been turned two or three times, will often give tongue. There is no mistaking it, and he is generally bounding through the jungle when he does it. So get into position at once, for if he bounds up to or past your machan you have no time to shake hands and be introduced; it is going to be a snap shot or nothing at all.

In all such cases there is one very important point. Get your eyes on your foresight at once and bring that onto the tiger; do not fix your eyes on the tiger and then try to find your foresight. Mark and practice this carefully in your machan when waiting for the beat to start. I once missed an enormous tiger through my eyes getting glued to him instead of onto my foresight. A tiger being large, you automatically see him, and if your eyes are fixed on the foresight you will easily bring that on to him and roll him over, no matter what pace he is going. But try the reverse, and you will realize what a difficult thing it is to find your foresight when your eyes are glued on a moving tiger. In the excitement you are apt to do this, so take timely warning.

*Tiger skin hanging to dry in the shade of a big tree.*

Remain at the ready until the beat is under your tree. Do not forget there may be more than one tiger in the beat, so after firing reload at once and again come to the ready. There may be a panther in the beat, and he has a sly, slinking way of coming out last.

I should think that in at least half of all the beats you may have you will find sambar, chital, or nilgai (blue bull) enclosed by the stops—that is, in the area enclosed for the beat. This must mean that the wind for them is wrong, and that they have settled down for their midday rest very close to the point of danger, quite oblivious to the presence of "Old Stripes," who may be sleeping within one or two hundred yards of them. If a tiger gives tongue in a beat, the stampede of all else is ensured. In such cases I have noticed that the stag always leads, followed by the does with their young, a regular pell-mell rush from what they know to be certain death. I have never seen a case where a tiger has killed a deer during a beat; it likely has happened, but the tiger is busy looking after his own skin, and just having had his feed his thoughts are in other directions.

When you fire at a tiger, every beater must at once climb the nearest tree, and no advance must be made until you give the order. You should have some prearranged signal with your shikaris, such as a blast on your horn or a whistle to mean all clear, but if the tiger is wounded and has broken back, pass the word along to the stops as well.

A wounded tiger breaking back toward the beat will charge and kill anyone he meets, so you must take instant precautions to protect your men. In dealing with a wounded tiger, you have no light problem before you, and if you have a man killed you will never forgive yourself. Hence my advice: Do not take long, risky, or uncertain shots. It is far better to wait.

There is one golden rule. If you "down" a tiger, he may appear to be dead, but no matter how dead he is, you must put a second shot into him. Make no mistake about this. You make once sure, doubly sure, and you do not destroy the skin in the least. Many a tiger thought to be dead has suddenly got up and gotten away, or has broken back and caused endless trouble, all for the want of a second, or third, bullet.

It is difficult to explain to anyone who has not had experience, the amount of lead a tiger will stand up to if not hit in what I might call the "instant knockout place"—that is, the heart or the brain. You may mortally wound him and he will go for miles, all the time ready and able to charge and kill anything that comes in his way or follows him up. He may have his entrails hanging out, but he will carry on. As long as he has a kick in him, he will fight to the last, and woe betide those who neglect precautions.

I have had a case of a tiger hit through both lungs with my first shot. My second went in at his shoulder, up through his neck, and out over his eye, carrying most of the jaw away . . . yet he carried on, and I had to ring him and follow up, and finally "do him in." I was firing a .475 high-velocity, softnose bullet, which in each case mushroomed to about the size of a halfpenny. Both were mortal wounds, but I had missed the heart and the brain, and he was still living after an hour.

If you have killed the tiger, do not let anyone touch him until you come down from your machan. If you can, take a photo of him from your machan; it is an interesting record of where he fell and the view surrounding him as seen from the machan. Then climb down and take other photos of him near at hand. If he is lying in long grass or an unsuitable place, have him carried to a clear spot. Photos are interesting records and should be in all shikar books in conjunction with the records in writing.

Do not wait until you get back to camp to measure him. A dead tiger stretches when carted about, especially if hanging over an elephant, and thus you would not get the true measurement in camp. Choose some flat place and put the tiger on his back, pull the tail straight, and put your foot on his chin and press the head down. Drive a peg in at the tip of the tail and at the point of the nose; remove the tiger, and the distance between the two pegs gives you his true length. For my own satisfaction I also measure a tiger from the tip of the nose to the tip of the tail by measuring round the curves and along the back. The latter method generally gives about eight to twelve inches more than the former. Measure also the following:

- Girth behind the shoulders
- Girth of forearms
- Girth at middle
- Girth of head
- Length of tail, tip to root.
- Height from main cushion of forepaw to middle of back between the shoulder blades

*The Pench River, with good tiger jungle on both sides.*

Have your shikaris present, and in front of them count the whiskers and claws. Natives are apt to steal these. All this completed, you now get your machan down from the tree, cover it with grass, and have the tiger lifted onto it. Get your men to procure three good, strong poles; these are slipped under the machan and lashed to it. Put two men onto the ends of each pole (equals twelve men), they lift, and the tiger is carried home to camp. Do not rope the tiger onto the machan, as the rope is apt to rub and damage the fur.

Having killed a tiger, invariably go and look at his kill afterward. You will see how he has dragged it and where—you'll also find the spot he lay up for his midday sleep. This will greatly assist you in a future beat at the same place, and it will teach you the lie of the jungle from the tiger's point of view. Even in a blank beat, you should inspect the kill.

On no account during a beat have a bar in front or round your machan as a rest for your rifle, for it is apt to hinder you and may even spoil the whole beat, as it once did for me. The large branch of a tree hung at an angle of about 20 degrees over the centre of a small nullah, forming an ideal lead. On this I built my machan and put up a strong rifle rest in front in the form of a bar.

While waiting for the beat to start, I tried my aim over the bar at what I thought every conceivable spot at which the tiger could come out or show himself in front of me, and when the beat started I felt there was no flaw or loophole. No. 3 stop on my left spoke, and shortly afterward I got a glimpse of a huge tiger crossing quietly over toward the right stops. It was just a glimpse, with no time to get a shot in.

The tiger was now in the neck of the bottle, and I began to count my chickens. No. 4 stop on my right spoke; then No. 3 clapped. Immediately there were two or three deep grunts, and then I heard crashing through the jungle as the tiger tumbled into the nullah twenty yards in front and came straight up the nullah toward me at a great, bounding pace.

I fired and hit him far back; he only winced and reduced speed to a quick trot. Before I could get in my second shot he was almost under my machan, about fifteen feet away, but, alas! owing to the confounded rifle rest, I could not get a shot down at that angle.

I admit I got annoyed and flurried, but I struggled to get round so as to take him in the rear. Through the meshes of my machan I could see him under me, only ten feet away! With all the hurry and excitement, not only was I unsteady but I was also late, so I made a bad miss as he disappeared into the jungles behind me.

Had it not been for the bar, I would have had an almost certain shot at fifteen feet, right down onto the tiger. I had forgotten the possibility of a shot at him below me, which was a really bad mistake. When he got at an angle of 45 degrees below my machan, he was safe: I could not touch him; he was in dead ground. All this I found out after the event, and it became just one more lesson learned, but never did I again have a rifle rest in a beat.

I think that was the biggest tiger I ever saw—he had great, massive shoulders and quarters on him but was considerably lighter in colour than is usual. It was all a grand sight. He fairly snookered me, and I hope he is living today. This is only one of the many disappointments and mistakes I could record, but I have no regrets; just a lesson learned and the memory of a really fine sight, one of India's biggest tigers in his jungle home.

An officer lately said to me that he much preferred scattergun shooting to big-game shooting. He had not the patience for the latter, nor was he able to compete with the disappointments one had when after big game.

Well, we are all built differently. Patience and the effort of waiting have never been strong points with me, but it is one of the worthiest traits in any man's character, and the jungles will teach it to you in a way almost nothing else will. So if you are of an impatient nature, there is all the more reason for adopting big-game shikar as your hobby.

As for disappointments, I have little sympathy for a man who cannot stand up to this and shake off all sorrow and regret at missing or losing an animal. You will miss a tiger, sure; you will mess up a beat, certain; but that is not the last and only tiger in the world. There are just as good fish in the sea as ever came out of it, so get down to facts and appreciate your mistakes, and in such circumstances you are allowed to use any language, so long as it is worthy of an officer and a gentleman.

Much of the joy and fascination of all shooting is in the mistakes you make. If you hit and captured all you fired at, it would be a poor game, and most shikaris would give it up tomorrow. Therefore make the jungles no "land of regrets," but one of solid determination, each disappointment making you more determined than ever to persevere and be master of patience and all disappointments. Appreciate the fact that a tiger can go one better than you on this or that occasion, and long may he live to fight again.

# Chapter Twenty

## James Best
### Tiger Days
### (1931)

James Best spent his career in the Indian Forest Service, the ultimate profession for an avid naturalist and hunter. He had had years of intimate contact with different forest animals, including many encounters with tigers. Best wrote several books in the 1920s and 1930s all centering on his forest adventures. His wife, Eva Best, often accompanied him and sketched plates for his books.

Best worked in central India, an area known for its extensive forests and wildlife, especially tigers. The area was also famous for its cultural heritage, especially its many tribal peoples and as a place for religious pilgrimages to the cities of Amarkantak and the Narmada River, the second holiest river in India after the Ganges. Because the region had so many tigers that came into contact with so many people, man-eating was inevitable. Not only did the cats prey on local villagers, but they even interrupted trade routes and religious pilgrimages.

The author describes one of the most notorious man-eaters, the "Terror of Ajwar," a tigress that terrorized the countryside and killed many people before being shot by Best's superior. The selection is taken from Tiger Days (1931) and is set in the Mandla district. Today Mandla is home to Kanha National Park, which protects more than a hundred tigers, one of the world's largest remaining tiger populations on earth.

### The Terror of Ajwar

The following story, remarkable in its truthful facts, has been written by me from notes collected from W. and others closely connected with the "terror," when I visited Ajwar shortly after the tigress had been killed. I was asked to report to the government my opinion on whether the tigress killed was indeed the notorious man-eater. As the story can show, I had no difficulty in sending in a definite report of my opinion.

Perhaps because we know it to be inevitable, the greatest fear in our lives is probably that of death, or maybe it is the pain often associated with death—particularly a violent one—that makes us so careful to delay its advent. Death in normal circumstances has, however, no such terrors as the unusual or the unexplainable, and what may be looked upon as almost commonplace in some countries would be abnormal and terrifying in others. If in an Indian district there should suddenly be a similar death toll from road accidents in the same area as is reported each year from London, there can be no doubt that the press of the world would take a little notice of it, probe into its causes, and suggest remedies for the evil.

But beyond a few passing remarks on the increasing death toll, the newspapers take no more than a brief notice of the fact in London. Carry the comparison further, and let the papers know that in the county of Dorset more than a hundred people are killed and eaten in a year by man-eating tigers—which, of course, very fortunately is not the case—and the press would have so much raw material at their disposal that there would be no need for other news for a long time. And noble lords seeking opportunities for a new political party to displace the old could, by organizing a successful tiger shoot, get quite a lot of votes. Yet there are districts in India where there are not only tigers living in every piece of wooded country but, indeed, some that live almost entirely on human flesh. I confess that, when on a Sunday afternoon I find gates left open, hedges smashed, cigarette papers left about, and people taking away basketloads of the roots of our beautiful Dorset wildflowers, I sometimes feel that a man-eating tiger would have his uses on my farm.

The Indian villager accepts the risk of sudden death from tigers and other wild animals in much the same way as we accept an equal risk in crossing a London street. I have in *Indian Shikar Notes* gone into the question of man-eating tigers and the reasons for their taking to the evil habit of preying on humans.

The Dindori Plateau in the Mandla district is a good example of two causes for the prevalence of man-eating tigers. In this sparsely populated and roadless country seldom visited by Europeans, the Baigas [forest tribes], with the help of poisoned arrows, pitfalls, and other traps, have so diminished the game as to deprive the tigers of their natural food, thus driving them to prey on that most common animal of all, man. The prevalence of man-eaters in this district has been well known for many years, and what can be more natural than for parent tigers to pass the taste for human flesh on to their offspring?

When I first knew the Dindori plateau, things had got so bad that it was pretty safe to say that in many places every tiger was a man-eater. Before the war there was a big settlement of pious men at sacred Amarkantak who ministered yearly to the needs of thousands of pilgrims who washed in and drank of the water of the holy Narmada at her source. Gradually the settlement diminished, and although the tigers did well during the pilgrimage, the permanent settlement at the springs ceased to exist, save for one naked and gray, ash-covered hermit who lived under the mulberry tree above the beautiful Kapildahra Falls.

I remember spending a long time discussing religion with this gentleman, who was an educated philosopher with sound views on the subject of the tendency of all forms of religion toward superstition and idolatry. It was possible for us to discuss beliefs without either of us getting angry, which is unusual for earnest people.

I was afraid the old man would be taken by a tiger and warned him of the risk he ran. His answer to my warning was such as was to be expected from a man of his views. Next time I went to Amarkantak he was gone.

Ajwar, of which I write, is a village some way from Amarkantak but on the same plateau and served by the same group of man-eating tigers. This neighbourhood had until the year 1920 been comparatively free from the pest, and held a good population of Baigas, Gonds, and nomad Banjara. In other parts of Mandla, too, the man-eaters were not particularly noticeable although, of course, a few pages of the official gazette contained offers of rewards for their destruction in the district and elsewhere.

In another chapter I have written of the very ancient pack route that connects the Mahanadi Plains with that of the Ganges up the Chakmi Pass of the Bilaspur district, which after passing through Dindori, Ajwar, and Batonda comes out into the Northern Plains near Birsingpur Railway Station. Efforts have been made to open up the Mandla district to cart traffic, but even now the number of wheeled carts in so large an area of country is probably restricted to half a dozen in the village of Dindori.

Pack transport still monopolizes the trade routes, and the picturesque Banjaras who own the pack animals are the only means of commerce with the outside world for the local inhabitants. Dindori, a few miles from Ajwar, boasts two or three shops owned by moneylenders and a native magistrate who dispenses justice. All was peace in this pleasant green forest country until one

*Beaters and a bag.*

day in the spring of the year 1920, when Ratnu, a Baiga of Kodwari village, took up his ax and water bottle of dried gourd, hung them over his shoulder, and set out from his home into the forest to collect those luscious petals of the mohwa flower that make so sweet a store of food and potent liquor.

He had not far to go, and he took his ax, not because he would want to use it for cutting wood but from the habit of never being without a useful tool, in the same way as an English boy usually carries a knife. When he reached the grove where the mohwa flowers strewed the ground and burdened the air with their heavy scent, he paused beneath a large camel-foot creeper as thick as a man's leg that had pulled itself up into a high tree. Holding onto this and gripping with toes and fingers he climbed high enough to collect a large bunch of leaves under his arm. When he came down, he sat in the welcome shade and deftly wove baskets from the leaves, pinning them together by the stalks with much skill. His task finished, and all the baskets ready for the collection of the flowers, he reached out his arm to take a pull at the water bottle, and as he raised the bottle to his mouth he was suddenly knocked forward. He gave a scream of terror as he smelled the putrid breath of the tigress that was gripping the back of his neck, and then he was dead—a matter of a second or two at the most. Such was the scene much as it actually took place, as evidenced by those who found his remains.

It is interesting, too, to imagine the feelings of the tigress. One of her canine teeth was missing and the others were worn to mere stumps, which made it difficult for her to kill her natural food in a country where game was almost extinct. She was frantically hungry and had cubs to feed as well. Returning to them ill nourished herself, with no food for her cubs, she fell to the temptation of slaying a man offered for so easy a killing. Then, too, imagine her doubts and fears after the excitement of the stalk and the death of her victim were over. Here at her feet lay one of those animals that instinctively she and her tribe had always dreaded. She paused before starting her meal, fearing that even dead men could hurt or retaliate. Looking round fearfully lest other men be about, she turned suddenly and ate in quick gulps from the buttock. Soon she had finished, not because she was satisfied, but because there was no more to eat; then, with guilty glances behind her, she slunk away into the forest.

After this the tigress grew more bold, for her natural dread of man had been virtually overcome, and she had found that when tackled from behind her new prey could be easily and safely killed. But she still feared man in open combat, and when she ventured into a village and seized a small child from its doorstep, a brave mother drove her off with no more dangerous a weapon in her hand than a bread basket and was able to drag the dead body of her child into the house. Until dawn the tigress roamed round the village, striking fear into the hearts of the people with her hungry roars.

By now all the village folk round about Ajwar were thoroughly frightened, as day after day more victims were reported. Those who had journeys to take did so in parties armed with bows and axes, and unless they strayed from the main body they were usually safe. But there was no real security, even close to the villages. Water had to be collected from the springs, usually some little distance from their huts, work had to be done in the forest clearings, and in a country where indoor sanitation is unknown, men and women were compelled to make solitary journeys to a covert outside the village at least once a day.

Then again, there would be periods of two or three months at a time when no victims would be taken. Then confidence would be restored while the tigress went elsewhere, until once more she would proclaim her presence and keep the villagers terrorized.

Two victims survived to give an account of their adventure. Nirpat, a Gond of Saristal, left his village in the morning to go to the stream that is within calling distance of the huts. He suspected no danger, and as he stooped to drink in a shallow pool he was knocked over and held firmly by the back of the neck. His wild screams for help were heard by Bora, a fellow Gond, who with a few others rushed out with loud shouts to rescue him. Three nasty marks were left in Nirpat's neck. Nirpat told me that until the tigress had been driven off, she held onto his neck so tightly that he could not see what manner of beast held him. Shortly afterward, Patpatia, a Gond of Dahonia, was attacked while grazing his herd of buffaloes. He too was rescued, but by the master bull of the herd; he came off with a cruel mauling of his neck and back that laid him low for many a day.

By the end of the hot weather the figure of victims was mounting at an alarming rate, and a special reward of five hundred rupees was offered by the government for the destruction of the tigress. The country is too remote and access too difficult to be reached by ordinary sportsmen, but district and inspecting officers whose duty it was to visit it made attempts at ridding the Ajwar Valley of its curse. Local tigers, no matter how innocent, came in for an uneasy time, more than one falling to the rifle. Others, when located, had their midday slumbers disturbed by noisy beaters.

Most hilly country is difficult to beat for tiger, and the sal forest round Ajwar is no exception. On a cold morning of 1922, I was following the course of a deep nullah during my inspection of the forest with W., the divisional forest officer. Far up the hill on one of the deep slopes of the nullah, a troop of monkeys was perched on the rocks and trees, cursing with loud cries some enemy below them.

Field glasses revealed two small, light-coloured animals passing along the face of the cliff. We split into two parties, and one went straight up in the hopes of a stalking shot, while the other tried to cut off a possible retreat. A tigress and two cubs got away between us to continue their terrible work, which reached its climax when Nana was taken.

Nana Bania was a shopkeeper and financier in the local centre of Dindori, who, there is no reason to suppose, was more popular with the members of the local forest villages than others of his calling. In the month of February, business took him over the pass along the pack route at Batonda to Birsingpur.

Being the proud possessor of four carts, he traveled in the comfort that befits one in his affluent position, and, after transacting his business, he started back on his journey home with a relative and four servants. Among other places, he rested at Ajwar, trusting to the daylight and the presence of the small village for safety. After man and beast had been satisfied with food and drink, all, except one of the servants who had been appointed watcher, took their midday sleep before continuing the journey toward Dindori.

About 4:00 p.m. Nana woke to find the faithless watcher asleep, and after waking him, he sent him out into the fields to cut grass for the cart bullocks. Later in the afternoon he strolled across the open valley to see what his servant was doing, but apparently could not find him. Nana never returned. Those who remained with the carts state that they heard a gurgling noise followed by that of rocks rolling down the side of the hill. At the time they thought little about it, not knowing that poor Nana had been killed and was being dragged by the tigress over the rocks up the hill into the forest. Later in the evening they became anxious at his absence, but gave up a halfhearted search under excuse of darkness. In the morning, helped by the Baigas, who at other times would be looked down upon as despised savages, they searched far enough to find Nana's shoes and to see the tigress.

Clearly any further hunt by a party armed only with axes was folly, so word was sent to the subinspector of police at Sharpur, who represented the armed forces of the Crown. He, supported by his constables, was able to form a stronger party to follow the trail with the Baigas. It is suspected that money was owed to the unfortunate Nana by the local Baigas, for they told me their tale with a twinkle in the eye, not as those lamenting the demise of a loved one in tragic circumstances, but rather after the manner of people relating some highly humorous event. After following the marks of the drag for some time, they saw the tigress pulling the remains of the body away. She growled at them and ran off with a leg in her mouth, behavior that one of the party afterward described rather flippantly as like that of a dog that has stolen a piece of meat.

The police were armed, but it was not until the evening that the remains of the moneylender were recovered. Two legs up to the trunk had been eaten, as well as one arm, but the tigress apparently had some honest feelings left: She stopped eating at the moneylender's waist, where his cash, amounting to some two hundred rupees, was kept in his belt. The metal may have frightened her.

Local humour was later tickled by a further outrage on the part of the tigress, which a few days subsequently carried off one of her victim's bullocks.

Next month, W. of the forest service was teaching an ill-trained staff at Ajwar how to make thinnings in sal forests. On the 17th he was camped at the top of the pass at Batonda, some twelve miles distant from Ajwar. Buffalo calves were ready to be tied up as baits for the tigress as soon as there should be any news to show where she was.

There is another village called Jata, about a mile away from Ajwar in the opposite direction to Batonda, and on the evening of the 17th the village watchman, or *kotwar,* of that place left his hut for a visit to the fields and was killed by the tigress. His body was rescued by some stout-hearted fellow villagers before the tigress had time to start feeding off it, and was kept in a house for the night while the terrified villagers listened to the roars of the famished tigress and dared not shoot, although armed with two guns.

At dawn a messenger ventured down the valley to W.'s camp at Batonda and brought the further news that on his way he heard a riot of monkeys going on at some animal near Ajwar. W. made a quick move to Ajwar, and at once the buffalo calves were sent to Jata to be tied up as baits in the hope that the hungry tigress would soon return to the village to take the bait and so enable W. to locate her the next day. It is curious that throughout the three years that the tigress spread terror through the valley, none of the Gypsy Banjaras were taken, although hardly a day passed in which those wandering people did not camp in or near Ajwar. It is possible that their fierce dogs kept the tigress away, or that the wary Banjaras gave her little chance of catching a lone victim.

While W. was waiting for his baits to be sent on to Jata, he sat taking his ease in a long chair on the veranda of the Ajwar rest house. Below him, some quarter of a mile away in the middle of the valley, the Banjaras were forming a good-size camp. The first thirsty rush for water over, the pack animals were unloaded and the sacks of grain heaped in a neat pile in the centre of the camp, while the animals began cropping the grass around.

Two o'clock is the hottest part of the day, and the road was deserted. Men and dogs in the camp were sleeping after the midday meal, and the women were bathing in the stream. Except for the occasional tinkle of the bullocks' bells and the merry chatter of the women in the stream, hardly a sound was to be heard.

*A cautious approach.*

The view from the rest house leads over the valley to the forest opposite, where the dark wall of woodlands stands out in marked contrast to the sunburned grass of the glen. Beyond its margin, the forest rises in soft lines to the hilltops. Nature was asleep, and so very nearly was W. as he lay back in his chair, thinking of his chances of at last coming to terms with the tigress and ridding the valley of its curse. Lazily his eyes took in the camp and the bathing women; then he lifted his glance over the valley and marked the place where he was, in a few days, to begin teaching his staff the first principles of forestry. The green forest not half a mile away was a relief to his tired eyes, and he let them rest lazily on it as he lay back half asleep.

Suddenly he started forward, for there creeping from the forest over the short grass toward the bathing women was the tigress. Robbed of her prey the previous evening, she was making another attempt to satisfy a famished stomach. It took half a minute for W. to reach the camp and rouse the men, who, in spite of the best intentions, much resented having their sleep interrupted, even to save their own women.

A goat was soon obtained from the village and tied up near the forest in the place where the tigress was last seen disappearing in a patch of high grass. A rude platform, or machan, was put up in a tree for the accommodation of W. so that he could watch the goat unseen and be away from his way-too-enterprising enemy. For four hours he watched—motionless—for any movement might give his position away to the tigress, who was certain to make a careful survey of the ground previous to stalking the goat. Flies are maddening enough at any time, but one fly, no matter how sluggish, can drive a man perfectly frantic. This is especially true for someone sitting in a machan, who must make no sudden movement for fear of warning his quarry.

Four minds were concentrated on the spot. The goat was comfortably eating grass because it knew that it was expected to bleat, and, being a contrary animal, did otherwise. The tigress was less happy, for she wanted to eat the goat badly, but having seen W. enter the tree and not come away, she preferred taking no risks. W. was as uncomfortable as it is possible for a man to be. No one who has not tried it has any idea how uneasy a person can be when he sits on a hard seat with the end of a sharp, broken branch sticking into his back for the space of some four hours. W. knew and so did the fly, which was the only one concerned in the little drama that was thoroughly enjoying itself. Few flies have had such chances—bare, hot knees and neck and no fear of disturbance gave great scope for enterprise and amusement—and the fly made the most of it.

Before darkness fell, W. decided on a move home, but he did not go unaccompanied. The goat, on being released, made a wild dash for home, all the while bleating madly. Then came W. closely followed by the fly, who by now had some friends joining in the sport. Last of all came the tigress. Unseen, she was waiting for her chance and yet fearful of the venture, for W. is a big man and his topee was strange and disconcerting. Gradually she crept nearer her unsuspecting prey. If she was to make the venture at all, it would have to be done soon, before the quarry was too far from the covert into which he must be dragged and hidden, and too near the camp and a possible rescue.

A patch of grass gave opportunity for a nearer approach before the final rush. She made up her mind in a second, and at full speed started to tear across the fifty yards toward W. Not a sound reached W., who assured me that he turned to look back casually and for no reason that he can remember. The nasty yellow, cruel eyes held him for the fraction of a second, then he put his rifle up. Unused to being faced by her game and that a six-foot man, the tigress threw herself back just before her anticipated spring, and then, cur that she was, she turned to flee. The first shot took her in the quarters, cramping her style, and so gave W. the chance of a flank shot that she took in the shoulders, and then she crumpled up. Blood was flowing on the grass, and the fly with its merry companions abandoned the trivial pleasures of an afternoon, deserted W., and settled down to the more serious business of feeding.

Who would not feel shaky after such an ordeal? But more trials were to come. Women, bringing their children, ran from the village to touch in homage the feet of the man who had rid their homes of the terror, and freed their lives of a dreadful menace.

Subsequent examination of the tigress showed one canine tooth missing and the remaining three to be mere rounded stumps. It was surprising that she had managed to keep herself alive as long as she did. Her teeth, when compared with the tooth marks on the necks of Nirpat and Patpatia, showed without need of reference to Sherlock Holmes that the destroyer had at last met her just reward.

## Chapter Twenty-One

# Reginald Burton
### The Tiger Hunters
### (1936)

Brig. Gen. Reginald George Burton comes from an established Anglo-Indian military family. His father, Major General E. F. Burton, was a decorated soldier and noted sportsman who was killed fighting brigands in the Deccan. The younger Burton, like his father, served a lifetime in India, with a short stint in the Caribbean.

Both Burtons exemplified the soldier-sportsman ideal, and both were accomplished writers. R. G. became an even greater authority on Indian field sports, as well as Napoleonic military history. Burton was an active hunter who shot in many different locales across the continent. He was also a keen naturalist who always had a special interest in tigers. Burton wrote one of the first natural histories of the animal—The Book of the Tiger (1933)—which became a standard reference for many years.

The following selection is a chapter from Burton's last book, The Tiger Hunters (1936). It is semibiographical in nature and describes adventures that took place over many decades in India. The hunt described here is Burton's first, in which he is accompanied by his shikari Bhima, as well as a subahdar [Indian captain] and local Muslim elder [shaikh]. Of particular interest is the descriptive aftermath of the hunt—bringing the carcass to the village and skinning the cat.

### The First Tiger Hunt

We were up with the sun next morning, and after an early breakfast started up the valley of Shaikh Falid to see if any of the buffaloes had been killed. Cautiously approaching the first place, we saw that the calf had disappeared, and at first we thought that it had been taken by the tigress, especially as her fresh tracks were on the path by which we had come. But the fact that there

*The author (seated right) at his hunting camp.*

was no visible kill, and no signs of a drag, made us suspicious. Bhima said that the animal must have gotten loose, as the unbroken rope that had secured it could be seen still tied to the tree where it was picketed. This was confirmed by tracks of the calf for some distance along the path leading back to camp, and we rightly concluded that it had gone back and rejoined Brook Sahib's herd—an example of the necessity of ensuring that the animals are securely picketed.

Farther up the valley we found more fresh tracks of the tigress, and on viewing from a distance the spot where the second calf had been picketed, we saw at once that it had been killed and dragged into the thicket beyond the water, the killer having leaped across a wide nullah with the victim in her jaws. There was a pool of blood, a broken rope, and the trail of a heavy body dragged through the grass. There could be no doubt about the tragedy that had been enacted in the night.

The other buffaloes were then visited and found to be untouched. We watered them at the pools where they were tied up and cut fresh grass for them when they were again fastened to trees or pickets. I could never feel reconciled to leaving these poor creatures to their fate. The sole consolation was that they had no knowledge of impending doom, while death generally came in an instant after the onslaught of the beast of prey. And when this resulted in a tiger's being shot, the buffalo served as the means of saving the lives of many prospective victims.

We hurried back to camp to make arrangements for the beat. Men were at once sent off to collect beaters from the adjacent villages, and as there were enough people within a mile or so of our camp, in an hour the whole party was ready to start for the scene of action. Bhima led the way, carrying his nine-foot spear over his shoulder, for he knew every inch of the jungle for many miles round his village, where we were encamped. Strict silence was enjoined when we entered the valley, for nothing disturbs game so much as the sound of the human voice. The beaters were halted by Nathu and Chandru half a mile short of the position of the kill, indicated by vultures hovering like black specks in the sky and descending by degrees to perch in the surrounding trees. The tigress was evidently on the spot to guard her prey from these scavengers, or they would have gone down to the kill instead of remaining perched in the trees.

We all halted with the beaters, and a dozen villagers known to Bhima as trustworthy for the purpose were selected as stops, together with such of our own men as were not required to stiffen and support the line. Leaving the beaters at the point of assembly, where they were to remain until Bhima and others returned after stops and guns had been posted, we now went on round one flank of the area of the beat, posting stops on the way, and took up positions in trees at a height of some twelve or fifteen feet from the ground. This was not for the sake of safety but in order that we should be concealed from the tigress, which would not look up but was liable to be alarmed if we remained on the ground, when she would probably break back or slink off without offering a shot. The *subahdar* [officer] with Shaikh Karim and the remainder of the stops went round the other flank and then rejoined the beaters. The tigress was thus enclosed in a limited area with the guns ahead, stops on either flank covering tributary nullahs and other places where she might attempt to break out, and the beaters forming the base of what was a rough triangle. The guns were posted so as to command the line toward which the tigress was to be driven, selected as her most probable line of retreat when she was disturbed. We commanded all the most likely ground.

We were now on the tiptoe of excitement and expectation, rifles loaded and cocked, spare cartridges handy in our pockets, and water bottles hanging on convenient branches within reach. The start of the beat was heralded by a blast of the *subahdar*'s whistle and a distant chorus of shouts. I grasped my rifle firmly, listening for every sound and watching for any movement. Perhaps the beating of my own heart seemed to me loudest of all. I heard a rustling among the dry leaves that carpeted the ground, and quite thought that the tigress was coming, but it was only a peacock running ahead of the beaters. It saw me at once as these birds always will; nothing escapes the keen sight of their bright eyes. It rose in flight, its long train of gold and green glittering in the sunlight. Then a sambar stag ran out of the cover and stood on a small hillock listening to the beat for a moment before galloping out of sight.

And now the beaters were coming nearer, and their cries could be more clearly distinguished. Then the *subahdar* called out from their midst, a hundred yards off: "There is the tiger! She is coming! She is coming!"

She came along rapidly; we could both see her crossing an open space in the jungle ahead of the beaters before she descended again and was lost to view in the main watercourse. Then a stop was heard tapping on a tree; there was an answering rush and a roar as the tigress broke into full view, trotting directly toward my post. Then she slowed down to a walk and came quickly toward me through a patch of grass and low bush, her sinuous striped body shining like molten gold in the light of the sun. I held my breath, trembling with excitement, but steadied myself as the beast approached.

Suddenly she came to a standstill about twenty yards off, apparently looking straight into my eyes, but she could not make me out, for I made no movement. Then she looked away, and I raised my rifle slowly and fired at her chest, knocking her backward. In a moment, before I could reload the empty barrel—and I had practiced this until I could do it with lightning speed—the tigress had disappeared in the watercourse.

I sounded my whistle twice, the agreed signal to stop the beat, and called out: "I am sure I have hit her, but she has turned back."

Just then a panther raced past Robert like a streak of yellow light, and he fired at it with no other effect than to make it gallop faster, if possible, and it was lost to sight in a moment.

By this time the beaters had all scrambled up trees while the *subahdar* with Bhima, Nathu, and Chandru were making their way round by a circuitous route so as to avoid any chance of meeting the wounded beast. They came round to my tree and I got down, having handed my unloaded rifle to one of the men; I reloaded it as soon as I reached the ground. Robert then descended in the same manner, and we assembled under my tree. The tigress had disappeared in a deep and narrow ravine, entirely hidden by undergrowth except for a few small open

*Chandru and Nathu, trusty shikaris and loyal friends.*

spaces. The shelving banks were overgrown with bushes and long grass. We all went to the spot where the tigress was standing when I had fired at her.

"That is the spot. See, there is blood!" I exclaimed, pointing to the ground.

I bent down to examine the track and picked up a large piece of a canine tooth, proving that the beast had been hit in the mouth. Leaving the men above, Robert and I followed a short distance on the tracks, when suddenly Robert called out: "There she is; there is the tigress!" at the same time raising his rifle.

But before he had time to fire, the animal, who was lying down about fifteen yards off, jumped up and disappeared round a bend of the watercourse.

We now rejoined the men on the high ground overlooking the ravine. To follow in that narrow and intricate way would have been to court certain disaster. The *subahdar*, with a spare rifle, and the shikaris went along the opposite and steeper bank, while we followed its course on our side. The shikaris threw stones into the bushes at the bottom of the ravine, and they had not gone twenty yards before the tigress charged out with a fierce roar and rushed up the steep hillside straight at Nathu. He stood his ground fearlessly, raising the long, iron-tipped staff he carried. He prepared to strike the beast as she came up to him, for his position was such that the *subahdar* could not fire for fear of hitting Nathu. But we on the opposite bank of the ravine at once opened fire, and under this fusillade the tigress turned back into the cover of the bushes, where we could see her well enough to make out that she appeared to be dead.

I was for going down at once to examine her, but Nathu first threw a stone to make sure that she was dead. The stone fell plump on her body, and as she did not move there could be no doubt that there was no life left in her. We went down to the dead beast, and now the beaters began to come up, for we had let them know that they might safely approach. The tigress was carried out into the open, and the tape proved that she was at least of average length— eight feet, three inches in a straight line from the tip of the nose to the end of the tail, and the tail was three feet long.

The first bullet had struck her in the mouth, knocking out several teeth and lodging in the back of the gullet; three other bullets had hit her well forward. Poles were cut and the body was slung on them and sent back to camp in charge of some of our men, including Chandru, who would see that the whiskers were not pulled out. These are used as a charm, while some say that they are cut into small pieces and given to enemies in food, causing death in the same way that ground glass is administered to poison people in India.

We now crossed over the hills into Chichkora, taking with us three buffalo calves and a young goat brought from camp. One of the calves was tied up in the place of the one that had escaped. But we first examined the kill, of which the tigress had eaten nearly the whole of both hindquarters. After killing the buffalo, she had dragged it to the margin of a nullah and then picked it up bodily and jumped across with the carcass in her jaws. She had killed it by seizing the throat from below, at the same time clasping the forequarters with her claws, as proved by the scratches on either side. The poor beast's neck was broken, probably by its own weight as it was borne to the ground.

Chichkhora was not as wide as the Shaikh Farid *khora,* but it was more densely overgrown with jungle and was traversed by a wider watercourse. Here were deep, cool recesses overgrown with jamun (wild plum) bushes in whose sequestered shade tigers could find those lairs they love so well, sheltered from the heat of the sun. There was much long grass, green where it grew by the water, but elsewhere dried by the heat of summer, and there was game in abundance. We put up more than one four-horned antelope, and a herd of spotted deer showed their dappled hides for a moment in an open glade. But we did not molest these creatures, although we would have been glad of some venison for our large camp and also for the peasants who were in need of food during this season of scarcity.

We soon found imprints of the great pads of the big tiger already reported by Bhima. These were imprinted in the soft mud on the margin of a pool where he had slaked his thirst during the past night. The pugs were clear-cut and fresh, as could be seen at once when we had the opportunity of comparing them with other tracks that were two or three days old. Numerous tracks of different dates showed that the big tiger was a permanent inhabitant of Chichkora. The buffalo calves were picketed, and the sun was already sinking toward the line of hills in the west when we turned our steps homeward.

We followed a narrow path down the valley, more trodden by wild animals than by human beings, though no doubt originally made by man. It was interesting to read the history of the night on this dusty pathway through the forest, for, strange though it may seem, animals prefer to walk in these tracks of human origin rather than through the jungle. No doubt the paths are easy to follow; there is no grass and bush to brush their sides or to wet their flanks with the dews of night. From the footprints impressed on the path one can plainly tell of all that have passed. A panther, a bear, two hyenas, some stags and

*Prime tiger country.*

four-horned antelope, and a porcupine, as well as small mongoose and other inferior animals had left their impress in the dust. Then there were footmarks of birds—peafowl, partridges, and little quail. Where tracks overlay others, it was easy to see which had passed first along the way.

Suddenly Bhima stopped and said: "Here it is, here is the *deo*."

This was the shrine of the jungle god, represented by a large upright stone, painted a brilliant red and sheltered by a little hut of branches and wattle, with a few red and dingy white rags fluttering from a stick at the top. The goat was dragged before the graven image and while facing the *deo* was anointed between its horns with country spirit, *daru* distilled from the fleshy blossoms of the mhowa tree. I had been told that the goat would do obeisance to the *deo*, whereupon the sacrifice would take place, for there was no Buddhist here to stay the hand of the slayer in accordance with the precept of the Master:

> Kill not, for pity's sake, and lest ye slay
> The meanest thing upon its upward way.

Certainly the goat did bow down, perhaps owing to the anointing, and it was immediately slaughtered, the blood being spilt before the shrine and a severed foot hung up within as an offering. But let us not call these simple people idolaters and worshipers of graven images, for symbols and images, and figures of man and beast, are connected with most religions. Here was no praying to any deity in human form, nor did these good and simple people imagine the stone itself to be a god. It was to them merely a symbol representing the Spirit of the Wild whose habitation was in that lonely valley. To those who were animists, such as the aboriginal Gonds, the Spirit was personified, or materialized, or expressed in the great beasts of Nature, the bison and the tiger who roamed these remote solitudes and represented in their mighty strength and armature the forces of the spiritual world.

When this ceremony was over, we went on our way, the men carrying with them the carcass of the sacrificial goat, for the meat was not left to be wasted on a symbolic deity. Did not Abraham of old in the same way offer burned sacrifice to Jehovah, and even prepare a human victim in his own son, until the angel came down to stay his hand! And as related elsewhere in this book, human sacrifices were within recent times offered up to the Hindu god in the shape of Shiva and Kali.

As we neared camp we became aware of a great noise, a beating of drums and the sound of wild, barbaric music. Approaching, we saw a procession headed by eight men who carried the dead tigress slung on long poles, followed by the village band with tom-tom and drum, with all the inhabitants and the returned beaters trailing after. The tigress was deposited on the outskirts of the camp, and the women of the village came up to the dead beast, some carrying infants astride of their hips and all bringing small copper coins or cowrie shells, the small change of the country, and some with red powder to place the caste mark on the forehead of the tigress. They salaamed to the dead beast and deposited their offerings on the body, where it was afterward collected by Bhima. Meanwhile Nathu had arrived and, standing by the tigress, described to the admiring crowd with voluble tongue and realistic gesture how he had driven the animal downhill "as if it were a goat" when it charged him, and how the first tiger had fallen to the rifle of the Baba Sahib whom he had taught to shoot when he was a baby.

In course of time all these people disappeared and Chandru and the syces [attendants] set to work to remove the skin. We were interested spectators of this operation, and lent a hand from time to time. A slit was made down the middle of the animal from chin to tip of tail and a cut down the inside of each leg to the pads. The skin was then gradually stripped off, special care being needed at the lips, nose, paws, and ears. It was then pegged out with bamboo slips with the hairy side underneath on the ground over dry cut grass in a shady place so that the sun should not melt the fat and cause hardening of the pelt. Care was taken not to stretch the skin unduly. When all the adhering flesh had been taken off, the skin was well scraped with flat stones and knives, a mixture of burned alum and saltpetre was well rubbed in, and arsenical soap was applied round the lips, nose, ears, and pads where there was most fear of the skin's going bad and the hair slipping in consequence. I had skinned animals in my early days in India, and we collected the skins of small creatures shot at home with catapults, so we were interested in seeing this great beast treated in the same manner.

Meanwhile the "lucky bones" were cut out of the chest by Nathu. These are clavicles or rudimentary collarbones found in all the cat tribe, about four inches long and hatchet-shaped in the tiger. They are much prized, and, as well as the claws, are often mounted in gold and hung round the necks of children to keep off evil. Great care was taken to collect all the fat from the tigress, which was boiled down in a pot over the fire and stored in bottles. The villagers also carried off not only bits of flesh and the liver but also the whole legs and quarters.

On being questioned, the *subahdar* said that the fat was most valuable as a remedy for rheumatism and to make men strong when rubbed into the patient. This is a universal belief throughout the whole of India, where the fat of tigers is everywhere highly prized. He added that the villagers would eat the flesh and especially the liver, the latter being supposed to impart to those who partook of it some of the courage of the tiger.

"But," said Nathu with Oriental flattery, which is really only politeness, "it is not necessary for the sahibs to eat tigers' liver, as they already possess the courage of the tiger."

Even so the Persian courtier said: "If the King says at midday, 'It is midnight,' reply: 'True indeed, behold the moon and stars!'"

Talking over the events of the day, we expressed wonder at the beauty and symmetry and size of the tiger, so much greater than we had thought. Bhima told us that when we killed the big tiger in Chichkora we would see that he would be twice the size, or at least twice the weight of the tigress, and I remarked that we would realize how much finer these animals are in their native wilds than in captivity, where alone I had previously seen them. All in camp were tired after the long day's work and excitement. Even Nathu's garrulous tongue stopped wagging before ten o'clock, and half an hour later the whole camp was asleep.

Chapter Twenty-Two

# Jim Corbett
## Man-Eaters of Kumaon
## (1946)

Maj. James Corbett was the most famous tiger hunter of all time, and perhaps the best. He was a keen naturalist who knew more about the cat's habits than anyone in living memory. He was also a great writer whose stories were popular worldwide and are still being reissued.

Corbett first became enthralled with tigers after seeing one as a child after it dashed out of a shrub a few yards from his home. As an adolescent he wandered the forested Kumaon hills, part of the lower Himalayas in northwestern India, perfecting his tracking and shooting skills. After a career working for the Indian railroad, which took him across the country, he returned to his mountain home. He spent his retirement hunting man-eaters and other rogues. Toward the end of his life he gave up hunting and helped with tiger conservation efforts. He left his beloved India after independence and moved to Kenya, where he died in 1955.

Corbett wrote six books. This chapter is from his first, Man-eaters of Kumaon (1946). The story is about a tiger named the "Bachelor of Powalgarh," who, because of his large size, was one of the most sought-after trophy tigers in the province. He wasn't a man-eater, but fears he would turn to eating cattle prompted Corbett finally to shoot the crafty old cat.

### The Bachelor of Powalgarh

Three miles from our winter home, and in the heart of the forest, there is an open glade some four hundred yards long and half as wide, grassed with emerald green and surrounded with big trees interlaced with cane creepers. It was in this glade, which for beauty has no equal, that I first saw the tiger who was known throughout the United Provinces as the "Bachelor of Powalgarh," who from 1920 to 1930 was the most sought-after big-game trophy in the province.

The sun had just risen one winter's morning when I crested the high ground, overlooking the glade. On the far side, a score of red jungle fowl were scratching among the dead leaves bordering a crystal-clear stream, and scattered over the emerald-green grass, now sparkling with dew, fifty or more chital were feeding. Sitting on a tree stump and smoking, I had been looking at this scene for some time when the hind nearest to me raised her head, turned in my direction, and called. A moment later the Bachelor stepped into the open from the thick bushes below me.

For a long minute he stood with his head held high surveying the scene, and then with slow, unhurried steps started to cross the glade, the newly risen sun lighting up his rich winter coat. He was a magnificent sight as, with head turning now to the right and now to the left, he walked down the wide lane the deer had made for him. At the stream he lay down and quenched his thirst, then sprang across and, as he entered the dense tree jungle beyond, called three times in acknowledgment of the homage the jungle folk had paid him, for from the time he had entered the glade every chital had called, every jungle fowl had cackled, and every one of a troupe of monkeys on the trees had chattered.

The Bachelor was far afield that morning, for his home was in a ravine six miles away. Living in an area in which the majority of tigers are bagged with the aid of elephants, he had chosen his home wisely. The ravine, running into the foothills, was half a mile long, with steep hills on either side rising to a height of a thousand feet. At the upper end of the ravine there was a waterfall some twenty feet high, and at the lower end, where the water had cut through red clay, it narrowed to four feet. Any sportsman, therefore, who wished to try conclusions with the Bachelor, while he was at home, would of a necessity have to do so on foot. It was this secure retreat, and the government rules prohibiting night shooting, that had enabled the Bachelor to retain possession of his much sought-after skin.

In spite of the many and repeated attempts that had been made to bag him with the aid of buffalo bait, the Bachelor had never been fired at, though on two occasions, to my knowledge, he had escaped death only by the skin of his teeth. On the first occasion, after a perfect beat, a guy rope by which the machan was suspended interfered with the movement of Fred Anderson's

*The legendary Jim Corbett in uniform.*

rifle at the critical moment, and on the second occasion the Bachelor arrived at the machan before the beat started and found Huish Edye filling his pipe. On both these occasions he had been viewed at a range of only a few feet, and while Anderson described him as being as big as a Shetland pony, Edye said he was as big as a donkey.

The winter following these and other unsuccessful attempts, I took Wyndham, our commissioner, who knows more about tigers than any other man in India, to a fire track skirting the upper end of the ravine in which the Bachelor lived, to show him the fresh pug marks of the tiger that I had found on the fire track that morning. Wyndham was accompanied by two of his most experienced shikaris, and after the three of them had carefully measured and examined the pug marks, Wyndham said that in his opinion the tiger was ten feet between pegs, and while one shikari said he was ten feet, five inches over curves, the other said he was ten feet, six inches or a little more. All three agreed that they had never seen the pug marks of a bigger tiger.

In 1930 the Forest Department started extensive fellings in the area surrounding the Bachelor's home, and, annoyed at the disturbance, he changed his quarters. This I learned from two sportsmen who had taken out a shooting pass with the object of hunting down the tiger. Shooting passes are issued only for fifteen days of each month, and throughout that winter, shooting party after shooting party failed to make contact with the tiger.

Toward the end of the winter an old *dak* [mail] runner, who passes our gate every morning and evening on his seven-mile run through the forest to a hill village, came to me one evening and reported that on his way out that morning he had seen the biggest pug marks of a tiger that he had seen during the thirty years of his service. The tiger, he said, had come from the west and, after proceeding along the road for two hundred yards, had gone east, taking a path that started from near an almond tree. This tree was about two miles from our home and was a well-known landmark. The path the tiger had taken ran through very heavy jungle for half a mile before crossing a wide watercourse and then joining a cattle track that skirts the foot of the hills before entering a deep and well-wooded valley—a favorite haunt of tigers.

Early next morning, with Robin at my heels, I set out to prospect, my objective being the point where the cattle track entered the valley, for at that point the tracks of all the animals entering or leaving the valley are to be found. From the time we started Robin appeared to know that we had a special job in hand, and he paid not the least attention to the jungle fowl we disturbed, the *kakar* (barking deer) that let us get quite close to it, and the two sambar that stood and belled at us. Where the cattle track entered the valley the ground was hard and stony, and when we reached this spot Robin put down his head and very carefully smelled the stones. On receiving a signal from me to carry on, he turned and started down the track, keeping a yard ahead of me. I could tell from his behavior that he was on the scent of a tiger, and that the scent was hot. A hundred yards farther down where the track flattens out and runs along the foot of the hill, the ground is soft; there I saw the pug marks of a tiger, and a glance at them satisfied me we were on the heels of the Bachelor and that he was only a minute or two ahead of us.

Beyond the soft ground the track runs for three hundred yards over stones before going steeply down onto an open plain. If the tiger kept to the track we should probably see him on this open ground. We had gone another fifty yards when Robin stopped and, after running his nose up and down a blade of grass on the left of the track, turned and entered the grass that was there about two feet high. On the far side of the grass there was a patch of clerodendron, about forty yards wide. This plant grows in dense patches to a height of five feet, and has widely spread leaves and a big head of flowers not unlike horse chestnut. It is greatly fancied by tiger, sambar, and pig because of the shade it gives.

When Robin reached the clerodendron, he stopped and backed toward me, thus telling me that he could not see into the bushes ahead and wished to be carried. Lifting him up, I put his hind legs into my left-hand pocket, and when he had hooked his forefeet over my left arm, he was safe and secure, and I had both hands free for the rifle. On these occasions Robin was always in deadly earnest, and no matter what he saw, or how our quarry behaved before or after fired at, he never moved and spoiled my shot or impeded my view.

Proceeding very slowly, we had gone halfway through the clerodendron when I saw the bushes directly in front of us swaying. Waiting until the tiger had cleared the bushes, I went forward expecting to see him in the more or less open jungle, but he was nowhere in sight. When I put Robin down, he turned to the left and indicated that the tiger had gone into a deep and narrow ravine nearby. This ravine ran to the foot of an isolated hill on which there were caves frequented by tigers, and as I was not armed to deal with a tiger at close quarters, and further, as it was time for breakfast, Robin and I turned and made for home.

*The author with the Bachelor of Powalgarh.*

After breakfast I returned alone, armed with a heavy rifle, and as I approached the hill, which in the days of the long ago had been used by the local inhabitants as a rallying point against the Gurkha invaders, I heard the boom of a big buffalo bell and a man shouting. These sounds were coming from the top of the hill, which is flat and about half an acre in extent, so I climbed up and saw a man on a tree, striking a dead branch with the head of his ax and shouting, while at the foot of the tree a number of buffaloes were collected.

When he saw me, the man called out, saying I had arrived just in time to save him and his buffaloes from a *shaitan* [devil] of a tiger, the size of a camel, that had been threatening them for hours. From his story I gathered that he had arrived on the hill shortly after Robin and I had left for home and that as he started to cut bamboo leaves for his buffaloes he saw a tiger coming toward him. He shouted to drive the tiger away as he had done on many previous occasions with other tigers, but instead of going away this one had started to growl. He took to his heels, followed by his buffaloes, and climbed up the nearest tree. The tiger, paying no heed to his shouts, had then set to pacing round and round, while the buffaloes kept their heads toward it. Probably the tiger had heard me coming, for it had left only a moment before I had arrived.

The man was an old friend, who before his quarrel with the headman of his village had done a considerable amount of poaching in these jungles with the headman's gun. He now begged me to conduct both himself and his cattle safely out of the jungle, so, telling him to lead on, I followed behind to see that there were no stragglers. At first the buffaloes were disinclined to break up their close formation, but after a little persuasion we got them to start. We had gone halfway across the open plain I have alluded to when the tiger called in the jungle to our right. The man quickened his pace, and I urged on the buffaloes, for a mile of very thick jungle lay between us and the wide, open watercourse beyond which lay my friend's village and safety for his buffaloes.

I have earned the reputation of being keener on photographing animals than on killing them, and before I left my friend he begged me to put aside photography for this once and kill the tiger, which he said was big enough to eat a buffalo a day, and thus ruin him in twenty-five days. I promised to do my best and turned to retrace my steps to the open plain, where I was to meet with an experience every detail of which has burned itself deep into my memory.

On reaching the plain, I sat down to wait for the tiger to disclose his whereabouts, or for the jungle folk to tell me where he was. It was then about 3:00 P.M., and as the sun was warm and comforting, I put my head down on my drawn-up knees and had been dozing a few minutes when I was awakened by the tiger calling; thereafter, he continued to call at short intervals.

Between the plain and the hills there is a belt, some half-mile wide, of the densest scrub jungle for a hundred miles round, and I located the tiger as being on the hills on the far side of the scrub—about three-quarters of a mile from me—and from the way he was calling it was evident he was in search of a mate. Starting from the upper left-hand corner of the plain and close to where I was sitting, an old cart track, used some years previously for extracting timber, ran in an almost direct line to where the tiger was calling from. This track would take me in the right direction. But on the hills there was high grass, and without Robin to help me there would be little chance of my seeing him. So instead of my going to look for the tiger, I decided that he should come and look for me.

I was too far away for him to hear me, so I sprinted up the cart track for a few hundred yards, laid down my rifle, climbed to the top of a high tree, and called three times. I was immediately answered by the tiger. After climbing down, I ran back, calling as I went, and arrived on the plain without having found a suitable place in which to sit and await the tiger. Something would have to be done and done in a hurry, for the tiger was rapidly coming nearer. So, after rejecting a little hollow that I found to be full of black, stinking water, I lay down flat in the open, twenty yards from where the track entered the scrub. From that point I had a clear view up the track for fifty yards, to where a bush, leaning over it, impeded my further view. If the tiger came down the track, as I expected him to, I decided to fire at him as soon as he cleared the obstruction.

After opening the rifle to make quite sure it was loaded, I threw off the safety catch, and with elbows comfortably resting on the soft ground waited for the tiger to appear. I had not called since I came out onto the plain, so to give him direction I now gave a low call, which he immediately answered from a distance of a hundred yards. If he came on at his usual pace, I judged he would clear the obstruction in thirty seconds. I counted this number very slowly, and went on counting up to eighty, when out of the corner of my eye I saw a movement to my right front, where the bushes approached to within ten yards of me. Turning my eyes in that direction I saw a great head projecting above the bushes, which here were four feet high. The tiger was only a foot or two inside the bushes, but all I could see of him was his head. As I very slowly swung the point of the rifle round and ran my eyes along the sights, I noticed that his head was not quite square on to me. I was firing up and he was looking down, so I aimed an inch below his right eye, pressed the trigger, and for the next half-hour nearly died of fright.

Instead of dropping dead as I had expected him to, the tiger went straight up into the air above the bushes for his full length, falling backward onto a tree a foot thick that had been blown down in a storm and was still green. With unbelievable fury he attacked this tree and tore it to bits, emitting as he did so roar upon roar, and what was even worse, a dreadful blood-curdling sound as though he was savaging his worst enemy. The branches of the tree tossed about as though struck by a tornado, while the bushes on my side shook and bulged out, and every moment I expected to have him on top of me, for he had been looking at me when I fired and knew where I was.

Too frightened even to recharge the rifle for fear that the slight movement and sound should attract the attention of the tiger, I lay and sweated for half an hour with my finger on the left trigger. At last the branches of the tree and the bushes ceased waving about, and the roaring became less frequent, and eventually, to my great relief, ceased. For another half-hour I lay perfectly still, with arms cramped by the weight of the heavy rifle, and then started to pull myself backward with my toes. After progressing for thirty yards in this manner I got to my feet and, crouching low, made for the welcome shelter of the nearest tree. There I remained for some minutes, and as all was now silent I turned and made for home.

Next morning I returned accompanied by one of my men, an expert tree climber. I had noticed the previous evening that there was a tree growing on the edge of the open ground, about forty yards from where the tiger had fallen. We approached this tree very cautiously, and I stood behind it while the man climbed to the top. After a long and a careful scrutiny he looked down and shook his head, and when he rejoined me on the ground he told me that the bushes over a big area had been flattened down but that the tiger was not in sight.

I sent him back to his perch on the tree with instructions to keep a sharp lookout and warn me if he saw any movement in the bushes. I then went forward to have a look at the spot where the tiger had raged. He had raged to some purpose, for, in addition to tearing branches and great strips of wood off the tree, he had torn up several bushes by the roots and bitten down others. Blood in profusion was sprinkled everywhere, and on the ground were two congealed pools, near one of which was lying a bit of bone two inches square, which I found on examination to be part of the tiger's skull.

No blood trail led away from this spot and that, combined with the two pools of blood, was proof that the tiger was still here when I had left and that the precautions I had taken the previous evening had been very necessary. When I started on my "get-away," I was only ten yards from the most dangerous animal in the world—a freshly wounded tiger. On circling the spot, I found a small smear of blood here and there on leaves that had brushed against his face. Noting that these indications of the tiger's passage led in a direct line to a giant semul tree *(Bombax malabaricum,* the silk cotton tree), two hundred yards away, I went back and climbed the tree where my man was. I wanted to get a bird's-eye view of the ground I should have to go over, for I had a very uneasy feeling that I should find him alive. A tiger shot in the head can live for days and can even recover from the wound. True, this tiger had a bit of his skull missing, and as I had never dealt with an animal in his condition before I did not know whether he was likely to live for a few hours or days, or live on to die of old age. For this reason I decided to treat him as an ordinary wounded tiger, and not to take any avoidable risks when following him up.

From my elevated position on the tree I saw that, a little to the left of the line to the semul tree, there were two trees, the nearer one thirty yards from where the blood was, and the other fifty yards farther on. Leaving my man on the tree, I climbed down, picked up my rifle and a shotgun and bag of a hundred cartridges, and very cautiously approached the nearer tree and climbed up it to a height of thirty feet, pulling the rifle and gun, which I had tied to one end of a strong cord, up after me.

After fixing the rifle in a fork of the tree where it would be handy if needed, I started to spray the bushes with small shot, yard by yard up to the foot of the second tree. I did this with the object of locating the tiger, which, on hearing a shot fired close to him or on being struck by a pellet, will either growl or charge. Receiving no indication of the tiger's presence I went to the second tree and sprayed the bushes to within a few yards of the semul tree, firing the last shot at the tree itself. After this last shot I thought I heard a low growl, but it was not repeated, so I put it down to my imagination. My bag of cartridges was now empty, so after recovering my man I called it a day and went home.

When I returned next morning, I found my friend the buffalo man feeding his buffaloes on the plain. He appeared to be very much relieved to see me, and the reason for this I learned later. The grass was still wet with dew, but we found a dry spot and there sat down to have a smoke and relate our experiences. My friend, as I have already told you, had done a lot of poaching, and, having spent all his life in tiger-infested jungles tending his buffaloes or shooting, his jungle knowledge was considerable.

After I had left him that day at the wide, open watercourse, he had crossed to the far side and had sat down to listen for sounds coming from the direction in which I had gone. He had heard two tigers calling, and he had heard my shot, followed by the continuous roaring of a tiger. Very naturally he

*Returning to the village with the Bachelor of Powalgarh.*

concluded that I had wounded one of the tigers and that it had killed me. On his return next morning to the same spot, he had been greatly mystified by hearing a hundred shots fired, and this morning, not being able to contain his curiosity any longer, he had come to see what had happened.

Attracted by the smell of blood, his buffaloes had shown him where the tiger had fallen, and he had seen the patches of dry blood and had found the bit of bone. No animal, in his opinion, could possibly live for more than a few hours after having a bit of its skull blown away, and so sure was he that the tiger was dead that he offered to take his buffaloes into the jungle and find it for me. I had heard of this method of recovering tigers with the help of buffaloes but had never tried it myself, and after my friend had agreed to accepting compensation for any damage to his cattle I accepted his offer.

Rounding up the buffaloes, twenty-five in number, and keeping to the line I had sprinkled with shot the previous day, we made for the semul tree, followed by the buffaloes. Our progress was slow, for not only had we to move the chin-high bushes with our hands to see where to put our feet, but we also had frequently to check a very natural tendency on the part of the buffaloes to stray. As we approached the semul tree, where the bushes were lighter, I saw a little hollow filled with dead leaves that had been pressed flat and on which were several patches of blood, some dry, others in process of congealing, and one quite fresh.

When I put my hand to the ground I found it was warm. Incredible as it may appear, the tiger had lain in this hollow the previous day while I had expended a hundred cartridges and had moved off only when he saw us and the buffaloes approaching. The buffaloes had now found the blood and were pawing up the ground and snorting; as the prospect of being caught between a charging tiger and angry buffaloes did not appeal to me, I took hold of my friend's arm, turned him round, and made for the open plain, followed by the buffaloes. When we were back on safe ground, I told the man to go home and said I would return next day and deal with the tiger alone.

The path through the jungles that I had taken each day ran for some distance over soft ground, and on this soft ground, on the fourth day, I found the pug marks of a big male tiger. By following these pug marks I found that the tiger had entered the dense brushwood a hundred yards to the right of the semul tree. Here was an unexpected complication, for if I now saw a tiger in this jungle I should not know—unless I got a very close look at it—whether it was the wounded or the unwounded one. However, that contingency would have to be dealt with when met, and in the meantime worrying would not help, so I entered the bushes and made for the hollow at the foot of the semul tree.

There was no blood trail to follow, so I zigzagged through the bushes, into which it was impossible to see farther than a few inches, for an hour or more, until I came to a ten-foot-wide dry watercourse. Before stepping down into this watercourse I looked up it and saw the left hind leg and tail of a tiger. The tiger was standing perfectly still with its body and head hidden by a tree, and only this one leg was visible. I raised the rifle to my shoulder, and then lowered it. To have broken the leg would have been easy, for the tiger was only ten yards away, and it would have been the right thing to do if its owner was the wounded animal, but there were two tigers in this area, and to have broken the leg of the wrong one would have doubled my difficulties, which were already considerable. Presently the leg was withdrawn, and I heard the tiger moving away. Going to the spot where he had been standing, I found a few drops of blood—too late, now, to regret not having broken that leg.

A quarter of a mile farther on there was a little stream, and it was possible that the tiger, now recovering from his wound, was making for this stream. With the object of intercepting him, or, failing that, waiting for him at the water, I took a game path that I knew went to the stream. I had proceeded along it for some distance when a sambar belled to my left and went dashing off through the jungle. It was evident now that I was abreast of the tiger, and I had taken only a few more steps when I heard the loud crack of a dry stick breaking as though some heavy animal had fallen on it. The sound had come from a distance of fifty yards and from the exact spot where the sambar had belled. The sambar had in unmistakable tones warned the jungle folk of the presence of a tiger, and the stick therefore could only have been broken by the same animal, so, getting down on my hands and knees I started to crawl in the direction from which the sound had come.

The bushes here were from six to eight feet high, with dense foliage on the upper branches and very few leaves on the stems, so I could see through them for a distance of ten to fifteen feet. I had covered thirty yards, hoping fervently that if the tiger charged he would come from in front (for in no other direction could I have fired), when I caught sight of something red on which the sun, drifting through the upper leaves, was shining. It might only be a bunch of dead leaves; on the other hand, it might be the tiger. I could get a better view of this object from two yards to the right, so, lowering my head until my chin touched the ground, I crawled that distance with belly to ground, and on raising my head saw the tiger in front of me. He was crouching down looking at me, with the sun shining on his left shoulder, and on receiving my two bullets he rolled over on his side without making a sound.

As I stood over him and ran my eyes over his magnificent proportions, it was not necessary to examine the pads of his feet to know that before me lay the Bachelor of Powalgarh. The entry of the bullet fired four days previously was hidden by a wrinkle of skin, and at the back of his head was a big hole which, surprisingly, was perfectly clean and healthy.

The report of my rifle was, I knew, being listened for, so I hurried home to relieve anxiety, and while I related the last chapter of the hunt and drank a pot of tea, my men were collecting. Accompanied by my sister and Robin and a carrying party of twenty men, I returned to where the tiger was lying, and before he was roped to a pole my sister and I measured him from nose to tip of tail, and from tip of tail to nose. At home we again measured him to make quite sure we had made no mistake the first time.

These measurements are valueless, for there were no independent witnesses present to certify them; they are, however, interesting as showing the accuracy with which experienced woodsmen can judge the length of a tiger from his pug marks. Wyndham, you will remember, said the tiger was ten feet between pegs, which would give roughly ten feet, six inches over curves, and while one shikari said he was ten feet, five inches over curves, the other said he was ten feet, six inches or a little more. Shot seven years after these estimates had been made, my sister and I measured the tiger as being ten feet, seven inches over curves.

I have told the story at some length, as I feel sure that those who hunted the tiger between 1920 and 1930 will be interested to know how the Bachelor of Powalgarh met his end.

## Chapter Twenty-Three

# James Sleeman
### From Rifle to Camera: The Reformation of a Big Game Hunter
### (1947)

Sir James Lewis Sleeman was a decorated soldier, a writer, and a sportsman. His long military career took him to the far corners of the British Empire. He fought in Europe in World War I and the South African Boer War and was stationed in India, New Zealand, and Africa.

Sleeman began his military and hunting career in India. He was posted in the Nepalese Terai, where he frequently shot tigers, bear, and other big game. These experiences were the basis of his first book on shikar, written in 1907. After that, most of his hunting took place in Africa. He did not hunt again in India until thirty years later, when he returned to the Terai for tigers.

This chapter is part of his last book, From Rifle to Camera, written in 1947 and subtitled The Reformation of a Big Game Hunter. In this story he shoots his last tiger and then decides to lay down his rifle for good. He is not antihunting, or even exceptionally conservation minded. His reasons are personal, and he states that "it is abnormal for a man to carry into old age a spirit of destruction." The book is really an autobiography and a memorial to his long hunting career. India was the site of his first hunt, and his last, in which, fittingly, he killed a trophy tiger. He left the Terai soon thereafter and never returned.

### The Last Tiger Shoot

It may seem somewhat illogical after what I have written that I should again participate in an ordinary big-game hunt, but that is not actually so. For while wild animal life can be approached by the aid of the motorcar in many parts of Africa, this, fortunately, is not the case with regard to tiger shooting in the deep jungles of India.

*The author and his first tiger, 1907.*

When, the following year, I went there for the fifth time, I therefore gladly availed myself of an opportunity to revisit the scenes that I had once known so well, being invited to shoot in the Nepal Terai, that mecca of tiger hunting, as a guest of the British Resident to the Court of the Maharaja of Nepal, Col. E. M. Bailey, CIE, an old friend and a good sportsman.

Following a long train journey, I was met toward evening on the edge of the jungle by a motor lorry, but I had traveled only a third of the way to the distant jungle camp when it broke down, and I had to wait in darkness for some hours before an elephant came to my rescue. There was more to it than that, for during the subsequent travel I ascertained from the mahout that, by an extraordinary coincidence, the elephant was one upon which I had shot my first tiger, thirty years before, while he was the son of the one who had served me so well on that occasion. This was to have a bearing upon what was to follow, for when my host was told, this notoriously staunch elephant was allotted to me for the shoot. It was a coincidence made the more remarkable in that this elephant was on its way to join the shoot after long travel.

The camp was pitched by the beautiful Sardar River, affording a view of snow-crested Himalayan Mountains in the far distance. At that season of the year much of it was dry, while many jungle-clad islands, temporarily approachable, formed ideal shelter for wild animal life.

Our six guns included Baron von Mannerheim, once regent of Finland, who proved a pleasant companion. With some twenty elephant and skilled shikaris and a block of jungle known to contain several tiger, it might appear to those unfamiliar with such hunting that it was merely a matter of days before success attended our efforts—especially as we had the enthusiastic help of those poor Indians resident on its outskirts to whom the loss of a few cattle spelled bankruptcy. For that reason, they were only too glad to provide the *puddahs,* or young buffalo, and, without that essential lure, few tiger could be accounted for in Indian jungles. If their use must ever cause a pang, a salve is afforded by the knowledge that most of them survive their nights of peril, while those few that fall victim thereby save the lives of hundreds of other animals if the tiger concerned is killed by means of their sacrifice. If the buffalo could reason, it would be different, but most *puddahs* spend their nights between sleep and abnormally generous feeding, blissfully unconscious of the part allotted to them.

In this connection it should be known that tiger, unlike lion, cannot be attracted by carrion but, as a general rule, eat what they kill. Given that a tiger kills on the average at least one animal per week during an adult life of perhaps fifteen years and that those Indians who live near the jungles cannot be armed (for then far greater animal suffering would result) and yet must be protected against an excessive increase of carnivora, what alternative offers? Perhaps the day will dawn when a synthetic *puddah* will be invented, or the atomic bomb will solve the problem, for there will always be found those prepared to use the latter for such purpose, of a type who would willingly shoot their own grandmothers for the gold fillings of their teeth, were it not a capital offense.

To revert to my story: Although we searched the deep jungle by day and placed our *puddahs* out by night, for all we saw of a tiger during the first week, there might not have been one in all India. By way of contrast, I once saw more than thirty lion in one day in Africa.

There are few sights that modernity has changed so little throughout the centuries as a tiger hunt in Nepal, which is full of intriguing interest.

Were it possible, for example, for my grandfather who had shot in these jungles over a century ago to have revisited the scene, he would have found little changed.

Our party, too, ran true to type, including a charming hostess, a "Heaven-born" (as senior Indian civil servants were once enviously called), and two eager young subalterns. All, with the exception of the baron and these latter, had previously shot tiger and were in consequence eager to see success come their way, for it was the shoot of a good sportsman. This meant much, seeing that there are some conducted shoots elsewhere in India in which the tiger are so astonishingly accommodating as to appear at the exact spot and moment laid down in the itinerary of distinguished visitors, and are invariably shot by those of the highest status, apparently being impervious to the bullets of all others. Those are shoots-de-luxe that offer the minimum of risk and discomfort while catering for those who pretend to an unconsciousness of how such amazing results are obtained, and who rest content with securing more tiger within a few days than fall to the lot of a skilled hunter in a working lifetime.

Yet this system of "Tiger on Tap" has to be used if tiger are to be shot according to a timetable. As proof of the difficulty of ensuring success when the shoot is genuine, the result of eight days of patient endeavour was nil, the subalterns having to depart disappointed.

Both shikaris and mahouts were by now depressed by failure and asked permission to propitiate the spirit who rules over such matters. A weird ceremony was held that night in the firelit jungle that, however seemingly futile, was destined to uphold the faith of the superstitious. For at crack of dawn came *khubber*, or information, of a tiger kill—that of a buffalo. This information was received with great exultation, for its pugs, or footprints, revealed that it was a large cattle-killing tiger, much feared in the neighbourhood both for his boldness and aggression—a type that too often turns to man-killing.

The kill had taken place close to a long and narrow jungle-clad island in a temporarily dry part of the riverbed, and soon our elephant had forded the deep channel that separated it from camp, and we were making toward it. Not long after, my mahout drew my attention to an immense tiger pug in the soft sand. We found where the tiger had dragged his kill into the jungle. To the uninitiated it might seem that the rest would be a foregone conclusion, seeing that we were so well provided with skilled shikaris and beating elephant. But such an impression would fail to take into account the high intelligence and resourcefulness of a tiger, its power of concealment, and the character of the cover it favours.

Now followed a long beat, during which the island was combed from end to end, a search so thorough as to make it incredible that the tiger could still be there. This opinion was made all the stronger by the elephant having given no sign of danger, such as they usually do by compressing air in their trunks and releasing it by hitting the tip against the ground, which produces a curious popping sound, not unlike the bursting of a series of paper bags.

But as, meanwhile, no sign had been found of the tiger's departure in the soft sand by which the island was surrounded, a second effort was determined upon—following a much needed lunch. That, too, proved equally fruitless until we reached the last remaining expanse of tiger grass. By now the day was drawing on, and it seemed that our search was doomed to failure. A ring of elephants was now thrown round this area of several acres in extent. To watch them separating alternately, one going to the right and the other to the left, and disappearing into a vast tangle of high grass or jungle, makes it seem impossible that they will ever join up again. How, indeed, the mahouts accomplish this remains as great a mystery to me as that by which they maintain such silent contact with one another although widely separated, when beating through dense jungle for hours on end, that at any given time they are able to re-establish union.

The height of the grass was such that all that I could see when the ring was completed were the two elephant on either side, which, like my own, were now engaged in trampling down the grass and leveling the light timber about them, in order to afford a better chance of a shot in the event of the tiger's being found. They did this with their customary cleverness, and when they had prepared the way, a "beating-up" elephant entered the "ring" opposite my elephant, carrying in addition to her mahout and head shikari a semi-naked youth standing astride her rump and holding on by a rope, ready to stimulate progress in emergency with a nail-studded club.

In such stupendous cover, a tiger will often sit as tight as a crafty old cock pheasant, and had that happened in this instance, we should have been none the wiser and thought it yet another case of drawing blank. More than a dozen times that day, this same elephant had been called upon to perform this uncongenial task without unpleasant results; consequently, she now proceeded on her way with an air verging between the blasé and the jaunty.

*The author and his last tiger, 1937.*

Scarcely had she disappeared, however, when there came a terrific "woof-woof," that characteristic challenge of a charging tiger, mingled with the shrill trumpeting of a badly frightened elephant and the approaching sounds of her rapid retirement.

There was a humorous side to the picture as she shot into the open, for the totally unnecessary human accelerator balanced on her agitated stern emerged like some grotesque May queen bedecked with pampaslike plumes. Although so aggressive as to have attacked without provocation, the tiger was prudent enough to stay his progress just before he must otherwise have showed. Soon I could see by the movements of the grass that he was returning toward the centre.

Female elephants are usually entrusted with the more dangerous tasks, being generally more reliable than the males, but this one had suffered such a shock that it was with difficulty that she could be persuaded to try again. Eventually, coaxing, plus the less pleasant attentions of the underclad "whipper-in," persuaded her reluctantly to re-enter the arena and to pass once more from sight. Within a few minutes, there was a repetition of the first act, the angry roar of the tiger, the shrill trumpeting of the elephant, and the rapid return to the open, until, when two further attempts had failed in the same way, it became clear that the tiger was determined not to make his appearance.

By now the sun was on the point of setting, and my host came up and invited me to enter the "ring" to try my luck alone, seeing that all else had failed and that little of daylight remained. Jumping at the chance and acting on the assumption that the tiger would think mine to be the beating elephant returning for a further dose of frightfulness, I followed the same line into the grass. I was soon greeted by the menacing challenge and crash of grass as the tiger charged. Although standing, with eye level fully seventeen feet above the ground, all that I could see of this were the grass plumes moving toward me a foot or so below. This time, however, there was to be no "strategic withdrawal," for my staunch elephant stood his ground like a rock. To save him from a mauling, I fired blindly in the direction of the tiger's coming.

To quote that overworked and inept journalese, as my shot "rang out," all noise and movement ceased, as if by some lucky fluke I had killed. Many have been the fatal accidents due to such fond imaginings! Even I, with experience of many similar happenings, felt a certain optimism when seconds lengthened into minutes without a sound from a direction so shortly before made sinister with evil melody. Time had now become the essence of the contract, for it was already growing dark in that formidable cover, and presently I made the mahout take his elephant slowly forward, in the hope that a dead tiger would be revealed. Within a few yards, bent and broken grass showed where its charge had ended, but that was all! Without the slightest sound or sign of movement, the tiger had gone!

Nothing now remained but to quarter the grass, and that we did until the tiger charged again, once more to be stopped by an undirected shot. By this time night was approaching so rapidly that I recall looking at my wristwatch and determining that, unless I could kill within a further ten minutes, the chase must be abandoned. For to wound a tiger in darkness might easily result in grave harm to my elephant, and perhaps create a future man-eater.

It was then that I recalled an admirable tip given by the best Scots gillie I have ever been out with: "When in doubt, look for colour" (that is, the curious tint of the red deer). Although the yellow body and black stripes of a tiger enable it to blend into such grass to an amazing degree, there is just a detectable difference, caused by its undershadow, and seizing upon this forlorn hope, I abandoned further movement and, foot by foot, gazed methodically up each narrow channel of grass from right to left. In few places was it possible to see farther than a few yards, except where the grass had been disturbed by the tiger's charge. When, however, I came to the last limited avenue of vision, I seemed to detect a faint difference of colour some twenty yards away, one so slight that I at first dismissed it from my mind as imaginary and turned to look elsewhere.

It has been my experience that one somehow senses when a dangerous animal is watching one closely, and this subconscious feeling soon became so strong that I was compelled to look back again. Was it merely a figment of desire born from anxious hope, or did I detect a slight movement? I thought I did and aimed at the suspected patch of shadow. Again I was undecided and had brought my rifle down when it suddenly resolved itself into a huge and angry tiger, coughing his hate and in full charge! Fortunately I was ready and hit him so hard that he fell over and lay as if dead. It is at such moments that the overly punctilious or the novice can make costly mistakes, for the former will refrain from putting in a further shot for fear of detracting from initial prowess, while the latter is prone to suffer from the impression that if a tiger stays motionless it is dead. Whole cemeteries could be filled with the mortal remains of those who have paid the price of such folly. Not being a member of that suicide club, I therefore gave him the second barrel, this time aiming at his head. The wisdom of this was shown by the tiger's responding by rising to his feet before falling dead, which showed that, although mortally wounded, he had retained sufficient vitality to be capable of doing great harm.

It was now so gloomy that only the fact that I was carrying a Leica Summar camera, with its wonderful 1.2 lens, enabled me to get a photograph, and even a few minutes later, that would have been impossible. That taken by my other camera, with a 4.5 lens, was little better than a blur.

Throughout this episode, those outside the high grass knew nothing of these happenings, but my host soon reached the scene. I was delighted to be told that though he had been present at the "ringing" of many a tiger, this was the first he had known killed within one by a solitary gun.

Next followed the Nepalese system of measurement, which is direct between point of nose and tip of tail. This is a disappointing method for those who are prone to exaggerate, for it reduces the size of a tiger that could, by the usual system of following the curves, be made to measure well over ten feet, to just a fraction under that length (in spite of the tail's being exceptionally short) but still within the record class. In perfect condition, he was not only the largest but also the finest tiger in my experience. Previous success with tiger does not, however, exonerate one in Nepal from the "blooding" ceremony, for now, although I had shot others before, I was called upon to endure having my face and ears smeared with blood by the head shikari.

Before me as I write hangs a frame containing two photographs, one of a radiant subaltern with his first tiger in 1907, the other of an aged former brigade commander with his last one, almost exactly thirty years later—one and the same person. It is an unusual record in an India that does not suffer old men gladly, and one that I think few Britons can claim.

This last experience of hunting had, however, shown me that, in the interim, my sympathy for wild animal life had grown to such a degree that throughout this shoot I had felt no desire to kill beyond that of ridding the neighbourhood of a menace, the fear of which overshadowed the existence of the Indians living near. Call it sentimentality, call it what you will, I prefer to think that it is abnormal for a man to carry into old age a spirit of destruction. Nor was the sensation new to me, for it had been growing upon me ever since my visit to Africa, and now, when I looked upon this tiger's fearful symmetry stretched out in death, it suddenly came to me that here was the opportunity to end my shooting career on a good wicket, so to speak, and to resolve to exchange the rifle for the camera at a propitious moment.

This resolution was quickly put to the test, for next morning came news of another kill, which culminated in the tiger concerned being located in high grass surrounded by light jungle. "Nothing succeeds like success" is an axiom well exemplified in tiger hunting, where shikari and mahout, naturally enough, are apt to place faith in those who have previously met with good fortune, even if accidental. Knowing this from past experience, and knowing also that my host was eager for Baron von Mannerheim to get the shot, I took particular pains to explain to the head shikari on the way out that I wished to be placed anywhere but where the tiger might be expected to appear, should it be located.

With an assurance that he had selected the negative position I desired, he departed to take charge of the drive. But I had served a long apprenticeship in such hunting, and, knowing my India, I had detected a suspicious glint in his eye, so when he had gone I invited the baron to take my place and had my elephant moved elsewhere. Scarcely had I done so when a tigress broke cover exactly where I had been stationed, falling dead to a magnificent shot from von Mannerheim's rifle.

Being now due to return to duty, I left that pleasant camp after dinner and traveled through the darkness on my faithful elephant and with two Nepalese puppies, saddened by the knowledge that I was leaving those fascinating jungles forever. On arrival at the railway, a tent was pitched for my shelter until the arrival of my train at dawn, after which my loyal mahout started back to camp, while my bearer went off to a neighbouring village, there to indulge in that interminable chatter that forms a great part of their lives and generally revolves about women, money, and water.

I was sitting outside my tent alone, and in somewhat melancholy mood, when, to my glad surprise, my elephant loomed silently out of the darkness, and I found that my mahout had returned in order to pay what he knew to be a last farewell to one who had hunted with his father before him. Dismounting, he salaamed, and expressed his sorrow at the parting in a simple and pleasing fashion—a regret shared by me, for he had proved a brave and reliable mahout, without whose aid I could not have got the tiger. One will travel far to meet the equal of an unspoiled Indian. This homage was quite genuine, for he had already his reward and now refused an additional gift.

Indeed this little drama played in the silence of the night affected us both, for I realized that never again would I revisit those scenes of yesterday. Twice had I shot tiger from this same elephant without his suffering a scratch, and I like to think that he remembered this, seeing that elephant are said never to forget. For when the mahout had remounted and was on the point of departure, the elephant stretched out his trunk and gave my arm the softest of caresses before lifting it in a last salaam. Then they melted into the darkness of the night like a dream, and my last contact with those glamorous jungles had ended. In the full blaze of an Indian hot-weather day had I first entered them thirty-four years before, and in the full zest of youth, and there was therefore something curiously fitting that I should be saying good-bye in the darkness of night. My feeling was akin to that at the fall of the final curtain on the long run of an attractive play.

### Chapter Twenty-Four

# Olive Smythies
## Tiger Lady
### (1953)

There were several notable female tiger hunters in British India, including Mary Hastings Bradley and Ingrid Sucksdorff. The best known, however, was Olive Smythies, who wrote two books on her many hunting adventures, as well as on nature and local culture. But, in her words, she most wanted to chronicle "her duties and life" as a forester's wife.

Olive came to India at age eighteen to marry Evelyn Smythies shortly before he embarked on his career with the Indian Forest Service. The couple spent the next thirty years posted in various places in the Himalayan foothills of northern India, including a stint in Nepal. Evelyn's job took him to many remote forest destinations, and Olive usually accompanied him. Hunting was always their favorite pastime, especially ghooming, or wandering in the forest on elephant back to see what creatures they would encounter. She was an intrepid adventurer and a keen hunter who shot many tigers and other big game during her stay in India.

This chapter is from Smythies's first book, *Tiger Lady (1953)*, which takes place in the Terai of northwestern India. She entitles it a "great adventure." Near tragedy is more accurate, though, as Olive almost lost her life to an angry, injured tiger who climbed up into her machan and came within inches of killing her. Yet she escaped almost unharmed.

### A Great Adventure

The Christmas following our return to India marked the greatest adventure of my life! We had invited a friend, Major Percy Dodd, to spend Christmas with us at Jaulasal, in the Haldwani Division. We met him at Lalkua, a small station on the O&T Railway, whence we traveled on two trolleys along the forest tramway to our bungalow at Chorgalia. The tramway runs through forest in which live all kinds of wild animals: elephants, tigers, leopards, and deer of several species that can sometimes be seen from the line. But on that day we were disappointed to see nothing except langurs and a variety of birds.

We spent the night at the forest bungalow at Chorgalia ("place of thieves") and next morning set out on two elephants to do the nine-mile march to Jaulasal along the Kandi Sarak, a road that runs for 150 miles along the foot of the hills from the frontier of Nepal to the Ganges. Here it passes through dense forests of sal interspersed with grassy savannas—some of the best country for big game in the whole of India.

Jaulasal is a really lovely place. The forest bungalow is on a low ridge from which one looks northward up a small valley down which a stream, that has risen in the hills nearby, runs in several small channels. Between the channels are copses of shisham and khair trees, and patches of tall grasses, a favourite haunt of tiger. Once, when *ghooming*, we shot one only one hundred yards from the ridge and within sight of the bungalow. To the south lies a large plain surrounded by dense sal forest where live innumerable deer.

Our guest, Major Dodd, had never shot a tiger, so we decided to set to work and get one for him. We tied up five or six buffaloes every night on the fire lines and jungle roads in a radius of three or four miles from the bungalow. At daybreak we visited one or two of these ourselves, hoping that if there had been a kill we might catch the tiger before he had left to lie up for the day. Forest guards and orderlies in pairs visited the remaining baits, which, if still alive, they brought home. The tigers in this part of the jungle obtain so much natural food that they often pass a buffalo bait untouched.

We had no kill till Christmas Day, although we knew from the footprints that there were several tigers about. On 25 December, forest guards brought news that a buffalo had been killed about three miles to the east on a fire line. We started off on two elephants loaded with machans and ropes. We all had rifles. Major Dodd and my husband were on one elephant, and I was on the other. As we were going up the forest road we met a blind beggar, and we gave him a rupee for luck.

We found that the buffalo had been dragged some way into the forest. We followed the drag cautiously and slowly, keeping a keen lookout ahead for any glimpse of the tiger, and found the carcass well hidden under shrubs. There was a good tree for the machan, which the orderlies began to put up as silently

*Olive and her husband Evelyn with their "ghooming" elephant.*

as possible. We moved off on our two elephants to divert the tiger's attention from these operations, in case he were nearby, and to find him if possible.

We had not gone far when the mahout stopped his elephant and we saw a tiger thirty yards away staring at us. Major Dodd took steady aim and fired, hitting the tiger in the brain. The beast fell where he stood, and we were able to load him up and take him back to the camp.

The next day Major Dodd had a telegram recalling him to his regiment, so the remainder of the shoot fell rather flat, especially as my husband was busy with his work. I decided, however, to wander out alone. On 29 December I saw nothing all day and felt distinctly bored. Then, the next day, a forest guard brought in news that a buffalo had been killed in the famous Riala beat (three miles to the west of Jaulasal, right up against the foothills), where many tigers have met their fate, and where I nearly came to a tragic end.

The buffalo had been tied near a small stream adjacent to some heavy jungle and terrific narkul grass—a perfect lie-up for a tiger. We decided to have a beat, and it was Evelyn's turn to have the number one machan. We were not very excited about it, and I remember spending a busy morning with the washerman and mending clothes.

After an early lunch we set out with our two elephants loaded with machan, and so on. A forest guard, orderlies, and a few coolies accompanied us. On nearing the place where the buffalo had been killed, my husband and I climbed down from the elephants. The machans, ropes, and rope ladder were loaded on the coolies, and we made our way on foot, making a large detour behind a ridge in order to avoid disturbing the tiger. We wore rubber shoes and walked as silently as we could, uttering not a word. I know I went on tip-toe most of the way, which is extremely tiring when kept up for half a mile. At last we reached the spot behind all the thick cover where we hoped the tiger was lying up.

The tiger invariably breaks cover here by a certain tree. In this tree my husband's machan was tied. Another tree was chosen for my machan, behind and slightly to the north, about fifty yards from tree Number One. Our orderlies were adept at tying up these seats. Our machans were made of four pieces of wood (like a frame for needlework, but about 2½ feet square), laced across with twine. They had iron rings at the four corners through which ropes were slung and tied to convenient branches on the tree. I watched the men erecting my machan—a task they performed with great care and with the minimum of noise. I did not know then that my life depended upon the quality of their work.

At last all was ready, and I climbed up a rope ladder to my machan, which seemed to have been placed unusually high. I hated climbing rope ladders, but again my life depended upon the fact that the machan was a good height above the ground. A few moments later the orderlies untied the ladder and I was left alone in the tree.

My husband also ascended to his place by the rope ladder, and sat with his back to me, facing the thick cover where we hoped the tiger lay. I could see my husband over my right shoulder.

The orderlies and forest guards climbed up trees to act as stops in case the tiger should try to break to the right or left. One man returned to the elephants to tell the mahouts that all was ready for the beat to begin.

I felt a little nervous and apprehensive as I waited. I scrutinized my tree to see if I could climb any higher should the tiger attack me, but realized that this was impossible. I had not camouflaged myself in any way with leaves, thinking it unnecessary to do so in a beat. I was armed with my .256 Mannlicher, not a suitable weapon for tiger shooting, but having accounted for four tigers with it I felt pretty confident so far as my weapon was concerned. My husband carried a .400-450 high-velocity double-barrel rifle.

A long time seemed to elapse before I heard the noise of elephants moving through thick grass. The beat was done with only two elephants. Our wonderful mahout, Bisharat Ali, was on one of them, quite unarmed except for the *gujbar*, an iron spike with a hook attached. With this weapon he controlled or punished the elephant by jabbing it into its head or ear.

The elephants came nearer and nearer, and I saw my husband raise his rifle and fire. The tiger had walked out of the grass well in front of the elephants, but I had not seen it. At the shot, the beast bounded back into cover, roaring and growling furiously, but quite uninjured.

For a long time the tiger lay up in the terrific grass and refused to move. When the elephants tried to advance he roared and demonstrated. Once he charged Bisharat Ali's elephant, but she stood her ground while Bisharat shouted and threatened with his iron hook. The other elephant did not possess such magnificent courage and fled from the scene until stopped by her mahout.

I heard the awful noise that was taking place and felt extremely worried. I imagined that the tiger had been wounded and was attacking the elephants, and realizing that the mahouts were unarmed I was fearful for their safety.

In order to force the tiger out of the grass, Bisharat Ali sent his elephant directly into a small tree, which cracked and fell almost on top of the tiger. The infuriated animal, moving fast and roaring loudly, bounded out toward my husband's tree. I saw my husband raise his rifle and fire, and then the tiger galloped off in a northeasterly direction. Whether the beast had been hit or not I did not know, for tigers will often dash off thus when fatally wounded. I took hasty aim and fired when the animal was crossing my front about fifty yards away. The tiger crashed over at my shot and lay rolling on the ground. I decided to try to finish him off with one shot and, taking careful aim at his neck, fired again.

The tiger was throwing himself all over the place, and the neck is indeed a bad target under those conditions. My shot proved as bad as my decision, and I missed him completely. Then I saw the tiger raise himself on his front legs, turn, and look straight at me. The next moment he charged at my tree, roaring hideously. I thought he must be dashing past, but to my intense horror I realized that he was climbing up the tree like a cat. I only just had time to stand up on my machan, which was slung out from the trunk of the tree.

While I was doing so, I pulled back the bolt of my rifle and slipped the third cartridge of my clip of five into the breech.

The tiger arrived up at the machan almost instantaneously and seized the front part of it in his teeth (if I had not stood up he would have had me by the legs), with one paw on the right of the machan and the other on the left, so that I had only a very small space to stand on at the back.

I felt too frightened to be afraid, if that can be possible. I thought that if I put my rifle in his mouth and fired, the beast would be killed forthwith. His mouth was open, so I pushed the rifle between his front fangs (the teeth marks were afterward found nine inches up the barrel) and pulled the trigger, and kept on pulling. But nothing happened. A misfire!

I felt as if I were having a nightmare. How could I cope with such a desperate situation? The tiger had one end of my rifle, and I had the other. The barrel of it was clacking about between his teeth, and as he roared blood spattered all over me.

I might, I suppose, have ejected the bad cartridge and loaded another, but it would not have been easy with the rifle swaying about. No doubt the clip would have jumped out, as it had a habit of doing. But in any event I was too confused by now to think of trying to load another cartridge. All I could think of was to withdraw the barrel from the tiger's mouth, if I could, and hit him on the head with the stock. I was about to try this when the tiger's paw, with which he had been scratching all this time on the right of the machan, came through the string seat, tearing a great hole in it. The next moment the beast had grabbed at my legs. To avoid his claws I stepped hastily backward, quite forgetting in my dilemma that I was in a tree. There was no question of throwing myself from the tree. I simply found myself with no foothold, and fell!

As I did so I imagined I was going straight into the tiger's mouth. I remember thinking, *Surely I am not going to be killed like this!* By now I was so terrified that I must have lost consciousness. I can recollect nothing of my fall, but I must have turned a complete somersault and landed on my feet. My body was not even bruised; only my left wrist, which I must have used as I reached the ground to break my fall, was sprained.

The next thing I remember is coming to my senses when I ran into a fallen tree. I think I must have straightened myself up immediately upon reaching the ground and run quite unconsciously, fortunately in the right direction. Now I was in control of my faculties again, I imagined the tiger would be after me, and I wondered whether to try to hide or whether to run on. I decided upon the latter course, and again fortune took me toward the tree where my husband was ensconced. I looked up and saw him staring at me with his eyes starting out of his head. I saw his mouth working, but no sound reached me.

I must now go back again and relate what my husband had been doing in the meantime. During my nightmarish adventure I had completely forgotten he was anywhere near me. When he had fired the second shot at the tiger and it had galloped off toward me, he had turned hastily in his machan (it will be remembered he had his back turned toward me), and in doing so had swept all his spare cartridges off the machan onto the ground. He had only one cartridge left in his rifle and one in his pocket.

He had seen me fire and had shouted "Good shot" as he saw the tiger fall. He had watched me fire my second shot, and then to his horror and amazement the tiger had charged me. He could scarcely believe his eyes when he saw the beast climbing my tree.

He realized, of course, that he must do something at once, and had fired at the tiger when it was halfway up the tree. His bullet had hit the tiger but had not wounded it mortally. Moreover, he had to take the risk of hitting me, which had unnerved him extremely. He had then to reload, and while he was doing this he saw me having my tussle with the tiger, my rifle in its mouth. He had fired again—his last cartridge—fully realizing that my life depended upon his shot. By the grace of God his bullet went true and found the tiger's heart.

I had not heard either of these shots. Just before he fired the last shot, my husband told me, he saw my headlong fall from the tree, and later the tiger fell almost on top of me. He could not see much of what happened on the ground because of the underwood and grass, and he did not know what was happening. He dreaded to hear my screams if the tiger were mauling me. His agony of mind can well be imagined. There he was, powerless to do any more, while I was on the ground, probably being killed by a tiger mad with fury. He yelled frantically to the mahouts to bring up the elephants.

When he saw me running toward his tree he was, of course, tremendously relieved to see that I was alive and apparently unharmed. He shouted that help was coming, and almost immediately I saw Bisharat Ali tearing up on his elephant.

All this time I expected the tiger to spring onto me at any moment. Usually I had to be helped onto an elephant by someone holding its tail to make a step for me, but Bisharat Ali gave me a hand, leaning down from where he sat on

*The author with the skin of the tiger that almost killed her.*

the elephant's neck. I put my foot on the elephant's knee, and the mahout hauled me up by way of the trunk.

I collapsed onto the pad, and, still thinking the tiger might be on us at any second, I told Bisharat to make off as quickly as possible down the stream. I was now unarmed, having left my rifle in the tiger's mouth. After going a little way we stopped. I was beginning to feel the reaction to the shock I had suffered. My teeth were chattering, and I was shivering violently. I was conscious of a sharp pain in my wrist.

Bisharat Ali was very concerned because my face was covered with blood. He feared that I had been scratched by the tiger, and I had to reassure him many times that the marks on my face were due to my falling over the tree, which had brought me back to consciousness, while the blood he saw had been spat over me by the tiger.

Meanwhile the other elephant brought my husband from his machan. He, too, needed much reassuring about the scratches and the blood. Had the scratches been done by the claws of the tiger, it would have been a serious matter for me: We were two days' journey from a doctor, and a tiger's claws are highly poisonous.

A stop, who had been in the tree near mine, had climbed to the topmost branch of his refuge and had witnessed the whole incident. He now shouted that he could see the tiger lying dead at the foot of the tree. My husband, having retrieved his lost cartridges, went over to make sure that this was so. I told him to leave the tiger where it lay, for I never wished to see it again. My request was ignored, however, and he had the tiger loaded up before he joined me on my elephant. We went back to the bungalow, where I had a large dollop of whiskey in my tea. The tiger, a male, measured nine feet, six inches round the curves.

In some ways I had been fortunate, but in others I had been most unlucky. I was fortunate in that the machan had held firm, for had the ropes broken under my weight and that of the tiger I should have had no chance of survival. Moreover, it was almost miraculous that I had not been injured when I fell fifteen feet backward. On the other hand it was most unlucky that I should have had a dud cartridge when the barrel of my rifle was in the tiger's mouth. And it was most unusual, if not unprecedented, for the tiger to climb to a machan.

My husband and I would have liked to keep the whole incident a secret, thinking that our friends might be scornful of the mess we had made of it all, but it proved impossible to keep the matter to ourselves. The mahouts and orderlies were very excited, and the tale spread far and wide.

We moved camp after a few days and reached the small railway junction of Lalkua, where the stationmaster gave a tea party to celebrate my escape. We had a splendid tea complete with gramophone recital in the station yard, and after tea our photographs were taken. Somebody who was at this show sent an account of the tiger hunt to a Calcutta newspaper. Reuters got hold of it and cabled the news to England, where it was published in several newspapers with, unfortunately, many inaccuracies. My husband's parents saw it in print before they received an account of the adventure from ourselves.

Numerous garbled and ridiculous versions of the story have been printed. For example, Count Apponyi, in his book *My Big Game Hunting Diary*, writes as follows: "The lady fired point-blank but missed. . . . After thrusting her rifle barrel into the tiger's mouth, and hearing that the cartridge had missed fire, she had in her horror thrown herself off the machan, because she feared the tiger would climb up, and she thought she would be safer on the ground." The truth is that I neither missed the tiger at point-blank range, nor did I intentionally throw myself out of the tree!

One of my husband's contractors asked for permission to hold a fete in honour of my deliverance from the tiger. This took place at Chorgalia. Hundreds of people were present, and my husband's little tramline ran a special train for the occasion. There were dancing girls, fireworks, a band, and food was given to the poor, and I was presented with a wonderful address framed in a gilt surround. Later a monolith was erected at Jaulasal near the range quarters on the Kandi Sarak, with the following inscription:

> This pillar is erected by the forest contractors and staff of Jaulasal Range in memory of the bravery displayed by Mrs. E. A. Smythies in her hand-to-hand fight with a tiger on 30.12.25, and in thankfulness for her deliverance from this great danger.

For some years after this adventure, if I had any nervous strain or became overtired, I had terrible nightmares and used to wake up screaming. Once I woke to find myself screaming in the corridor of a Swiss hotel. I hastily returned to my room, but heard many doors opening as people came out of their rooms to see who was being murdered. Another time I awoke screaming in some seaside lodgings. The landlady was so alarmed that she jumped out of bed and sprained her toe against a wardrobe! These reactions, fortunately, lasted only a few years, after which period I completely recovered and shot several more tigers.

### Chapter Twenty-Five

# Kenneth Anderson
### Nine Man-Eaters and One Rogue
### (1954)

Kenneth Anderson's renown as a tiger hunter and writer is second only to that of Jim Corbett. In some ways he was the more significant in the annals of tiger hunting. He wrote more books than any other hunter (eight) and witnessed the rapid changes in hunting after Indian independence in 1947. Regulations became so lax by the late 1960s that the tiger almost became extinct, leading to a total hunting ban in 1968.

Anderson remained in India after independence, when most Europeans left for good. He worked as a civil servant in the city of Bangalore, near the Western Ghats. The Ghats were Anderson's hunting and naturalist getaway, and he spent as much time there as he could. Many of his adventures take place in the same locales as had G. P. Sanderson's almost a century earlier. Like Sanderson, Anderson was called upon by the government to shoot man-eating tigers and cattle lifters. Most of his writings recount those experiences.

Anderson gave up hunting completely toward the end of his life and died in 1973, the year that Project Tiger, which gave total protection to the animal, was established in India. This chapter is from his first book, Nine Man-Eaters and One Rogue *(1954)*. Here Anderson stalks the notorious Jowlagiri man-eater who terrorized the Salem district of southern India for many months before Anderson finally ended her career.

### The Man-Eater of Jowlagiri

Those who have been to the tropics and to jungle places will not need to be told of the beauties of the moonlight over hill and valley, which picks out in vivid relief the forest grasses and each leaf of the giant trees and throws into still greater mystery the dark shadows below, where the rays of the moon cannot reach, concealing perhaps a beast of prey, a watchful deer, or a lurking reptile, all individually and severally in search of food.

All appeared peaceful in the Jowlagiri Forest Range, yet there was danger everywhere, and foul play was afoot. A trio of poachers, who possessed between them two matchlocks of ancient vintage, had decided to get themselves some meat. They had cleverly constructed a hide on the sloping banks of a water hole and had been sitting in it since sunset, intently watchful for the deer that, sooner or later, must come to slake their thirst.

The hours wore on. The moon, at the full, had reached mid-heaven, and the scene was as bright as day. Suddenly, from the thicket of evergreen saplings to their left, could be heard the sound of violently rustling leaves and deep-throated grunts. What could be there? Wild pig, undoubtedly! A succulent meal, and flesh in addition that could be sold! The poachers waited, but the beasts, whatever they were, did not break cover. Becoming impatient, Muniappa, the marksman of the trio, decided to risk a shot. Raising his matchlock, he waited till a dark shadow, deeper than its surroundings, became more evident, and fired. There was a snarling roar and a lashing of bushes, followed by a series of coughing whoofs and then silence.

Not pigs, but a tiger! Fearfully and silently the three poachers beat a hasty retreat to their village, there to spend the rest of the night in anxiety as to the result of their act. But morning revealed that all was apparently well, for a male tiger just in his prime lay dead, the chance shot from the ancient musket having sped straight to his heart. So Muniappa and his friends were, for that day, the unsung and whispered heroes of the village.

But the next night produced a different story. With sunset came the urgent, angry call of a tigress seeking her dead mate. For it was the mating season, and this tigress, which had only just succeeded in finding her companion the night before, was decidedly annoyed at his unaccountable absence, which she quite rightly connected with the interference of human beings.

Night after night for a week she continued her uneasy movements, calling by day from the depths of the forest and in darkness roaring almost at the outskirts of the village itself.

Young Jack Leonard, who was keen to secure a trophy, and who had been summoned to the village by an urgent letter, arrived on the morning of the eighth day and acquainted himself with the situation. Being told that the tiger wandered everywhere, and seeing her many pug marks on the

*The author with his trusty companion Nipper.*

lonely path to the forest bungalow, he decided to try his luck that evening, concealing himself by five o'clock behind an anthill that stood conveniently beside the path.

The minutes passed, and at 6:15 P.M. dusk was falling. Suddenly there was a faint rustle of leaves and a loose stone rolled down the bank a little to his right. Leonard strained his eyes for the first sight of the tigress, but nothing happened. The minutes passed again. And then, rapidly moving along the edge of the road toward him, and on the same side as himself, he could just discern the form of the tigress. Hastily transferring the stock of his rifle to his left shoulder, and leaning as far out from his sheltering bush as possible, so that he might see more of the animal, Leonard fired at her chest what would have been a fatal shot had it carried a little more to the right.

As it was, Leonard's bullet plowed deeply into the right shoulder, causing the beast to roar loudly before crashing away into the jungle. Bitterly disappointed, Leonard waited till morning to follow the trail. There was abundance of blood everywhere, but because of the rocky and difficult country, interspersed with densely wooded ravines and close, impenetrable shrubbery, he failed to catch up with his quarry.

Months passed, and the scene changes to Sulekunta, a village deeper in the forest and about seven miles from Jowlagiri, where there was a little temple occasionally visited by pilgrims from the surrounding region. Three of these had finished their devotions and were returning to their home: a man, his wife, and son aged sixteen. Passing under a wild tamarind tree, hardly a quarter-mile from the temple, the boy lingered to pick some of the half-ripe acid fruit. The parents heard a low growl, followed by a piercing, agonized scream, and looked back to see their son carried bodily in the jaws of a tiger, as it leaped into a nullah bordering the lonely path. The aged couple bravely turned back and shouted abuse at the marauder as best they could, only to be answered by two more shrieks from their only son; then all was silent.

Thereafter, death followed death over a wide area, extending from Jowlagiri in the extreme north to the cattle pen of Gundalam, thirty miles to the south; and from the borders of Mysore State, twenty miles to the west, to the main road to Denkanikottai, for about forty-five miles of its length. Some fifteen victims, including three girls, one just married, had fallen prey to this monster when I received an urgent summons from my friend, the subcollector of Hosur, to rid the area of the scourge.

Journeying to Jowlagiri where the subcollector told me the trouble had begun, I pieced together the facts of the story, deducing that this was no tiger but a tigress, and the one that had been robbed of her mate by the poachers and later wounded by Leonard's plucky but unfortunate shot. From Jowlagiri I tramped to Sulekunta in the hope of coming across the fresh pug marks of the marauder, but I was unlucky, for no kills had occurred at that place in recent days, and what tracks there were had been obliterated by passing herds of cattle. Moving on to Gundalam, twenty-three miles away at the southern limit of the affected area, I decided to pitch camp since it was at this cattle pen that the majority of kills had been reported, seven herdsmen being accounted for in the last four months.

Three fat buffalo calves had been very thoughtfully provided as bait by my friend the subcollector; I proceeded to tie them out at likely spots in the hope of securing a kill. The first I tethered a mile down the river bordering Gundalam, at that time of the year a mere trickle of water at a point where the river was joined by a tributary named Sige Halla, down which the tigress was reported to keep her beat. The second I tied along the path to the neighbouring village of Anchetty, four miles away. The remaining calf I secured close to the watershed, whence both herdsmen and cattle obtained their daily supply of drinking water. Having myself attended to the securing and comfort of these three baits, I spent the next two days in tramping the forest in every direction, armed with my .405 Winchester, in the hope of picking up fresh pug marks, or perhaps of seeing the man-eater herself.

Early in the morning of the second day I located the footprints of the tigress in the soft sand of the Gundalam River. She had descended in the night, walked along the river past the watershed—and my buffalo bait, which, as was evident by her footprints, she had stopped to look at but had not even touched—and up and across a neighbouring hill on her way to Anchetty. There the ground became too hard for further tracking.

The third morning found me searching again, and I had just returned to camp, preparatory to a hot bath and early lunch, when a group of men, accompanied by the headman of Anchetty, arrived to inform me that the tigress had killed a man early that morning at a hamlet scarcely a mile south of the village. Hearing restless sounds from his penned cattle, he had gone out at dawn to investigate and had not returned. Thereafter his brother and son had followed to find out the cause of his absence, and at the outskirts of the cattle pen they had found the man's blanket and staff and, indistinct in the hard earth, the claw marks of the tigress's hind feet as she reared to attack her victim. Being too alarmed to follow, they had fled to the hamlet and thence to Anchetty, where, gathering strength in numbers and accompanied by the headman, they had hastened to find me.

Forgoing the bath and swallowing a quick lunch, we hastened to Anchetty and the hamlet. From the spot where the tigress had attacked and—as was evident by the fact that no sound had been made by the unfortunate man— had killed her victim, tracking became arduous and slow, owing to the hard and stony nature of the ground. In this case, however, the profusion of thorny bushes among the shrubbery assisted us, for, on casting around, we found shreds of the man's loincloth impaled on the thorns. Had the circumstances not been so tragic, it was instructive to learn how the sagacious animal had endeavoured to avoid such thorns and the obstruction they would have offered.

Some three hundred yards away she had dropped her burden beneath a thicket at the foot of a small fig tree, probably intending to start her meal. Then she had changed her mind, or perhaps been disturbed, for she had picked her victim up again and continued her retreat toward a deep nullah that ran southward toward the main Cauvery River, some thirty miles away.

Thereafter tracking became easier, for the tigress had changed her hold from the man's neck and throat, which accounted for the lack of blood spoor. Now she held him by the small of his back. Drops of blood and smears across the leaves of bushes and thickets now made it comparatively easy for us to follow the trail, and in another hundred yards we found the man's loincloth, which had completely unwound itself and was hanging from a protruding sprig of wait-a-bit thorn.

Continuing, we reached the nullah where, in the soft, dry sand, the pugs of the tigress were clearly imprinted, with a slight drag mark to one side, evidently caused by one of the man's feet trailing downward as he was carried. As there was no need of a tracker and numbers would create disturbance, apart from needless risk, I crept cautiously forward alone, after motioning to the rest to remain where they were. Progress was of necessity very slow, for I had carefully to scan the heavy undergrowth on both banks of the nullah where the tigress might have been lurking, waiting to put an end to her pursuer.

Thus I had traversed two bends in the nullah when I sighted a low outcrop of rock jutting into the nullah bed itself. Keeping as far as possible to the opposite side of the rock, I increased the stealth of my approach. Closer scrutiny revealed a dark object on the far side of the rock, and this duly proved to be the body of the unfortunate victim.

The tigress had already made a fair meal, having consumed about half her prey in the process, severing one leg from the thigh and one arm. Having assured myself that she was nowhere in the vicinity, I returned to the men, whom I summoned to the spot to help construct some sort of place where I might sit up and await the return of the assassin to its gruesome meal, which I was confident would be before sunset that day.

A more unsuitable spot for sitting up could hardly be imagined. There was a complete absence of trees on which a hide or machan could be constructed, and it soon became evident that there were only two possibilities. One was to sit close to the opposite bank of the nullah, from where the human victim was clearly visible. The other was to ascend the sloping outcrop of rock to a point some ten feet above the bed of the nullah where a natural ledge was formed about four feet from its upper edge. The first plan I rejected as being too dangerous since I was dealing with a man-eater, and this left me with the prospect of sitting upon the rock ledge. From there I could view not only the cadaver but also the whole length of the nullah up to its bend in the direction from which we had come, and for about twenty yards in the other direction, where it swung abruptly to the right.

Working silently and quickly, at a spot some distance up the nullah, whence the sound of lopping would not be heard, the men cut a few thorny branches of the same variety as grew in the immediate vicinity of the rock, so as not to cause a contrasting background. These they deftly and cunningly arranged below the ledge so that I would not be visible in any direction from the nullah itself. Fortunately, I had had the forethought to bring my blanket, water bottle, and torch, although there would not be much use for the last of these during the major portion of the night as the moon was nearing full and would rise comparatively early. By 3:00 P.M. I was in my place and the men left me, having been instructed to return the next morning with a flask of hot tea and sandwiches.

The afternoon wore slowly on, the heat from the blazing sun beating directly on the exposed rock and bathing me in sweat. Looking down the nullah in both directions, I could see that all was still and that nothing disturbed the rays of shimmering heat that arose from the baked earth. Absence of vultures could be accounted for by the fact that, in the position the tigress had left it beneath the sharply sloping rock, the body was hidden from the sky. About 5:00 P.M. a crow spotted it, however, and by its persistent cawing soon attracted its mate. But the two birds were too nervous of the human scent actually to begin picking the kill.

Time wore on, and the sun set as a fiery ball beneath the distant rim of forest-clad hills. The crows flapped away, one after the other, to roost in readiness on some distant tree in expectation of the morrow, when, overcome by hunger, they would be more equal to braving the feared smell of human beings. The cheering call of the jungle cock broke forth in all directions as a farewell to the dying day, and the strident *ma-ow* of a peacock sounded from down the dry bed of the stream. I welcomed the sound, for I knew that in the whole forest no more alert watchman than a peacock could be found, and that he would warn me immediately of the tigress's approach, should he see her. Now was the expected time, and with every sense intently alert I awaited the return of the man-killer. But nothing happened, the peacock flapped heavily away, and dusk rapidly followed the vanquished day.

Fortunately, the early moon had already risen and her silvery sheen soon restored a little of my former range of vision. The birds of the day had gone to roost by now, and their places had been taken by the birds of the night. The persistent *chuck-chuck-chuckoo* of nightjars resounded along the nullah, as these early harbingers of the night sought their insect prey along the cooling banks. Time passed again, and then a deathly silence fell upon the scene. Not even the chirrup of a cricket disturbed the stillness, and my friends the nightjars had apparently gone elsewhere in their search for food. Glancing downward at the human remains, I thought that one arm reached upward to me in supplication, or perhaps in a call for vengeance. Fortunately the head was turned away so that I could not see the frightful contortion of the features that I had noticed earlier in the afternoon.

All at once the strident belling of an alarmed sambar broke the silence and was persistently followed by a succession of similar calls from a spot I judged to be about half a mile away. These were followed by the sharp cry of spotted deer, and echoed up the nullah by a restless brain-fever bird in his weird call of *brain-fever, brain-fever,* repeated in a crescendo. I breathed a sigh of relief and braced my nerves and muscles for final action. My friends, the nightwatchmen of the jungle, had faithfully accomplished their task, and I knew that the tigress was approaching and had been seen.

The calls then gradually died away. This meant that the tigress had passed out of the range of the callers and was now close-by. I strained my eyes on the bend to the right, twenty yards down the nullah, around which, at any moment, I expected the man-eater to appear. But nothing happened. Thirty minutes passed, then forty-five, by the hands of my wristwatch, clearly visible in the moonlight. *Strange*, I thought, *the tigress should have appeared long ago. She would not take forty-five minutes to cover half a mile.*

And then a horrible feeling of imminent danger came over me. Many times before had that obscure sixth sense, which we all possess but few develop, stood me in good stead in my many wanderings in the forests of India and Burma and on the African veld. I had not the slightest doubt that somehow, in spite of all my precautions, complete screening, and absolute stillness, the tigress had discovered my presence and was at that moment probably stalking me preparatory to a final spring.

In moments of danger, we who know the jungle think quickly. It is not bravery that goads the mind to such quick thinking, for I confess that at that moment I was very afraid and could feel beads of cold sweat trickling down my face. I knew that the tigress could not be on the nullah itself or below me, or I would have seen her long before. She might have been on the opposite bank, hidden in the dense undergrowth and watching my position, but somehow I felt that her presence there would not account for the acutely growing sense of danger that increasingly beset me. She could only be above and behind me.

Suddenly it was borne home to me that the four-foot wall of rock behind me prevented me from looking backward, unless I raised myself to a half-crouching, half-kneeling position. That position, though, would make a steady shot almost impossible, apart from completely giving away my position to any watcher on the opposite bank or on the nullah bed itself. I cursed myself for this lack of forethought, which now threatened to be my undoing. As I hesitated for another second, a thin trickle of sand slid down from above, probably dislodged by the killer, now undoubtedly very close above me and gathering herself for a final spring.

I hesitated no longer. I forced my numbed legs to raise me to a half-crouching position, simultaneously slewing the cocked .405 around till the end of the muzzle was in line with my face. Then I raised myself a fraction higher till both my eyes and the muzzle came above the ledge.

A fearful sight revealed itself. There was the tigress, hardly eight feet away and extended on her belly in the act of creeping down the sloping rock toward me. As our eyes met in surprise, we acted simultaneously: the tigress to spring with a nerve-shattering roar while I ducked down again, at the same moment contracting my trigger finger. The heavy blast of the rifle, level with and only a few inches from my ears, mingled with that demoniacal roar to create a sound that often till this day haunts me in my dreams and causes me to awaken, shivering with fear.

The brute had not anticipated the presence of the ledge behind which I sheltered, while the blast and blinding flash of the rifle full in her face evidently disconcerted her, deflecting her aim and deviating her purpose from slaughter to escape. She leaped right over my head, and in passing her hind foot caught the muzzle of the rifle a raking blow, so that it was torn from my grasp and went slithering, butt first, down the sloping rock, to fall dully on the soft sand below, where it lay beside the half-eaten corpse. More quickly than the rifle, the tigress herself reached the nullah bed, and in two bounds and another coughing roar was lost to view in the thickets of the opposite bank.

Shocked and hardly aware of what had happened, I realized that I was unarmed and helpless, and that should the tigress return on her tracks, there was nothing I could do. At the same time, to descend after the rifle would undoubtedly single me out for attack if the animal were lying wounded in the bushes of the opposite bank. But anything seemed preferable to indecision and helplessness, so I dived down the slope to retrieve the rifle and scramble back, expecting at each second to hear the awful roar of the attacking killer. But nothing happened, and in less time than it takes to tell I was back at the ledge.

A quick examination revealed that no harm had come to the weapon in its fall, the stock having absorbed the shock. Replacing the spent cartridge, I fell to wondering whether I had hit the tigress at all, or if I had missed her at ridiculously close range. Then I noticed something black and white on the ledge behind me and barely two feet away. Picking it up, I found that it was the major portion of the tigress's ear, which had been torn off by my bullet at that close range. It was still warm to my touch, and being mostly of skin and hair, hardly bled along its torn edge.

To say that I was disappointed and chagrined could not describe one-tenth of my emotions. I had failed to kill the man-eater at a point-blank range, failed even to wound her in the true sense. The tearing off of her ear would hardly inconvenience her, beyond causing slight local pain for a few days. On the other hand, my foolish miss would teach her never to return to a kill the second time. That would make her all the more cunning, all the more dangerous, and all the more destructive because now she would have to eat when she killed, and then kill again when she felt hungry, increasing her killings beyond what would have been otherwise necessary. She might even alter her sphere of activities and remove herself to some other part of the country where the people would not be aware of the arrival of a man-eater and so fall still easier prey.

I cursed myself throughout that night, hoping against hope that the tigress might show up again, but all to no purpose. Morning, and the return of my men, found me chilled to the marrow, disconsolate, and disappointed beyond expression. The hot tea and sandwiches they brought, after my long fast since the previous forenoon, followed by a pipeful of strong tobacco, somewhat restored my spirits and caused me to take a slightly less critical view of the situation that, after all, might have been far worse. Had it not been for my sixth sense, I would undoubtedly have been lying a partially devoured corpse beside that of the previous day's victim. I had something to be really thankful for.

Approaching the spot into which the tigress had leaped, we cast about for blood spoor but, as I had expected, found none beyond a very occasional smear from the damaged ear against the leaves of bushes, left as the tigress had retreated from what had turned out for her a very surprising situation. Even those we eventually lost some distance away, so that it was an unhappy party of persons that returned to the hamlet and Anchetty, and eventually Gundalam, to report complete failure.

I remained at Gundalam for a further ten days, persistently tying out my buffalo baits each day, although I had little hope of success. Whole mornings and afternoons I devoted to scouring the forest in search of tracks, and nights were spent in sitting over water holes, game trails, and along the bed of the Gundalam River in the hope of the tigress showing up, but all to no avail. Parties of men went out in the daytime in all directions to secure news of further kills, but nothing had happened. Apparently the tigress had deserted her haunts and gone off to safer localities.

On the eleventh day I left Gundalam, tramping to Anchetty and Denkanikottai. From there I traveled to Hosur where I told my friend the

*The author and the Jowlagiri man-eater.*

subcollector of all that had happened and extracted from him a promise that he would tell me immediately of further kills should they occur, as I now felt myself responsible for the welfare of the people of the locality. Then, leaving Hosur, I returned to my home at Bangalore.

Five months passed, during which time I received three letters from the subcollector, telling of vague rumours of human tiger kills from distant places, two being from across the Cauvery River in the Coimbatore district, one from Mysore State territory, and the fourth from a place still farther away.

Then suddenly came the bad news I had feared but had hoped not to hear. A tiger had struck again at Gundalam, killing the eighth victim there and the next evening had snatched, from the very door of the little temple at Sulekunta, the old priest who had attended to the place for the last forty years. The letter concluded with the request to come at once.

Such urgent invitation was unnecessary, for I had been holding myself in readiness for the worst, and within two hours I was motoring to Jowlagiri.

Arriving there I was fortunate in being able to talk to one of the party of pilgrims who had almost been eyewitnesses to the death of the old priest of the temple. Apparently a party of men had been on pilgrimage and, as they approached the temple itself, were horrified to hear the low growl of a tiger, which then leaped into the forest from the roots of a giant peepal tree that grew some thirty yards away.

Bolting for shelter into the temple itself, they were surprised to find it tenantless and looking out were aghast to see the body of the old priest lying within the folds of the gnarled roots of the old peepal tree that directly faced them. After some time and very timidly, they approached in a group to find that the old man had apparently been attacked in, or very near, the temple, and then had been carried to this spot to be devoured. The tiger had already begun its meal, consuming part of the skinny chest, when it had been disturbed by the pilgrim party.

I particularly inquired as to whether my informant, or his companions, had noticed anything wrong with the tiger's ears, but obviously they had all been too frightened to observe any defects.

I hurried to Sulekunta with my party of three and arrived near dusk. I must confess that the last two miles of the journey had been very uncomfortable, traversing a valley between two steeply sloping hills that were densely clothed with bamboo. But we heard and saw nothing beyond the sudden trumpeting of a solitary elephant, which had been inhabiting those parts for some time and had been a considerable annoyance to pilgrims, whom he apparently delighted to chase if they were in small parties. But that is another story.

There was no time to make a proper camp, so we decided to sleep in the deserted front portion of the temple itself, a proceeding that I, and very decidedly my followers, would have declined to do under normal circumstances. But nightfall and the proximity of a man-eater are apt to overcome all scruples and principles. I stood guard with the loaded rifle while my three men frenziedly gathered brushwood and rotting logs, which lay in plenty nearby, to build a fire for our warmth and protection, for on this occasion there was no friendly moon and it would soon be dark. Under such circumstances, attempting to sit up for the man-eater in the hope of its passing near the temple would have been both highly dangerous and futile.

Soon we had a bright fire blazing, on the inner side of which we sat, away from the pitch-black jungle night, which could easily have sheltered the murderer, all unknown to us, within a distance of two feet. Listening intently, we occasionally heard the deep, belling boom of sambar, and I could discern the harsher note of a stag, but these did not follow in persistent repetition, showing that the animals had not been unduly alarmed by any such major foe as the king of the Indian jungle. After midnight we arranged to keep watch in twos, three hours at a time, and I elected, with one of my companions, to take first turn. The other two were soon asleep.

Nothing untoward happened, however, beyond the fact that the solitary tusker, who had approached near enough to catch a sudden sight of the fire, trumpeted once again and crashed away. A *kakar*, or barking deer, uttered its sharp cry around 2:00 A.M., but as this was not continued I decided that it had been disturbed by a wandering leopard. Three o'clock came, I awoke the two sleeping men, and in turn I fell into a dreamless sleep, to awaken to the early and spirited cry of a gray jungle cock, saluting the rising sun.

Hot tea, made with water from the well nearby, and some food gave us new life and heart, after which I walked across to the giant peepal tree and inspected the remains of the old priest. The vultures by day, and hyenas and jackals by night, had made a good job of him, for nothing remained but a few cleanly picked bones. At the sight I fell to reminiscing about the old man who had tended this temple for the past forty years, looking daily upon the same view as the one I now saw, hearing the same night sounds of sambar, *kakar*, and elephant as I had heard that night, and was now but a few bones, folded in the crevices of the hoary old tree. For the next hour we cast around in the hope of finding pug marks and perhaps identifying the slayer, but although we saw a few old trails, I could not with any certainty classify them as having been made by my tigress.

By 9:00 A.M. we left on the long twenty-three-mile trek to Gundalam, where we arrived just after 5:00 P.M. There, upon making inquiries about the recent killing, I gleaned the first definite information about the slayer from a herdsman who had been attending to his cattle at the same watershed where I had tied my buffalo bait on my last visit. This man stated that he had had a companion with whom he had been talking and who had then walked across to a nearby bush to answer a call of nature. He had just squatted down when, beyond the bush, the devilish head of a tiger arose, with only one ear, soon to be followed by an evil, striped body. The man had shrieked once when the fangs sank into the face and throat, and the next instant tiger and victim had disappeared into the jungle. Here at last was the information I had been dreading, but somehow wanting, to hear. So, after all, it was now confirmed that the killer was none other than my old enemy, the tigress, who had returned at last to the scene of her former depredations, and for whose return and now vastly increased cunning I was myself responsible.

Everywhere I had heard reports that no cattle or buffaloes had been killed by this beast, so I did not waste time, as on the previous occasion, in setting live baits, realizing that I had an adversary to deal with whom I could only hope to vanquish in a chance encounter, face to face. For the next two days I again searched the surrounding jungle, hoping by luck to meet the killer, but with fear and dread of being attacked from behind at any moment. Pug marks I came across in plenty, especially on the soft sands of the Gundalam River, where the familiar tracks of the Jowlagiri tigress were plainly in view, adding confirmation to the thought that by my poor shot, some five months ago, I had been responsible for several more deaths.

At midday on the third day a party of men arrived in a lather, having covered the thirty miles from Jowlagiri to tell me of a further kill—this time the watchman of the Jowlagiri Forest Bungalow—who had been killed and half-eaten the previous afternoon within a hundred yards of the bungalow itself. Hoping that the tigress might retrace her steps toward Sulekunta and Gundalam, as she was rumoured never to stay in the same place for more than a day after making a human kill, I left with my men at once. Our numbers were augmented by the party from Jowlagiri, who, although they had virtually run the thirty miles to Gundalam, preferred the return tramp of twenty-five miles to Sulekunta protected by my rifle rather than return by themselves.

Again we reached the temple of Sulekunta as daylight was fading and, as the nights were still dark, repeated our campfire procedure within the temple itself. Our party had now been increased to twelve, including myself, a number that, although it made us feel safer, was far too many for my personal comfort.

This time, however, we were not to spend a peaceful night. The sambar and *kakar* were restless from nightfall, and at 8:30 p.m. we heard a tiger calling from a spot I judged to be half a mile away. This was repeated an hour later from quite close, and I could then easily distinguish the intonations of a tigress calling for a mate. The tigress had also seen the campfire and become aware of the proximity of humans. Obviously hoping for a meal, she twice circled the temple, her repeated mating calls being interspersed by distinctly audible grunts of anticipation.

All this gave me an idea by which I might possibly succeed in keeping her in the vicinity till daylight, at which time only could I hope to accomplish anything. Twice I gave the answering call of a male tiger and received at once the urgent summons of this imperious female. Indeed, she came to the edge of the clearing and called so loudly as almost to paralyze us all. I was careful, however, not to call while she was in the immediate vicinity, which might have aroused her suspicions. At the same time I instructed the men to talk rather loudly, and not overstoke the already blazing fire, instructions that were doubtlessly most unwelcome. I hoped by these means, between mating urge and appetite, to keep the tigress in the vicinity till daylight.

She called again, shortly before dawn, and, congratulating myself on my ruse, I hastened down the path toward Jowlagiri as soon as it became light enough to see. There, but a quarter-mile away, stood the tamarind tree beneath which the boy had been killed over a year ago, and which I had already mentally noted as an ideal sitting-up place, requiring no preparation.

Reaching the tree in safety, I clambered up some twelve feet to a crotch that was reasonably comfortable and provided a clear view of the path at both ends. Then, expanding my lungs, I called lustily in imitation of a male tiger. Nothing but silence answered me, and I began to wonder if after all the tigress had moved on at dawn. A new anxiety also gripped me. Perhaps she was near the temple, waiting for one of the men she had marked down the night before to come out of the building.

Before departing I had very strictly enjoined my companions not, on any account, to leave the temple, but I felt anxious lest any of them disobey me. Knowing their need to answer to a call of nature, perhaps, or to get water from the well that was temptingly near worried me.

I called a second time. Still no answer. After a short interval, and expanding my lungs to the bursting point, I called again. This time I was successful, for my voice penetrated the intervening forest and was picked up by the tigress, who immediately answered from the direction of the temple. I had been right in my surmise; the wily animal had gone there to look for a meal.

After a few minutes I called a fourth time and was again answered by the tigress; I was overjoyed to find that she was coming in my direction in search of the mate she thought was waiting. I called twice more, my last call being answered from barely a hundred yards away. Leveling the rifle, I glanced along the sights to a spot on the path about twenty-five yards away. I judged she would take less than thirty seconds to cover the intervening distance. I began to count, and as I reached twenty-seven the tigress strode into full view, inquiringly looking for her mate.

From my commanding height in the tree, I saw that her missing ear was clearly visible, and I knew that at last, after many tiring efforts, the killer was within my power. This time there would be no slip. To halt her onward movement, I moaned in a low tone. She stopped abruptly and looked upward in surprise. The next second the .405 bullet crashed squarely between the eyes, and she sank forward in a lurching movement and lay twitching in the dust. I placed a second shot into the crown of her skull, although there was no need to have done so. Actually, this second shot did considerable damage to the head and gave much unnecessary extra work to the taxidermist.

The dreaded killer of Jowlagiri had come to a tame and ignominious end, unworthy of her career, and although she had been a murderer, silent, savage, and cruel, a pang of conscience troubled me as to my unsporting ruse in encompassing her end.

There is not much more to tell. My eleven followers were elated at the sight of the dead marauder. Soon a stout sapling was cut, to which her feet were lashed by strong creeper vines, and we commenced the seven-mile walk to Jowlagiri, staggering beneath the burden. Because of the man-eater's presence, no humans were afoot until we almost entered the village itself. Then word went round, and throngs surrounded us. I allowed the people a short hour in which to feast their eyes on their one-time foe while I retired to a tree some distance away, where hot tea soon refreshed me, followed by some food and two comforting pipes of tobacco. Then I returned to the village, where willing hands helped me to lash the tigress across the rear seat of my two-seater Studebaker, to begin my homeward journey with the comforting thought that I had lived down my error and avenged the deaths of many humans.

### Chapter Twenty-Six

# Kesri Singh
## One Man and a Thousand Tigers
### (1959)

Col. Kesri Singh's parents must have had a premonition about their son's future when they named him "Kesri," which means tiger in Punjabi. He comes from a long tradition of native shikaris whose familiarity with local peoples, forests, and wildlife made them indispensable guides for Indian nobles and later Europeans. Singh become well known as one of the few native Indians to write about his hunting exploits.

He spent most of his career working for the game department in the princely state of Gwalior in west-central India. It was there that he learned about tigers and their particular habits in this dry and arduous land, making him an expert tracker and hunting guide. His favorite client was the maharaja of Gwalior, Madho Rao Scindia, who shot more than seven hundred tigers in his career, many with Singh's help. The colonel himself shot over two hundred. After the maharaja died, Singh headed the police department in neighboring Jaipur until his retirement. He devoted his remaining years to writing books about his illustrious hunting career.

This chapter is from his most famous work, One Man and a Thousand Tigers *(1959).* Here he recounts stories about how well tigers can camouflage themselves, making them appear and disappear like ghosts. Sometimes other types of ghosts made their appearance, something that neither Singh nor anybody else could explain.

### Tigers and Ghosts

All sorts of legends and ghost stories have gathered round the tiger. It could hardly be otherwise. All over the world the largest, most dangerous animals, those that seem to the husbandman to embody the forces of the wilderness, naturally attract a special, fearful, interest.

*The author organizes a tiger beat.*

But tigers are made particularly mysterious by the ease with which they can appear and disappear. For such large animals, the effectiveness of their camouflage, even at close range, is fantastic. Anyone who has seen tigers only in captivity can have hardly an idea of the way a colour scheme that looks, by itself, so bold and ostentatious will vanish into a comparatively sombre jungle background of high grass, scrub, or forest. Tigers are masters at freezing in a suitable position, not a whisker stirring. So long as one remains still, even the most experienced hunter may fail to take in the banded, visually broken-up shape a few yards away. Indeed, as has happened to me more than once, he may smell his tiger before he sees him.

I remember once organizing a small drive for the maharaja of Gwalior that finished in an unexpected manner. As so often is the case, the beat was to be along a ravine. A tree growing up from among a cluster of karoonda bushes on the floor of the dry watercourse provided an obvious place for a machan, and some time before the shoot was due to take place I had one large enough to accommodate three guns lashed to the branches. This tree grew quite close to the bare and sandy right bank of the ravine, and on the day of the shoot I gave orders for a ladder to be placed between the bank and the machan so that my employer and his two companions could get up without having to force a way through the karoonda.

When the guns had settled into position and the ladder had been withdrawn, the maharaja looked at his watch and, realizing it would be a quarter of an hour before I gave the signal for the beaters to start, lit a cigarette. He was a very heavy smoker, but smoking when waiting for game is never a good practice and after a few puffs he threw his cigarette away. Still glowing, it landed on the back of the tiger who was lying quietly in the bushes directly under the machan. After a few moments the heat penetrated the fur and the indignant animal, springing out of the bushes with a roar, rushed into the farther jungle. As none of the rifles were loaded, no one could take a shot at the vanishing form.

The curious thing is that all three men on the machan were thoroughly experienced shikaris, and the tiger must have been perfectly visible from above. Yet until he moved, none of them had the slightest notion of his presence.

A similar incident occurred some years later at Ramgarh, where the maharaja of Jaipur brought Lord Wavell for a shoot. I had been given very little notice of the event, which had to be wedged in between various public functions. I had been told, of course, that the viceroy was to pay a visit to the state and that there would be tiger shooting, so I had, accordingly, had baits put out and watched by shikaris at various places. But now I suddenly learned that he was lunching with the maharaja at the Ramgarh shooting lodge the following day, and would have time for only one beat, which must take place in the immediate neighbourhood and before lunch.

Fortunately, a tiger killed a bait quite near the lodge on the night before the viceroy's arrival, so there was a good chance that everything might go reasonably well after all. But about an hour before the drive was due to start and as I was making my last-minute dispositions, I noticed a disquieting sign. Some way outside the area to be beaten a number of monkeys were jabbering and calling in the peculiar tones they use when some big hunting animal is close at hand. It looked as if the tiger had already strayed far from the kill.

With the machans sited, the fields of fire arranged, and beaters, stops, and shikaris all briefed, it was impossible to change our plans completely at short notice—that is how accidents happen. However, there was a reasonable chance that the monkeys were being excited by a panther or a second, intruding tiger, so I decided to go into the jungle inside the prescribed area to see if I could get a glimpse of the beast that had taken the bait buffalo. The risk was that by doing this I might disturb him and actually cause the very misfortune I suspected, but it was the only way to find out if he was still there. I did not intend if I could help it to beat a patch of empty country while the tiger, so to speak, watched from the other side of the touchline. Having posted stops and warned them what I was going to do, I entered the jungle and began to walk very slowly and quietly toward the kill.

I had not gone far when I saw the tiger slowly getting to his feet in a patch of low brush on the other side of a stretch of more or less clear ground. I at once turned about, and as soon as I was a few hundred yards off I hurried away to the lodge to tell the maharaja and the viceroy to come to the machans at once, as the tiger was on the move.

As soon as I had seen the guns into position I gave the sign, and the beat began. The line of men moved steadily forward, but there was no sign of a tiger or any other large animal. Finally, to my surprise and annoyance, all the beaters reached the line on which they had to halt, so as not to be in danger from shooting, without anything having broken cover. Yet it was impossible for the tiger to have moved in front of them without exposing himself, and almost impossible that they should have passed him.

I was standing near the machans, and everybody seemed to be looking at me with long, anxious faces when a deafening, coughing roar from close-by sent all our hearts into our mouths. A second later the tiger leaped out of a thicket only a few paces from one of the machans and tore away behind them. Lord Wavell tried a snap shot but missed, and the next moment the beast was gone for good.

What must have happened was that the tiger, having been disturbed by my untimely prying, had gone straight up the line of the drive, not swerving (because of the stops already in position) until, after crossing the open in front of the firing line, he had reached the cover by the machan trees. There he had ensconced himself in a thicket near the machan soon after occupied by the viceroy. Coming up to move the guns into position before the drive, we must have passed within a few feet of him. Seeing the men climbing, he had realized that there was danger and had broken cover only after a long and anxious wait—and then with a maximum of dash and noise to disconcert his enemies. The ruse had succeeded very nicely.

If their suspicions are aroused, tigers often show a kind of cautious inquisitiveness that, combined with the extreme quietness with which they can move, sometimes produces an uncanny effect. I shall not forget a moonlit night when I lay behind a little screen about six feet from the top of a sloping sandy bank. Below me, at the bottom of the bank, lay the body of a buffalo killed by a tiger the previous night. The full moon was directly behind me. All at once, and without any accompanying sound whatsoever, the tiger's silhouette was cast on the sand a little way before me. It was a moment before I had traced the outline with my eye and grasped that the beast was directly above. I remained perfectly still, almost relaxed, certain I had come to the end of my hunting and that the long tally of tigers I had killed was now, as it were, to be balanced. There was a low growl, and the shadow moved back over me. When at last I craned my head around, there was only the moon.

But far odder incidents than this are likely to befall anyone who spends a great deal of time looking for tigers. I see from my records that it was in April 1943 that I went to Baswa to destroy a cattle-lifter reported to have attacked and killed several persons in the district. Baswa is a prosperous little place largely because it has a station on the main Jaipur-Delhi Railway. But there is no motor road there, and communications are not easy in the area round about. I therefore sent ahead a small advance party including a couple of riding camels. As soon as I could get away, I followed them and was met with the disagreeable news that there was no fresh information about the tiger from any quarter. The shikaris had not been able to pick up a fresh track or establish any sort of picture of the animal's normal habits.

It was in fact three days before I could get any sort of clue as to the tiger's whereabouts. Then news came that he had killed a cow near a temple of Vishnu, at the foot of a large hill about four miles east of where I had pitched camp. I set off at once on a camel and carefully inspected the site. There were no inhabited buildings in the vicinity of the temple, which was surrounded by big, shady trees and, on one side, by the remains of a mud wall that had no doubt once enclosed some sort of court or compound. Near the temple was a small cistern fed by a spring.

I found the remains of the cow about two hundred yards away; it had evidently been killed the previous night and was only half-eaten. No one had seen or heard anything till the carcass was found in the morning. The place was served by a single priest who told me that fear of the tiger had for some time caused him to leave the temple long before dark and return well after daylight.

No pug marks could be found in the hard ground near the kill, but after much trouble a few were discovered on the hillside. From these I concluded that, after feeding, the tiger had gone over to the opposite slope where there was a good deal of cover. After this I rode round the area on another search for information, questioning everybody I could find. The only useful piece of knowledge I could glean was that the tiger, if he were in the neighbourhood of the temple, would be certain to drink at the spring. He had done so on several occasions. Accordingly I bought a goat and returned to the temple.

What was left of the cow was dragged near the spring, and the goat tied up in the shade nearby. The roof of the temple was flat, with a parapet about a foot high: It was plain that it would make a better place to shoot from than a machan in one of the trees. Some big stones were carried up and put on the parapet so as to form a kind of battlement and allow me to aim without exposing myself too obviously. Then, having sent off the shikaris with the camels in plenty of time before dusk, I settled down with a rug, rifle, thermos flask, and some sandwiches to await events.

I had brought a goat not only because time was short, and one was easily available, but also because tigers are especially fond of goat meat. In addition, the bait was only fifteen yards from a particularly stable and convenient shooting post, and although the tiger was reported to be a powerful cattle killer and no doubt capable of killing and tearing loose such a small animal very quickly, I was confident I should have time enough to knock him over if he would only be tempted.

About half-past nine I heard a sambar calling somewhere high on the hill, warning that a hunter was on the move. Ten minutes later by the luminous dial of my watch a jackal gave tongue, much nearer. Then the goat began to bleat intermittently. From that moment I should have kept every faculty concentrated on the scene below, but in fact my attention was almost immediately caught by something on the roof. I saw it moving on my left, out of the tail of my eye. It was a large, common rat.

When I slowly turned my head to look at it, it came closer so that at first I thought it must still be unaware of my presence and moved my hand sharply to scare it away. At this gesture it dodged back into the shadows, but after perhaps half a minute I became unpleasantly conscious that I was being watched from

*Elephants prepare to take their positions.*

behind. Keeping my head below the level of the parapet I cautiously looked round, and there, sure enough, was the little humped form, quite near and looking almost silvery in the moonlight. I realized that it was likely to distract my aim. The only things I had to throw at it were my cartridge bag and the Thermos, and even the bag would have been impossibly noisy. While I was turning this absurd difficulty over in my mind and vainly longing for a stick, a fantastic thing happened.

The rat, which had been keeping perfectly still, suddenly scuttled round till it was on my right, and then made a rapid, squeaking dart at my hand, which was on the edge of the rug, causing me to draw back and grab my cartridge bag. It was ridiculous, shaming. There was I, with a weapon that would stop a rhinoceros, held at bay by a rodent weighing a few ounces. So much for the resourceful shikari. My sense of humour was not working; I was annoyed and, to be frank, curiously disquieted.

The rat would not go, but kept scuffling back and forth in the shadow under the parapet. It occurred to me that my handkerchief might frighten it away; animals are often startled by white objects. Circumspectly, I pulled it out and, holding it low, flapped it. The rat seemed unimpressed. But the next second I had forgotten its existence. There was the beginning of a loud bleat,

*The trophy is brought to camp.*

abruptly choked, from below, and immediately afterward a loud twang, as of a parting rope. I was just in time to see a tiger slip from under the shadow of the trees, the white shape of the goat hanging from its mouth, and vanish over the mud wall.

When I drew back from the parapet there was no sign of the rat. Reckoning that there was still a chance the tiger would return to drink, I decided to stay where I was and keep a strict lookout. But not even a jackal came to the dead cow, and the rest of the night passed entirely without incident.

However, in the morning a surprise was waiting. Pug marks of the tiger were plain in the dust round the place where the goat had been tied, and it was perfectly obvious that they could not be the tracks of the man-killer. He was known to be a grown male, and these, both from their size and the oblong rather than round impressions of the toes, could only have been left by a tigress.

Getting back to camp I was met by a party of peasants with the news I had been dreading. While I had been waiting for him at the temple, the man-killer had broken into the communal cattle pen at a village some miles in the other direction and killed a good cow in full milk. Some of the men, desperate at the thought of the loss, had tried to drive him off, and one of them had been badly mauled. Far from pleased with life, I got back on my camel.

At the village my spirits began to rise a little. I found there was a good tree growing near the pen and soon had a machan put up into it. I also inspected the dead milker and gave orders for the carcass to be moved to a suitable spot outside the enclosure, about forty feet from the tree. Not much had been eaten by the disturbed tiger, and there seemed a good chance he might this time come back to his kill. Anyway, I knew of nowhere else to wait for him: A wandering tiger is always a chance quarry.

Late in the afternoon I returned to the village and climbed onto the machan. Everything went like clockwork. Just before nine o'clock the cattle thief stalked into the moonlight and after examining the kill and taking a good look round settled down to feed. Successful assaults on men had made him careless or he would have been less easy about a carcass that had been shifted so far. As soon as his attention was engaged, I shot him dead. I then got down from the machan, and leaving a shikari to skin him returned to camp and bed in a much improved frame of mind.

More investigations round the temple area disclosed that the tigress that had escaped me quite often came to the spring to drink. She had never been known to take a domestic animal before and was very shy of human beings. I made no further attempt to shoot her. As for the rat, I have never seen one behave in such a way before or since, and do not propose to try to account for its behaviour here. However, I may add that though (as the reader may have noticed) I am not a man of punctilious observance, I do not believe it was right to expose a live bait or shoot an animal at a shrine dedicated to the Preserver, and should not have done so had the motive been sport and not the urgent destruction of a man-killer. Certainly I am glad that providence prevented me killing without cause a beast that must have come in the first place to drink at the temple spring.

It is an old story that the unquiet spirits of those a man-eater has devoured will sometimes help a hunter to avenge them. No such experience has ever befallen me, but the late maharaja of Jodhpur, Sir Umaid Singh, a most brilliant and fortunate shikari—he is one of the few ever to have been caught and knocked down by a rogue elephant who yet lived to tell of it—is said to have once been warned in this way. This is his story.

A machan had been built in a tree overlooking an open step-well where a flight of crumbling stairs, now seldom used, ran down to the water. A man-eater was reported to drink at this place, and the maharaja several times sat up for him. One night he had begun to give up hope and relax his watch when a man, apparently, in a white cotton garment and conspicuous in the moonlight, climbed up the steps of the well and, reaching the top, turned round and pointed back at the water. Then he walked quietly away. He was followed out of the well by the man-eater, which must have been there since nightfall, and was now killed without trouble. Sir Umaid Singh did not tell me this anecdote himself.

A more remarkable instance concerns a man-eater that lived in the Ada Bala Hills. A professional shikari who lived in the same range volunteered to destroy this animal, which had already eaten several persons of various ages and sexes. After making a study of the tiger's habits he built a machan in a *salar* tree close to a water hole and about fifteen feet from the ground. A buffalo was sacrificed for the common good, and one evening before a night when a full, early moon could be expected, it was tied up by the drinking place. The shikari mounted the machan long before dusk.

Man-eaters, if they live long enough, become very experienced in the ways of men. This one, when he approached the water hole and saw the buffalo conveniently tied to its stake, became suspicious. No doubt, too, having a predilection for human flesh he was in no great hurry to fall on a tough animal when there seemed a chance of getting its owner. He therefore retired into a nearby thicket and waited.

After a while he must have become conscious of the shikari up in the machan. At all events, sometime after midnight he went quietly to the foot of the tree and then with a sudden rush—his claw marks were visible on the trunk—clambered up and seized the unfortunate man, who was probably dozing. Next morning the shikari's clothes and some fragments of his corpse were found nearby. The buffalo had not been touched.

After this no one could be found to tackle the man-eater. Months went by and six more villagers were killed, but in spite of a comparatively substantial reward no volunteer could be found in the whole region. But the news traveled, and finally an enterprising sportsman from some distance away decided to come to see what was happening. On taking a good look round the place he was disconcerted to find that there was no other reasonably promising site for a machan except the very tree from which his predecessor was said to have been dragged. The tiger seldom or never returned to his kills, and the only foreseeable thing about his conduct was his liking for this particular drinking place.

The new arrival had a machan built nearly five feet higher than the first. An examination of the tree trunk did not lead him to suppose that this would put him beyond the tiger's reach, but knowing himself to be a good shot he was reasonably sure of being able to knock the animal down before he could get so far. He also obtained a fat buffalo calf that he thought might be expected to appeal to any tiger, one that even an old tiger would be able to kill without great difficulty.

No one came with him, so, having picked a suitable evening before a moonlit night, he walked alone down to the water hole and climbed up to his perch. Having loaded his rifle and having made himself as comfortable as the situation allowed, he began his watch. Nothing happened. The calf chewed its cud quietly; no jackal or lapwing broke the silence with its warning. The man stared and stared into the pattern of moonlight and shadow.

He was startled by a sharp blow between the shoulder blades. He rocked a little in the machan and at once saw the tiger directly below, crouched and looking up, ready to spring. Although his attention had wandered and he had been on the edge of a doze, being an experienced game shot he brought his rifle to his shoulder almost without thinking and fired straight down. The tiger collapsed at the foot of the tree, and at the same moment the hunter felt three light, congratulatory pats on his shoulder. He twisted round, but he was quite alone. There was no branch that could have so touched his back, and no wind to move one even had it existed.

The man who killed this tiger told me the story himself. He is not a man who cares to attract attention, and I am very far from suspecting him of a vagrant imagination. He believes, of course, that the dead shikari warned him. So should I, no doubt, if it had happened to me. As it is, I am content to put it down here, like everything else in this book, as simply another tiger story.

## Chapter Twenty-Seven

# Robert Ruark
### Use Enough Gun
### (1966)

Robert Ruark was one of America's most popular journalists in the 1940s and 1950s. Today he is almost unknown, except to big-game hunters and hunting aficionados, to whom he remains a legend.

Ruark wrote on many popular topics. His hunting stories began with childhood reminiscences in his native North Carolina. Once he became famous, he fulfilled his lifelong dream of going on an African safari. After that first trip, he published Horn of the Hunter *(1953)*, which established him as a safari hunter and writer. This was followed by a number of books and articles on Africa and hunting. Although fascinated by Africa, Ruark did hunt on other continents. He made only one trip to India, in the early 1960s, with two other Americans and his wife, whom he always called "Mama."

This excerpt is part of a chapter from Use Enough Gun *(1966)*, in which he recounts one of his biggest hunting mistakes—letting a trophy tiger escape. Ruark never found tiger hunting much sport, but he remarked, "A dead tiger is the biggest thing alive, and I have shot an elephant. A live tiger is the most exciting thing alive, and I have shot a lion." The book was published posthumously in 1965, after Ruark's untimely death from liver failure at age forty-nine.

### Use Enough Gun

This is going to be the story of a mistake. I suppose everybody has made a big one, but I reckon nobody ever made a sillier one than the one I made. You might say it is unique in the history of hunting mistakes. There never was a hunter or a fisherman who didn't have one great big silly to hang on his wall, but this silly of mine is the all-time world's record. This is a silly with pearl handles, and a built-in moral. I may as well tell you about it because it has already made me foolishly famous from Calcutta to Nairobi, and was last seen headed for New York.

If some of the first part of this sounds like bragging, it is meant to because I was bragging to myself, and that is what caused me to make the mistake. If I hadn't been bragging, I wouldn't have made the mistake. Pride goeth *after* a fall. It was like this:

The Madhya Pradesh of India was beautiful last spring, cool and crisp at night, bright and breezy-warm by day. Mama and I were hunting out of a hill camp near a place called Gondia, a few hours out of Nagpur. We were hunting tigers and wild bison, or gaur, and sambar stags and chital deer. We were living very comfortably in a *dak* bungalow [resthouse] that the Indian Forest Service owned, and it was like living in a country club. There was a big kerosene-fed refrigerator, two cooks, a *dhobi* to wash your clothes, and a couple of personal servants to wait on you. There was Swedish beer and Gordon's gin and Coca-Cola and more fancy canned goods than you can buy on Madison Avenue. The food, from curry to corn flakes, was elegant.

The hunting was so easy it was pathetic. We hunted along good country roads out of Jeeps. There were about a thousand wild aboriginals—Gonds and Baigas—in the immediate neighborhood, so we had more game scouts, beaters, and bearers than we needed. The countryside was lovely. They call it jungle, but it is about as jungly as Westchester County in the fall, full of evergreen trees and bright scarlet trees and tall, green sort-of-poplars. The thickest part of this jungle wasn't half as tough as quail country in Carolina.

Down the road a piece, a couple of friends named Jack Roach and Charlie Vorm were shooting out on another block. Jack comes from Houston, Texas, and Charlie is an Indiana man. They are both old hands at tigers and at the large African stuff. Nice neighbors to have around, but not people you would like to make a damned fool out of yourself in front of.

Charlie shot himself a very good old cattle-lifting tiger within three hours after arrival at his block. The tiger came slowly and easily and walked right under Charlie's machan, his roost in the tree. Charlie is an old, cool customer, and he let him come on until he was directly underneath, and then he shot him in the back of the neck. He gave him the other barrel, although the tiger didn't need it at all. A couple of days later he shot another tiger, and he was all ready to go home.

*A young Robert Ruark.* (Photo courtesy of Trophyroombooks.com)

Jack was having bad luck. They'd been hunting all spring in Assam and here but hadn't shot anything until now. And Jack couldn't seem to see a tiger. But it wasn't troubling him much because back home in Houston, in his automobile agency, he has a full mount of a snarling ten-foot-four-incher that may be the best trophy the Jonas boys ever handled. Apart from a certain impatience on Jack's part, we were a relaxed community . . . because this place was loaded with tigers.

Tigers are peculiar. They have an awful lot of house cat in them. They love human habitation. They are at ease and very daring about contact with humans. They will live in country that otherwise would not produce a rabbit in the way of game, because while they will kill for fun, they do not hunt for fun. They like to kill it easy and eat it close-by. And since every little village of Gond or Baiga has its work buffaloes, milch cows, and spans of oxen, for a tiger this is heaven on earth. He doesn't have to run his legs off chasing sambar. He just saunters down the road and clobbers the first tender-looking bullock he comes across. And if he's really feeling in a high, joyous mood, he may kill half-a-dozen just to watch 'em fall. In my vicinity, one tiger slew seven buffalo in a matter of minutes, and spectators saw him dancing up and down on the carcasses like a leopard in a hen house. And in the road exactly in front of my *dak* bungalow, one single tiger killed five horses apparently just for fun.

There were thirteen tigers, all big males but one, feeding in my block, which was about ten miles square. The Suphkar block has been famous for as long as men have shot tigers, and it has been shot over by two hundred years of maharajas and viceroys. The day I got there two tigers had killed and were feeding, but both consumed their kills and left the area. My shikari, a big, mustachioed Muslim from the Punjabi, name Khan Sahib Jamshed Butt, was blithe.

"My dear," he said, "in one, two days we must shoot a tiger. In a week we must shoot two tiger. In ten days we must shoot three tiger."

For five days we beat and sat up at night over kills before I shot my first tiger. Three days later I shot my second. It seemed to me I had the tiger situation solved. The good Lord knows they are easy to beat, if your shikari knows his business, and how anybody could ever miss one I don't know because you shoot them at under fifty yards and they offer as much target as a Jersey bull. Tigers? Phooey. Nothing to it.

I started hunting some other things, including a big panther that was as large as a small tigress and was killing the buffaloes we had staked out for their baits. I never saw this panther. He didn't get that old and that big by being stupid. We sat up for him night after night, using his most recent kills as bait, and a little, brave black goat named Babu Sahib to *baa* and lure the cat, but we never saw a hair of him. He'd just slink down the road a bit and kill another buffalo.

The other hunting was pretty good. We shot some peacocks and jungle fowl and doves. We shot some pigs. I shot two sambar stags, neither one very good in the horns, and I shot them both running and broke both necks. I shot a very good chital buck and busted his neck, too. I was collecting peacocks at a couple hundred yards with a scoped Hornet, and was feeling very fine about the whole business and pleased with myself.

One day Khan Sahib and I were away the hellangone off trying to shoot a blackbuck and a bear, without any luck, and I got something in my eye and ordered the little expedition back home to the *dak* bungalow, where Mama and the beer lived. When we got back, there was Brother Vorm come to call, to tell us about his two tigers, and there was also the game ranger in a high state of excitement over a very big, very old rooster tiger that had killed a tame buffalo that morning and had been driven from the kill without having had a chance to feed off it. The ranger had built a machan on the scene and was hoping we would come home in time to get to the platform before dusk. He said he was sure the tiger would return. I welcomed Brother Vorm, made myself a sandwich, and we took off. My eye had suddenly quit hurting.

The kill wasn't far away, about a mile in the Jeep, with about another mile to walk. The jungle there was very thin, but you had to ford a small river to get to where the tiger had killed the buffalo. The buff was lying in the middle of an open field, and had not been fed on. The cat had broken his neck and there were talon marks on his flanks, but he was untasted. On the far side of the field there was a rising ridge of thicker bush and a spring of water. The tiger was almost certain to be nearby.

The game ranger had built his machan just at the edge of the field. Khan Sahib and I went through the usual business of crawling up the shaky ladder, and receiving the guns and blanket and the canteen and the flashlamp apparatus. It was almost night when we got settled down for the longest wait in the world. The day had cooled and the peafowl were beginning their nightfall cries, which are as harsh as any sound in the world. The male says *meeoww,* like a human imitating a cat badly, and the females answer *halp!* like an old maid in a melodrama.

I was no newcomer to jungle nights in trees by now. We had sat up five nights waiting for the panther. We had sat up two nights over other tiger kills. We had sat up a very short time in the late afternoon waiting for a bull gaur to come down to water from the top of a mountain he lived on, and on him we had been very lucky. Before I began to fidget I heard the stones being dislodged as he came slowly down the mountainside, and in a very short time

*Ruark at home with his tiger.* (Photo courtesy of Trophyroombooks.com)

I could see his plumed tail switching against the flies and his dainty, oddly delicate little white-stockinged feet as he picked his way down the hill. I let his mountainous body come good and close and walloped him twice with my

.470, just where the neck joins the shoulder. He turned tail over tip, rolled down the trail, and came to a halt, very dead, right at the bottom of the tree in which we were roosting. That had been painless. It takes luck to shoot this huge wild ox, and we had spent less than half an hour in the process.

But apart from that I was hating night work. For one thing I have never liked the idea of night shooting. You can't see the animal clearly and the light distorts him. Unless you kill him dead in his tracks, he's off, wounded, and you dare not go after him until dawn, which gives him an entire night to suffer, unless he is very badly hit. And sitting in any sort of night blind is the toughest work in the world.

I am a chain smoker, and you can't smoke. I am a fidgeter, and you dare not fidget. You can't cough, sneeze, clear your throat, scratch, or belch. If you move one limb, the rasping of the trouser cloth is louder than a kid running a stick along a paling fence. Your feet go to sleep and your legs cramp. Ants crawl up the tree and bite you. Mosquitoes chew you.

I believe there is nothing quite like a jungle at night to refresh your memory on what a short distance man has come from ape. There you sit in a tree, like a monkey, in a night full of fear and awful noise. The ravens just at dusk are ghoulish enough, with their grave robber's chuckle and maniac's laugh. The peacocks are unbelievably loud. The monkeys chatter and grunt and bark.

Just when night comes black around you, there is absolute silence, and then the little noises start. A bird hits a six-note soliloquy like a Swiss bell-ringer. The last dove up gives a suicidal moan and goes to sleep. Then the crickets start, and a lot of night birds you'll never see or know chime in. Then there are pops and grunts and groans and crashes. Over there a sambar stag bells, a cheetah barks and is answered by a barking deer. Monkeys scream. A tree falls, and it sounds like a cannon shot. A mile away, on a road, some frightened, probably drunken Gonds are singing their way home in the dark. Then there are little pitters and patters and slithering sounds in the bush around you. And in your tree you sit, your nerves sharp-whetted.

You do not know if the tiger will come. He has never come before. You have never shot at a tiger at night because only the Indians would think of classifying this truly noble beast as vermin, shootable at any hour with any means in any numbers. In Africa they won't even let you go after a wounded leopard with a camp lantern when night falls.

But you know that if this tiger does come, he will be the biggest and last tiger you will ever shoot. His pug marks place him at least ten foot, four, and the record for the area is ten four, back through the memory of the oldest shikari in the Gond village. And you are leaving in a couple of days, anyhow, to look for wild water buffalo.

And you wait. You think about heaven and hell and your liver. You think about the money you owe and the sins you've committed and wonder if cigarettes really do cause cancer. Not that you wouldn't swap a mild case of cancer for one pull at a cigarette right this minute. You think about the work you ought to do and haven't done. You reflect that you are treading on the toes of forty years of age, and that your life is about two-thirds finished. You think about where you've left things but can't remember where you put them. While maintaining absolute immobility, your whole nervous system jumps at each new hoot, each giggle from a far-distant hyena, each rustle and crash. A thin sliver of moon edges up and the night gets colder and the mosquitoes knock off. The wind veers and blows the smell of the dead buffalo right at you. After a day in the sun he smells like hell.

Four or five thousand years pass, and you say to yourself, *Well, I wonder how much longer we'll give this old so-and-so,* and then your stomach rumbles with a horrible noise, and you start thinking about a very cold, very dry martini, and a hot Madrasi curry, and tender slabs of cold, boiled peacock with mustard mayonnaise, and a big cup of coffee with a double-dip of brandy in it, and the fire roaring and cold, crisp, clean sheets on the bed. Khan Sahib's belly growls louder than yours, louder than a tiger, and you can see that his innards are thinking, too. They are thinking about four or five pounds of mutton and a mountain of rice, a cup of tea, and some sweet, sticky cakes. Your feet are completely numb now. There is a dreadful ache in your back. But now you nod, halfway between sleep and daydream. . . .

You do not know how long you've dozed, but suddenly a hand clamps your neck, pressing gently. It is black dark where the dead buffalo lies, black as night and tree shadow can make it. You strain your eyes to the popping point but you can't see anything. You can hear, though. You can hear the awfulest assortment of noises you ever heard. The old *bagh* has come to the kill while you dozed. And he is very busy getting himself stuck all the way into that kill.

First you hear him shaving the rear end of the dead buffalo, biting off the thick hair as close and clean as a barber would shave it. Then you can hear the gurgling whoosh as he hauls out a whole section of entrails. Then you can hear him grunt and hear the ripping of teeth into flesh as he tears off huge, twenty-five-pound hunks of flesh, swallowing them without chewing—gurgling and growling and belching as he gobbles.

This is the hardest part of it, the waiting when the cat has come, the waiting when you want to shoot more than you've ever wanted anything, the waiting while the cat gets so deeply interested in his dinner that he is impervious to all life around him. The waiting takes ten minutes. A ten-year stretch in jail would pass more swiftly. Munch. Crunch. Rip. Tear. Burp. Growl. Gurgle.

And now Khan Sahib's fingers gradually relax and leave your neck. The icy-cold steel of the big double rifle slides through your hands, and slowly, very, very slowly, you ease the gun from its leaning position on the limber branch, out and over the branch, out toward the tearing, crunching sounds, and the butt is snug against your shoulder, the steel freezing against your face. An arm slides past your back, and all of a sudden the black is white as a powerful hand lamp comes alive across your shoulder and makes a brilliant pathway through the night to where Shere Khan, Bagh Sahib, is taking his dinner.

The tiger looks upward into the light. He has eaten a quarter through the rear end of the buffalo. His great clear yellow eyes reflect the yellow tongue of the torch and seem to strike splinters from the beam. His face is as big as a bushel basket. His huge ruff, his sideburns and old man's whiskers, his long white beard, are clotted with blood. His mouth, with those three-inch fangs, is a bloody smear, through which the teeth gleam when he snarls. He snarls at the light, as at an enemy come to steal his meal. He looks up the tree to me.

Does anybody ever really remember exactly when he shot or where he shot or how he chose the spot to shoot at or the time to do it? All I know is that I put the bead somewhere on his neck behind the ear and squeezed. The big Westley Richards, which I trusted so much, roared and possibly kicked, but I never felt it.

The tiger never left his crouch over the dead buffalo. He never moved his head. His chin dropped an inch and came to rest on the buffalo's flank. He did not flex his forearms. He did not kick. He was stone dead on the body of his victim, his eyes closed in the strong light of the torch. I raised the gun again to give him the other half, the finisher, the tenderizer.

"No, sahib," Khan Sahib said. "Don't shoot again. He is dead. He is as dead as the last one. The neck shot is deadly. Do not spoil the hide. Nobody ever killed a tiger any more dead."

"Great," said I, and the conceit mounted.

Khan Sahib shook me by the hand and beat me on the back and danced up and down so that the machan shook under his feet. He said I was about the greatest one-shot sahib since the invention of gunpowder. I agreed with him freely. I told him that without doubt he was the greatest shikari ever to deserve the patronage of such a miraculous sahib as I. I lit a cigarette and gave it to him. Then I lit one for myself, and looked at my tiger lying dead in the light, snugly pillowed on the rump of the dead buffalo. I took the little flask of emergency ointment and had a long pull at it. I toasted the tiger. I toasted Khan Sahib. I toasted me.

Old Three-Tiger Ruark. One-shot Bob. Some people miss 'em. Some people wound 'em. Not the Boy Genius. He shoots them in the neck. Poor Old Charlie Vorm back in the *dak* bungalow. Only two tigers, one of them little and one of them female. Wonderful Magnificent Me. Wait'll I tell the boys around the Norfolk Bar in Nairobi. You know anybody else shoots three tigers in a week and always in the neck?

Khan Sahib was hollering for the natives to come and let us down out of the tree. It would take them half an hour to get through the black jungle. I gave Khan another cigarette. I lit one myself and had another small toast to the tiger.

I thought about that house I was going to build someday, a man's house where a big Cape buffalo, two lions, two leopards, a rhino, the 110-pound tusks of an African elephant, a champion waterbuck, and other bric-a-brac like elands and Grant gazelles and impalas and gaurs and chitals and Spanish stags would blend very nicely with three hand-shot tigers, and always in the neck. Why shoot 'em twice when you can kill 'em with one bullet? Old Charlie Vorm'll think I missed, and he'll drop dead when we dump about ten-foot-four of tiger on the bungalow's front porch.

I was on the third cigarette and Khan Sahib had turned off the torch. I had just run for president and had been elected. You could hear the natives talking as they came to let us down out of the tree and admire our tiger. I had just been re-elected to a second term as president and had won the water-boiling contest at the Campfire Club when I heard an awful roar.

Khan Sahib Jamshed Butt flicked on the light. He flicked it on just in time to see my dead tiger's tail disappear into some high, dusty-yellow grasses, and now all we had on the ground was a quarter-eaten domestic buffalo. "That, the Raven said, and nothing more."

At least fifteen minutes had elapsed from the shooting until the disappearance, but the tiger had got up and gone away. I knew right then I would never see that tiger again, although all common sense told me that this was a death flurry and he would be dead in the bush fifty yards away, and we would take the buffaloes and find him in the morning.

The reason I knew we wouldn't see him was that I was remembering my friend Harry Selby, who in my book is the best professional hunter in the world. I could hear Harry's English schoolboy voice saying: "When it's big and it's dangerous, shoot it once and shoot it twice and then when you're absolutely certain it's dead, shoot it again. It's the dead ones that get up and kill you."

I remembered all the things we'd shot together—the lions and the elephant and the leopards and the rhino and the buff—always the extra pop for precaution. I then remembered that Khan Sahib, too, had always said the rule of thumb on tigers was to kick in the extra bullet. Hell, the extra bullet doesn't cost much, and you can sew up the extra hole it makes. Forty-five years this man has hunted tigers, and he not only breaks his own rule, but commands me to help him break it. "Don't shoot, sahib," he says. "Don't spoil the skin."

Good old One-Bullet Bob. The new president of the jerk factory. The loser in the flapjack-flipping contest in the Campfire Club. All his Abercrombie and Fitch buttons cut off, and his Merit Badges burned. And now to face Mama and Charlie Vorm.

We explained to the Gonds and the game ranger and crawled down out of the tree and walked a mile through pitch-black jungle that now contained, in addition to cobras, a wounded tiger. I didn't care if I got snake-bit. I would have welcomed a charge from the tiger. Nothing happened, of course. And I must say that Mama and Brother Vorm were quite polite. But I didn't sleep much that night, and when I slept I dreamed about a long line of bullets, dancing and laughing at me like the performing cigarettes in the television shows.

The next day we got up very early and took a herd of buffaloes to hunt the wounded tiger. That's how you do it, you know. You use the tiger's mortal enemy as a bird dog. About twenty-five buffaloes go milling along in the wake of the tiger's blood spoor. If he's hurt bad, he'll find a hidey-hole and lie up, and the buff smell him and go mad with fear and anger. Then the tiger charges the buffalo and you shoot the tiger. This is, if you don't get trampled by the fear-crazed buffaloes, each of which weighs two-thirds of a ton.

We found the bright slashes of blood on the grass and trailed him a quarter-mile to a long, grassy ravine with a mountain on each side of it, and then he quit bleeding. We looked for him high and looked for him low for two days, Khan Sahib nearly delirious with malaria and remorse, and me just sick at heart. No tiger. There wasn't ever going to be a tiger because what I had clearly done was crease him on the spine. The bullet had gone all the way through the fleshy neck, touching the spine and knocking him out briefly, but not hitting bone and inflicting no more damage than a hatpin. He didn't even bleed after that quarter-mile because the wound closed tight. We wore out the buffaloes and ourselves, but that tiger was well again and long gone.

Well, there's the shameful story. I don't remember ever hearing of anybody else who had a prize tiger dead on the ground for fifteen minutes and lost the tiger, and Khan Sahib said that he never heard of it before either. It just goes to show you, that vanity will murder you, and the most horrible mistake a hunter can make is to start counting his bullets.

I redeemed myself a little bit the next week, in a place called Raipur, when I shot a stampeding wild water buffalo neatly through the neck and dropped him stone dead. I am sorry I can't furnish any pictures of this particular beast, whose horns probably measured around ninety inches from tip to tip.

You see, when we were looking for the wounded tiger, the boy who was carrying the cameras fell into the creek and waterlogged both Rolleiflexes, ruining the lens because he was afraid to confess his accident, and we didn't find out about the dunking until both cameras were wrecked. The next time, I intend to spend that other bullet. It comes out cheaper in the end.

# Glossary

## A

Amarys – covered/canopied howdah
Anku – hook on a mahout's gujbar

## B

Baiga – forest tribe of central India
Babu – honorific title, gentleman; also office clerk
Bagh – tiger (Hindi language)
Banjara – nomadic tribe; Gypsy
Bhaun – primitive rocket used to scare/drive game during hunting
Batta – special pay for soldiers in the field. Given by the East India Company and native armies prior to the Raj
Bhil – forest tribe of central and west India
Bund – type of jungle
Bundobust – planning/organization (of a hunting trip)

## C

Chagal – water bag
Chamar – person or caste that skins animals
Chapatti – flat unleavened bread eaten in northern India
Chatta – umbrella

Chaud – small grassy clearing
Chital *(Axis axis)* – spotted or axis deer
Chinkara *(Gazella gazella)* – Indian gazelle
Chobdar – tent, door attendant
Coolie – laborer

# D

Dak bungalow – forest rest house
Dak runner – mail courier
Daru – liquor made from mohwa tree flowers
Dhaman – snake
Dhobi – clothes washer
Durbar – ceremony

# E

Ekka – two-wheeled cart

# F

Frash – servant who pitches a tent

# G

Ganja – cannabis
Gara – a kill
Ghat – mountain; steps
Ghooming – casual hunting forays on elephant back
Griffin; griff – novice; new recruit in the British military
Gond – forest tribe of central India
Goonda – lone male elephant
Guddi elephants – trained elephants not outfitted with howdahs/pads
Gujbar – steel or brass goad used to steer elephants

# H

Huli – tiger (Kanara language)
Hamadryad *(Ophiophags hannah)* – king cobra
Harcara – messenger
Hayla – young buffalo
Hazur – sir; formal Indian name
Hircus – horns made from sheep horn
Hogla – marshy area
Homgay *(Pongamia glabra)* – Indian beech tree
Howdah – platform or box mounted on elephant back for tiger shooting

# J

Jaghire – village district where revenues are assigned to single person (jaghite)
Jamun *(Syzgium cumini)* – tree producing edible fruits
Járdya – illness; giardia
Jat – Hindu tribal group/caste found near Delhi
Jheel – swamp; watery depression
Jemadar – orderly

# K

Kahouse – seat in a palanquin
Kakar *(Muntiacus muntjak)* – barking deer
Keddah – enclosure used to trap wild elephants
Khidmutgar – waiter
Khora – a place, often undefined or mysterious
Khubber – information on game
Kole balloo – old jackal
Koonkie – a tame elephant used to capture wild elephants
Koorpie – grass cutting chisel
Korku – forest tribe of central India
Koss – two miles

Kotwar – village watchman
Kukri – Nepalese knife

# L

Lalla – member of a rural caste; clerk
Langur *(Semnopithecus hypoleucos)* – common gray monkeys

# M

Machan – treetop platform for shooting tigers and other game
Mahseer *(Tor khudree)* – a large fish belonging to the carp family
Markhor *(Capra falconeri)* – wild mountain goat
Mewatic – soldier
Mukna – tuskless male elephant
Mohwa *(Bassia latifolia)* – oak–like tree whose flowers and fruits are eaten
                and distilled into liquor
Munshi – teacher
Murghi – chicken; chicken dish
Musselman – Muslim

# N

Naie – dog
Nautch girl – dancing girl
Nilgai *(Boselaphus tragocamelus)* – largest Indian antelope
Nullah – rocky ravine or riverbed
Nurri – jackal

# P

Paharia – forest tribe
Palanquin – chair or bed carried on two poles by bearers
Pedda Puli – big tiger

# Glossary

Peepal *(Ficus religiosa)* – large forest tree with important religious significance
Poojaree – priest
Potail – village headman
Puddah – young buffalo used for bait
Pug – footprint
Pugaree – turban; head cloth
Puli – tiger (Telugu language)

# R

Resai – quilt
Ressaldar – military commander of native cavalry
Rhidmitgar – footman
Roga – illness; giardia

# S

Sahib – honorary title; sir
Sal *(Shorea robusta)* – large forest tree of northern and eastern India
Salai *(Boswellia serrata)* – shrub–like tree used for resin and incense
Sambar *(Cervus unicolor)* – largest Indian deer
Shaitan – devil; bad person
Shikar – hunting; hunting trip or expedition
Shikari – native hunting guide
Subahdar – Indian army equivalent to an officer
Swary – soiree; social gathering
Syce – attendant

# T

Terai – woodland/grassland complex found in the Himalayan foothills
Topee – pith helmet
Tulwar – curved steel sword

# V
Vizier – official

# Z
Zaminder – landowner of high position
Zenana – women's quarters

# BIBLIOGRAPHY

Anderson, Kenneth. *Nine Man-Eaters and One Rogue.* London: Allen and Unwin, 1954.

Bacon, Thomas. *First Impressions and Studies from Nature in Hindostan; Embracing an Outline of the Voyage to Calcutta, and Five Years Residence in Bengal and the Doab from MDCCCXXXI to MDCCCXXXVI.* London: William H. Allen and Co., 1837.

Baden-Powell, Robert. *Memories of India; Recollections of Soldiering and Sport.* Philadelphia: David McKay, 1915.

Best, James. *Indian Shikar Notes.* London: John Murray, 1931.

——. *Tiger Days.* London: John Murray, 1931.

Blane, William. *Cynegetica: or Essays on Sporting.* London: John Stockdale, 1788.

Burton, Reginald. *The Tiger Hunters.* London: Hutchinson and Co., 1936.

Campbell, Walter. *My India Journal.* Edinburgh: Edmonston and Douglas, 1864.

Corbett, James. *The Man-Eaters of Kumaon.* New York: Oxford University Press, 1946.

Cumming, Gordon. *Wild Men and Wild Beasts.* Edinburgh: Edmonston & Douglas, 1871.

Ellison, Bernard. *H.R.H. The Prince of Wales's Sport in India.* London: William Heinemann, 1925.

Forsyth, James. *The Highlands of Central India.* London: Chapman Hall, 1871.

Glasfurd, Alexander. *Rifle and Romance in an India Jungle.* London: John Lane, 1905.

Gouldsbury, Charles. *Tiger Land.* London: Chapman and Hall, 1913.

Johnson, Daniel. *Sketches of Indian Field Sports.* London: Longman, Hurst, Rees, Orme & Brown and T. Fowler, 1822.

Mundy, Godfrey. *Pen and Pencil Sketches.* London: John Murray, 1832.

Napier, Edward. *Scenes and Sports in Foreign Lands.* London: Henry Colburn, 1840.

Pollock, Arthur. *Sporting Days in Southern India.* London: Horace Cox, 1894.

Rice, William. *Tiger Shooting in India.* London: Smith, Elder and Co., 1857.

Ruark, Robert. *Use Enough Gun.* Long Beach: Safari Press, 1999.

Sanderson, George. *Thirteen Years Among the Wild Beasts of India.* London: William H. Allen & Co., 1878.

Singh, Kesri. *One Man and a Thousand Tigers.* London: Robert Hale, 1959.

Sleeman, James. *From Rifle to Camera.* London: Jarrolds Publishers, 1947.

Smythies. Evelyn. *Tiger Lady.* London: William Heinemann, 1953.

Stewart, Arthur. *Tiger and Other Game.* London: Longmans, Green and Co., 1928.

Watson, Alfred. *King Edward VII as Sportsman.* London: Longmans, Green and Co., 1911.

Williamson, Thomas. *Oriental Field Sports.* London: Edward Orme, 1807.

Woodyat, Nigel. *My Sporting Memories.* London: Herbert Jenkins, 1923.